RECOMMENDATIONS.

FEW works ever have reached the reader with so many and important recommendations, as the one now laid before the community. It will be seen, that the English, French, and German press, no less than the most learned Rabbis of this country are unanimous on the subject. Please read.

Opinion of the Rev. Dr. Isaac M. Wise.

WHEN this book appeared in the German language in 1853, Dr. Wise wrote for the *Asmonean*, in which paper he reviewed it thoroughly. We extract the following passages:

Wegweiser fuer rationelle Forschungen in den Biblischen Schriften.—The above is the title-page of a work written in the German language, by the Rev. ISIDOR KALISCH, Rabbi of Cleveland, Ohio, which is now in the press, and of which we possess proofs of the first sheets. Being promised the other sheets as soon as having passed the press, we commence making some remarks on the subject matter. Before doing so we beg leave to observe, that the author of the book is a classical scholar gifted with a sound critical judgment, which we believe the numerous articles from the pen of Mr. KALISCH that have appeared from time to time in our paper have already made apparent to our readers.

* * * * * * * *

The author shows in the first chapter, that the writers of the New Testament admit the Divinity of the Bible. He next argues from the Mosaic record of Creation, which he explains at some length, to be agreeable to the results of modern science, which being written in strict accordance with the nature of things as the science of all centuries has explored them, is a proof of the Divine legation of Moses. Next he argues from the prophecies contained in the Bible, and from the

Moral Law promulgated therein, which our author says are to be final and sufficient to all ages of mankind The matter on which our author argues is conspicuously displayed, and the argument is clear and held in a popular style. He is led by this argument upon the assertion of Christian theologians, that the New Testament superseded the Bible; he enters upon a philological definition of the terms "*New Testament*" as used by Paul in his Epistle to the Hebrews viii, 8, 15, which results in a proof that Paul either misunderstood Jeremiah (xxxi, 31,) or willingly mistranslated the words ברית חדשה. After a few more arguments from the Mosaic records to the effect, that the Bible is the ultimatum in moral laws, he enters upon a minute criticism of the gospel story according to Matthew. Here the author displays not only an intimate knowledge of the Greek, but a sound critical judgment and a less biased mind than FREDERIC STRAUSS. This critical expositon is new, original, and ingenious, betokening a long, patient and impartial enquiry.

* * * * * * * *

In the critical exposition of the Gospel according to Matthew, the author adopts two plans; he points out the mistakes committed by the writer, and the contradictions which that book embodies; and then he examines the moral and religious doctrines contained therein, pointing out their respective sources in the Bible and in the rabbinical literature. He succeeds in establishing two important facts; first, that the book can not be of a Divine origin on account of the mistakes and contradictions contained therein; and secondly, that the moral part of the book has no claim to originality, being a mere synopsis of what has been written previously to Matthew. The logical deduction of these facts is, that Christianity is an inaccurate synopsis of Judaism, which by no means supersedes the latter, it only confirms the superiority and Divinity of the latter. Our author is very minute on this subject, and treats it with considerable earnestness, without irony or sarcasm, developing an extensive knowledge of our national literature, and handling the subject matter with such respect as is due to a subject of such importance, and also to the feelings of the community. This part of the work is very elaborate and should be read by every Jew and Gentile; it throws light upon a vital question of religious interest, which is eminently calculated to give an impulse to new and extensive researches. The Pharisees are most unmercifully attacked by Matthew; and it is, indeed, remarkable, that the doctrines and maxims of the same party are carefully copied in the Gospel not only according to Matthew, but also in the three other Gospels. Our author has done well to devote a considerable space of his work (from page 93 to 110) to an exposition of the religious and moral doctrines of the

Pharisees, which the reader will recognize at the first moment as the basis of Matthew's Gospel.

The author also received the following kind letter:

Rev. Sir:—I have not changed my favorable opinion of your book, which I consider a valuable contribution to American theological literature. Much credit is due to Rev. Dr. Mayer, for his accurate and ingenious translation of the book into the English language, and to you for the valuable additions and improvements which enrich the English edition. God bless you,

ISAAC M. WISE.

To the Rev. Isidor Kalisch, Rabbi of Milwaukee, Wisconsin.

At the request of the Rev. I. Kalisch, Rabbi and Preacher at Cleveland, Ohio, I have much pleasure in stating that I have carefully read a book lately published by him called *Wegweiser fuer rationelle Forschungen in den Biblischen Schriften*, and that I deem it a valuable and useful addition to our literature on this subject. As a polemical work, its style and modĕ of treating the argument are unobjectionable, while at the same time it evinces a great acquaintance of the controversy in question, and praiseworthy research into those original sources of information, Biblical, Rabbinical and Non-Israelite, which are the safest guides when consulted in a spirit of fairness and with critical discrimination, acute but dispassionate. I therefore readily recommend the book as deserving of encouragement and entitled to the attention of every well-intended and reflecting Israelite, and especially to such fathers of families as may at times feel at a loss how to reply to the eager questions of their children in a manner that shall carry conviction to their young minds, and strengthen their attachment to their faith. M. J. RAPHALL, Dr.

[From *La Lien D'Israel.*]

Guide pour servir a des recherches rationnelles dans les ecrits bibliques, ou, que nous apprend, d'une part, le Christianisme primitif; de l'autre, le Mosaisme, par Isidor Kalisch, rabbin et predicateur. (Cleveland, Ohio, 1853.)

* * * * * * * *

Par contre, vous voudrez bien m'accorder un petit espace dans votre journal; pour rendre compte de l'ouvrage (precedent) de notre collegue d'Amerique. Ce livre merite d'autant plus d'estime que dans ses attaques les mieux fondees et les plus profondes, et dans tout l'abandon que comporte la liberte americaine, il ne laisse pas d'etre ecrit d'un ton calme et rassis. De sorte que meme le lecteur chretien peut le prendre entre les mains, sans avoir a craindre une provocation a la polemique. Dans un long traite intitule: *Hathora min hoschamaim*, M. Kalisch donne des preuves irrefragables de l'origine divine de la loi de Moise et des prophetes. Il est vrai que le Christianisme lui meme reconnait cette origine, comme il resulte des aveux des ecrivains evangelistes, conf. St. Luc. xvi, 17; St. Mathieu, v, 17; *ibid.* xlv, 4 et ailleurs. Mais la critique rationnelle ne doit fonder ses assertions que sur l'autorite de la raison; c'est pourquoi notre auteur ajoute encore cinq autres preuves.

1) Les donnees de la Bible sont d'accord avec les resultats les plus recents des sciences naturelles. A cette fin, M. Kalisch commente le premier chapitre de la Genese, et montre, mot par mot, comment la cosmogonie mosaique s'accorde avec la science la plus exacte.

2) La division zoologique de la Bible n'est pas moins remarquable, vu qu'aucune cinquieme espece d'animaux n'a ete ajoutee aux quartre indiquees par Moise.

3) La realisation historique de tout ce que Moise et les prophetes ont predit prouve egalement l'origine divine de la Thorah.

4) Ceci est demontre par la morale si pure et si simple de la Bible.

5) Enfin, les prophètes nous montrent leur veracite en ne disant rien d'obscur, rien d'equivoque, rien de ce qui ressemble aux oracles paiens, en prononcant clairement leurs predictions et en les signant. De plus, ces predictions se realiserent toutes dans leurs temps respectifs.

Mais on dira peut-etre que cette Thorah divine et vraie ne fut donnee qu'a un peuple d'esclaves, que ce peuple a perdu la force de sa mission, que, par cette raison, il aurait besoin d'une loi meilleure et nouvelle en remplacement de la Thorah.

A cela, l'auteur repond par les quatre refutations suivantes:

a) Le peuple esclave mourut tout entier dans le desert, et la loi de Moise fut donnee pour etre observee par un peuple libre.

b) Les notions les plus claires et les plus elevees sur Dieu et sur la morale se trouvent dans les ecrits mosaiques, et non-seulement le Nouveau-Testament ne les a pas perfectionnees, mais encore il les a tres-souvent obscurcies.

c) Les prophetes, sur les predictions desquels le Nouveau-Testament se fonde tout entier, nous garantissent la duree eternelle du peuple Israelite.

d) La barbarie et la corruption regnerent parmi toutes les nations qui ne possederent pas la loi de Moise, et meme le Christianisme n'a pu vaincre le paganisme que par le fer et le feu.

Ici l'auteur fait une revue retrospective des temps ou florissaient l'inquisition, les auto-da-fe, les jugements de Dieu, les persecutions religieuses d'Espagne, etc.

Cette introduction complete est entierement terminee; l'ouvrage proprement dit commence. C'est tout simplement un commentaire critique sur l'evangile de St. Mathieu. L'auteur commente chaque chapitre, chaque verset, chaquo mot, et montre ce qu'il y a de faible dans cette partie du Nouveau-Testament, en la controlant contradictoirement, au moyen de la legislation mosaique, par la critique historique et des extraits du texte meme de la Bible. Souvent aussi, il nous fait voir l'ignorance en matiere philologique, dont se rendent coupables les ecrivains du Nouveau-Testament. Avec cela, l'auteur met a profit largement et judicieusemeut les sources judaiques, a savoir le Talmud et le Misdrasch. Il a encore le merite de nous montrer que les passages les plus sublimes et les plus instructifs du Nouveau-Testament se trouvent deja dans l'Ancien. En ajoutant a ce que je viens d'appendre que cet ouvrage si estimable (in 8o, contenant 292 pages) sera suivi par une traduction anglaise, j'ose exprimer le vœu de voir le savant autenr essayer de proceder a des recherches critiques de cette nature, sur les autres ecrits du Nouveau-Testament. Quant au livre en question, je ne puis que le recommander tres-vivement a la lecture de tous les amis de la verite.

D. L. LEVYSOHN, *predicateur.*

Ich habe mit vielem Vergnügen das Werk des Rev. J. Kalisch „Rationelle Forschungen in biblischen Schriften" gelesen, und empfehle dasselbe auf's Freundlichste meinen jüdischen Glaubensgenossen. Es zeigt von ernster Forschung, gründlichem Fleiße, und lebendiger Begeisterung für die Sache unsrer Religion. Die Aufgabe der Wissenschaft ist es, die Schwächen in den verschiedenen Religionssystemen nachzuweisen, das schroffe Gegenüberstehen dadurch zu beseitigen, und dadurch die so sehr gewünschte allgemeine Verständigung zu erzielen. Das Werk des Herrn Kalisch ist hiezu ein ernster Beitrag, und unsre jüdischen Brüder, die von Christen oft aufgefordert werden, über die Bibel ihnen Rede zu stehen, werden in demselben Vieles finden, das ihnen zu Nutzen kommen wird. Ich hoffe und bitte daher, daß das Werk Anerkennung und Unterstützung finden möge.

Rabbi Dr. Lilienthal.

Mit innigem Vergnügen entspricht der Unterzeichnete dem Wunsche des Herrn Rev. Isidor Kalisch in Cleveland, Verfasser des Werkes betitelt: „Wegweiser für rationelle Forschungen in den biblischen Schriften," dasselbe allen Freunden der Wissenschaft, insbesondere seinen resp. Gemeindegliedern, als ein lehrreiches, mit großer Bibelkunde und talmudischem Wissen ausgestattetes polemisches Werk zu empfehlen, und zu dessen weiterer Verbreitung die Hand zu bieten.

Der Verfasser legt in demselben eine freisinnige Auffassung der jüdischen Grundlehren mit Offenheit dar, und bekämpft die dunklen Deutungen mit Klarheit, welche dem Prophetenthume ein so mysteriöses Gebiet anweisen wollen, worauf das Christenthum seine Begründung fußt.

Sprache und Inhalt sind so leicht faßlich, daß es selbst das jüngere Geschlecht mit Nutzen und Vergnügen lesen wird, und die Anschaffung desselben in jedem Familienkreise mit sicherer Zufriedenstellung empfohlen werden kann.

Dr. L. Merzbacher.

RECOMMENDATIONS.

(Aus **Klein's Jahrbuch**.)

„Wegweiser für rationelle Forschungen in den biblischen Schriften." Von **Isidor Kalisch**, Rabbiner und Prediger zu Cleveland. (Cleveland, Ohio, 1853, 8.) Ein kräftiges Werk, wie es vielleicht nur in der freien Atmosphäre Amerikas entstehen kann; in Deutschland, dem blühenden Lande der Mucker und der deutschen .... Gründlichkeit wird es ein jüdischer Gelehrter nicht wagen, ein solches Werk ans Tageslicht treten zu lassen. Es ist eine Kritik des Evangeliums Matthäi und bildet in seiner Tendenz einen merkwürdigen Gegensatz zu dem vorher gedachten Werke. Es soll jetzt in englischer Sprache erscheinen. Ausführlicher hierüber berichtete ich im Universum, XI. Jahrgang, p. 24.

(Aus dem **Hausfreund**, eine christliche Zeitschrift.)

„Wegweiser für rationelle Forschungen in den biblischen Schriften von **Isidor Kalisch** Rabbiner und Prediger, Cleveland, Ohio, Druck von Ernst Scheufler, 1853." Wir machen nur im Allgemeinen auf dieses Buch aufmerksam, das sich als ein solches beurkundet, welches ein gründlicheres Studium der biblischen Schriften, besonders der des alten Testaments fördert. Interessant besonders erscheint die Darstellung des Zusammenhangs des Alten und Neuen Testaments, und die Entwickelung neutestamentlicher Vorstellungen und Ereignisse aus alttestamentlichen Wahrheiten und Thatsachen ermittelt und erläutert durch die ältern rabbinischen und talmudischen Schriften. Eine weitere Besprechung des Buches behalten wir uns vor.

A GUIDE

FOR RATIONAL INQUIRIES INTO

THE BIBLICAL WRITINGS.

BEING AN EXAMINATION OF THE DOCTRINAL DIFFERENCE BETWEEN JUDAISM AND PRIMITIVE CHRISTIANITY, BASED UPON A CRITICAL EXPOSITION OF THE BOOK OF MATTHEW.

By Rev. Isidor Kalisch,

Rabbi and Preacher of the Congregation Bene Yeshurun,
MILWAUKEE, WISCONSIN.

TRANSLATED, FOR THE AUTHOR, FROM THE GERMAN.

CINCINNATI, OHIO:
Printed by BLOCH & CO., Publishers of The Israelite and Deborah.
1857.

TRANSLATOR'S PREFACE.

When about three years ago, the Undersigned took it upon himself, in compliance with the request of his friend and colleague—the author of the present volume—to lay a translation of it before the English reading Public, it was not contemplated to introduce it by means of a "Translator's Preface," to the favors of its new readers, since the recommendations accompanying it, and the criticisms with which the Original was received, superseded the necessity of adding new encomiums, and multiplying the recommendations. But the "Signs of the Times," that have lately shown themselves also, on the horizon of this glorious Republic, admonish the Undersigned to reconsider his original resolve, and write a Preface.

It can not be denied, unless we are determined to offer a deaf ear to the loud preachings and proclamations of history, that the great political bankrupt under which the Monarchies and sham Republics of Europe have been, and still are suffering, and which has led to oppression and persecution, to revolutions and reactions, and their most melancholy results for the people of that continent, has been caused by that unfortunate "*Union of State and Church,*" and its mother, that most absurd of all doctrines, the doctrine of "*Christian State.*"—What is it that gave birth to this latter doctrine? The opinion preached from the pulpits, taught at school, proclaimed aloud everywhere, that whatever perfection there may exist in morals, politics, &c., &c., they can be derived only from the doctrines of Christianity; hence, if men are desirous of establishing a perfect Commonwealth, it must be founded upon "*Christian*" principles, in other words, it must be a "*Christian State.*" But it happened that as far as the history of all so-called "Christian" States has shown, they invariably trampled one of the most prominent lessons of the founder of Christianity under foot—the lesson, "render unto Cæsar the things which are Cæsar's, and unto God the things that are God's," and then, instead of holding State and Church seperate from each other, they blended them into one, to their mutual destruction;—they violated, by depriving all those who did not profess Christianity or a certain form thereof, of some of their inalienable rights, the great doctrine—generally supposed to be a Christian one, although it is far older than Christianity—: "do unto others as ye wish to be done to;" and really abolished thus the highest moral law so frequently repeated and enjoined upon his followers, by Jesus: "love thy neighbor as thyself!" That such States, even if we suppose for a moment that the moral doctrines upon which they are said to be founded are really Christian doctrines, present very un-Christian States, needs no further demonstration. It would be, indeed! supererogatory, on our part, farther to show, what illiberality and intolerance, bigotry and fanaticism, with all their pernicious consequences, have been exhibited in such Christian States,—the cöndition of Europe is the best demonstration.

Should these United States—with such examples before them, not take the most watchful care, lest they run into the same danger? As yet, the sacred soil of this glorious Republic has not been profaned by the practical execution of such pernicious doctrines;—as yet, our MAGNA CHARTA is unsullied by such fanatical "*Christian*" laws;—as yet, the greatest and wisest of all political rules, the separation of State and Church, is a living law in this country. I say, "as yet." For attempts have been frequently made already, to christianize also our Constitution, to make our government a Christian one; and thus lay "the foundation for that usurpation of the divine prerogative in this country, which has been the desolating scourge of the fairest portion of the old world." What else are the so-called Sunday-laws of several States but attempts to make the Sabbath of the Christians, by means of legal enactments, *the* Sabbath of the land? And are such laws not a direct violation of the very first principle of our government,—"which is a civil and not a religious institution,"—a rebellion against the very spirit of our Constitution, which "recognizes in every person the right to choose his own religion, and to enjoy it freely without molestation," forcing, as they do, a considerable number of the citizens of this country to celebrate a day as a religious one, against their own religious views, sentiments and creed? In some States bigotry has failed in this godless attempt; in others it has succeeded, because the injured parties neglected to appeal for restitution into their rights, to the highest tribunal of the land where, it cannot be doubted, they would have gained a victory both for themselves and the divine principle of Freedom of Conscience and Religion.—Another attempt of this kind was the petition addressed to the U. S. Congress, in the year 1829, "to stop the Mails on the Christian Sabbath." It met a most glorious repudiation by not even being admitted to a discussion on the floor of that venerable body, upon the famous report of Col. Johnson of Kentucky, who warned them against establishing "the principle that the legislature is the proper tribunal to determine what are the laws of God," by adopting "the sentiment of the petitioners." For, says the report, "among all the religious persecutions, with which almost every page of modern history is stained, no victim ever suffered, but for the violation of what government denominated the law of God. To prevent a similar train of evils in this country, the Constitution has wisely withheld from our government the power of defining the divine law. It is a right reserved for each citizen; and while he respects the equal right of others, he can not be held amenable to any human tribunal for his conclusion."

I will not disturb the peace of the defunct Order of the Know-nothings, who in their turn declared "Christianity an element of our political system," went a step farther, by excommunicating the Catholics, and proved by their speedy annihilation the correctness of their name: they ought to have known, that no community or association or public body, whatever name it may bear, of whatever nature it may be, can exist for a length of time, if it be founded upon exclusiveness, illiberality and fanaticism. Their sudden downfall should be a warning example for all future time.

I come now to the latest attempt, at Christianizing our government —an attempt which, assuming the garb of philosophical and legal learning, couched in the most sophistical sort of theological demonstration, and displayed with the most imperturbable coolness, the most specious persuasion and sanctimonious impressiveness, is rather dangerous, and deserves a more lengthy attention on our part. We allude to the work entitled: "*The American citizen: His rights and duties, according to the spirit of the Constitution of the United States. By John Henry Hopkins, D. D., L. L. D., Bishop of the Protestant Episcopal Church in the Diocese of Vermont.*"

I must acknowledge that after a careful perusal of the first five chapters of this work—and these alone we have to consider here—I was at the loss, whether I should rather admire the boldness with which Bishop Hopkins displays his doctrines, or pity the man who could so far disregard the intelligence of his fellow-citizens, as for a moment to suppose that they would suffer themselves to be gulled by his honeyed sophistries; yes, upon reflection I accorded him my most ardent sympathy. For considering that he is a high dignitary of a Church which rules a mighty empire on the European continent, while here, in this land of liberty, it exercises no more political influence than the Church of the Mormons, it must be mortifying for him to share the fate of his Church, to be Bishop only within its precincts, and beyond it, nothing more than the humblest laborer! Why, how sweet would it be to be entitled to a seat in the "Upper house" of the United States by virtue of his office! Thus, it is but natural that he should endeavor, as far as in his power lies, to get also in this country, an " Established Church." But while we sympathize with our Christian brother for his grief and mortification, we must beg him to excuse us when, in all charity, we call his arguments specious, fallacious, jesuistical. Because the Constitution of the United States prescribes an official oath, it requires Religion;—and because that oath is a Christian oath, therefore, " every man who takes it is legally presumed to be a Christian, on the general ground of a conscientious belief in the Gospel system;—*ergo:* our government is a Christian one,—hence, and as the Common law is established by the Constitution, "the very idea of a jury of Turks, Jews, or infidels, would be regarded, in law, as a pure absurdity;"—hence again, none but Christians (of course, Protestant Episcopal Christians) can hold offices, none be even tolerated in the land, except the Jews, merely because " they were also allowed to establish their Synagogues in England, and a few were even existing in the United States, before the Constitution was adopted, whose rights were questioned by no one." —Such is Bishop Hopkins' line of argument. Well feeling the great gap between his first proposition, that the Constitution of the United States requires an oath, and the second, that this oath is a Christian one, since the Constitution prescribes no certain religious form for it, he resorts to arguments that are really incompatible with sound reason and common sense. To recur for proofs to the Old Common Law, is too preposterous to deserve any notice; if we take this as our authority in the interpretation of the Constitution of the United States, we could soon argue away its most beautiful principles. But to say that the prescribed oath is a Christian one, because the framers of the Constitution happened to be Christians, is an argument unworthy of the learning of our author. We would say, and we trust, with far more logical force: even because the framers of the Constitution, although they were Christians, did not Christianize the oath of office, they intended to make our government a merely civil one, which should have nothing at all in common with a certain form of religion. All these framers intended by this oath was, to recognize, by implication, the existence of a God, but not to establish a certain mode of worshipping that God. Nay! the very copious extracts from their writings, which the author presents to us to prove his assertion, show nothing more than that they believed in a Divine Providence, without teaching their fellow-citizens that the Constitution recognized but a "Christian" Divine Providence.

"The recognition of Christianity," says an eminent Jurist of South Carolina, " and especially of the triune form of Christianity, in the Constitution of the United States as the national religion, is at war with one of the fundamental principles of that instrument, that of religious liberty, and religious equality, in all men, whether Jew or Gentile, Mahomedan or Pagan, Trinitarian, Unitarian, or Deist; and is, of course, utterly inadmissible." Of course, our Rt. Reverend author will not endorse such a truly republican doctrine. And how could he? who, after having placed the Turk and Jew on the same level with the infidel, boldly asserts: "a belief in the essential truths of Christianity is *the grand foundation of all judicial oaths*," &c., &c. Hence, when the foundation of Christian belief is taken away, the oath is stripped of all its validity." Did the author not feel the blush of shame in his episcopal countenance, when he penned this wholesale slander? Does he really and sincerely believe that no oath but that of a Christian can be held valid? Is he so fanatically uncharitable as to believe that the Mahomedan is not as conscientiously afraid of the words of the Koran (Sure v, 91, ii, 225): "God will punish you for what ye solemnly swear with deliberation," as any Christian with regard to the Third commandment? But this we would tell our author, that his Christianity is not as liberal as the Mahomedan Law, saying: "The oath of an Unbeliever (non-Mahomedan) hath full credibility and validity, as long as he hath made it with an appeal to the name of God.*) And that this law is practically sanctioned, may be seen from the fact, reported by the Newspapers, that a very short time ago a Mussulman of Constantinople was convicted upon the exclusive evidence of Englishmen.—As far as we Jews share in the slander of the Rt. Rev. author, I would ask him the following questions: Has he ever seriously reflected upon the many cases of murders, thefts, divorces, &c., &c., with the reports of which the daily papers, especially of the enlightened New England States, are filled? Has he ever observed how many Jews were among the guilty parties? Has it not forcibly struck him, how seldom a Jew—and the papers always take good care to point out *his* religion—is implicated, and then only in minor offences? Now, considering that we can boast of no City or other Missions, of no Bible Unions, or any other medium of instructing our correligionists in their duties, than our Schools and Synagogues, must he not come to the conclusion, that the Jews' religion must be somewhat divine, when it can make its professors such moral citizens? And must it not be supposed that men, who so conscientiously comply with the sixth, seventh and eighth commandments, will hold the third and ninth equally sacred? Verily! if the excellency of a Religion is to be judged from the moral influence which it exercises over its professors, it is not "Christianity," but Judaism, "which is alone authoritative, because it is alone divine."

Dr. Hopkins must pardon us when we tell him now, that we do not thank him for the expression of his "own deep veneration towards the posterity of Israel," and that we can not, but with some doubt, receive his asseveration. "The honor in which I hold the Jews is most

*) Das Moslemische Recht, aus den Quellen dargestellt von Nicolaus v. Tornauw. Leipzig 1855.

genuine and sincere, for it is a part of my religion." We Jews have long since learned to know what such protections are—sugared pills containing the most deadly poison." The one offered here reminds me most forcibly of the arch-Jesuit of Bavaria, Professor Dr. Dœllinger, who as a member of the Diet, in 1844, voted against the emancipation of the Jews "from mere love for themselves, because he knew that Judaism would die in the embrace of Christianity."

Thus far bigotry, created by religious selfishness and nurtured by sectarian narrowmindness, may lead men in illiberality and fanaticism, and it is the duty of every *good* citizen to upset the evil at its very beginning in this country. The following volume—the first of the kind in the English tongue, with the exception of a few fugitive pamphlets—having undertaken that noble task, I introduce it with joy to the English reading Public of all denominations. For my coreligionists it may be regarded as a well stored armory, whence they can supply themselves with many a strong weapon wherewith to defend their Religion against attacks from without;—my Christian brethren may learn from the following pages, that "Christian" is not altogether synonymous with "perfect," as their preachers and teachers may endeavor to make them believe, and that there is not one great moral truth found in their religious system, which was not, long before the coming of Christ, taught by Judaism in all its wide ramifications. But I would especially request my Christian colleagues, to bestow a careful perusal upon the work of my friend; it will teach them that we do, by no means, find fault with them for preaching and disseminating their Christianity as much as possible; we thank them for their exertions; for they thereby pave the way for the speedier spread of the true knowledge of God, the universal worship of the One in Unity, the God of Israel, and the acceleration of that great day on which "this one will say, I am Jehovah's, and another shall call himself by the name of Jacob, and another again shall with his own hand subscribe unto Jehovah, and surname himself by the name of Israel;" but we must protest against, and shall with all our power endeavor to repel every attempt at infusing their peculiar religious notions into our civil government, as godless, fanatical, blasphemous, and destructive of the very life's principle of our Constitution.

As regards the text of the following translation, the Undersigned would state, that it is only so far his, as it extends over the German original published in the year 1853; all later additions were translated by another, or others. He would further remark, that he is not accountable for typographical errors (which not seldom assume the nature of orthographical blunders), as he could not himself superintend the correction of the proofs, the book being printed in a city far distant from his own place of residence. M. MAYER.

CHARLESTON, S. C., May, (1857) 5617.

AUTHOR'S PREFACE.

THE Revolution which the inquiring mind stirred up, not long since, in the religious domain of German Christendom, and which manifested itself with inspiring enthusiasm, now, under the name of Apostolic-Catholic Christianity, and then, under that of Friends of Light or Free Protestant Congregations, and may be regarded, as it were, as the appearance of Elias before the universal enlightenment, purity of faith and peace, as the fore-runner to a true victory and the realization of the law of reason, the Messianic kingdom of reconciliation and the universal sovereignty of the spirit,—this Revolution shows beyond all doubt, that sound reason makes the most strenuous efforts in the very heart of Europe, to dethrone blind belief, and its vassals, that usurped their power to bury the nations in profound ignorance. A similar phenomenon is perceptible also in our country, the land of free America. The perseverance with which old confessional views are clung to, is but external. For the different religious systems, the forty-three forms, in which Christianity exhibits itself, in this new world, furnish irrefutable proof of the profound interest for truth, and the ardent desire for internal perfection which is perceptible in all phases of society. Nay, we hesitate not to add, that Christianity is rather dissolved in so many forms, because one sect not only disavows, but very often repudiates as objectionable what another holds to be fundamental, so that nothing is left to be believed in, by the calm thinker, after having attentively heard all parties; an internal conflict is thus created, produces a longing for something better, and causes that development of individual reason, together with the general struggle of the spirits of which we have just spoken.

To contribute my share towards the furtherance of these noble efforts, the success of which will be rewarded with the palm of moral perfection and immeasurable blessings, I have undertaken to publish this book. It is true, the consideration that three almost unconquerable captains, antiquated custom, vanity and selfishness, fight the battles of the mighty tyrants, Obscurantism and Fanaticism, might cause us to despair of conciliation and victory; but a glance at both the ancient and modern history of the nations which shows us that they accomplished almost incredible ends in political affairs as soon as they roused themselves, fills us with some hope that they will throw their weight of gigantic power into the balance of the highest spiritual progress also, in their religious affairs; as we see it done already by most of the nations in both the new and the old world. For it is not an all-demolishing sectarian spirit, that now permeates the nations of Europe and America; no! it is their much advanced civilization that acknowledges no other authority than that of reason. Joyfully do I avow this principle, and have proven, beyond all doubt, and cavil,—aside from any remarks upon Christianity,—that Mosaism had reached, long before the appearance of the founder of Christianity, that degree of perfection, which causes the divine nature to permeate man's inward part; wherefore, there is no reason why the moral law of Christianity should presume to be superior to that of its mother, and that the Mosaists have not yet completely fulfilled their mission in the great drama of the history of Mankind; all of which has hitherto been lost sight of in similar works. I have furthermore endeavored to examine and correctly to exhibit, according to the lessons of Holy Writ, and the most ancient and renowned theological authorities, the Doctrine of the Redemption of the world, or the coming of the Messiah, and the ideas concerning the Resurrection of the Dead, or the Day of Judgment. And lastly, as regards national law, I have clearly shown that a rational, republican form of government is recommended, as the best possible one by the Law and the Prophets, and may be attained too, although this is so readily denied in monarchical countries, by proper laws and institutions.

Our time being so propitious, as I have shown above, I hope that this small contribution towards the victory, so important for the whole human race, may not prove a useless task.

I. KALISCH.

התורה מן השמים

INCONTROVERTIBLE PROOFS OF THE DIVINE ORIGIN OF THE LAW OF MOSES AND THE PROPHETS.

All Christian sects, however diverse their dogmas may be, agree in this, that the five books of Moses, and the writings of the Prophets possess the character of an immediate Divine revelation. [1] It is natural, that no controversy could arise on this point, since Jesus, as well as his Apostles, did not only recognize the authenticity and divinity of the old Biblical writings, by frequently quoting and referring to passages therefrom, as being the revealed will of God; but because they express this opinion in unequivocal terms. For instance, (in Luke xvi, 17,) "It is easier for heaven and earth to pass, than one tittle of the Law to fail." Or: (Matth. v, 17,) "Think not, that I am come to destroy the Law, or the Prophets; I am not come to destroy, but to fulfil." And: (Matth. xv, 4,) "For God commanded, saying, Honor thy father and mother; and, He that curseth father and mother, let him die the death." (Vide Exod. xx, 12; xxi, 17.) Furthermore: "Say I these things as a man? Or saith not the Law the same also? For it is written in the Law of Moses, Thou shalt not muzzle the mouth of the ox that treadeth out the corn. Doth God take care for the oxen? Or saith he it altogether for our sakes? For our sakes, no doubt, this is written." (I. Cor. ix, 8—10.) "God, who at sundry times and in divers manners spake in time past unto

[1] See: Forma Concord. epitom. I. and III. Apolog. Art. I. page 92.

the fathers by the Prophets." (Hebr. i, 1.) See also: Acts iv, 24 and 25; xxviii, 25; Hebr. vi, 13, 14.—Hence it might appear to be superfluous, to expatiate upon the credibility of the old Biblical writings; but in an argumentative work, such as the present, I deem it requisite, to produce some rational proofs, that the Lord revealed, by direct communication, a supernatural knowledge of things to Moses and the Prophets.

As regards the Divine mission of Moses, the history of the Creation, as related by him,—even if he did not tell us anything else that is remarkable,—would be sufficient to lead us to the belief, that he was truly a messenger of God. Before, however, entering into a minute elucidation of this my assertion, I would briefly present the views of the greatest modern naturalists, concerning the History of the Creation, as contained in Genesis. In the "Popular Natural History of the three Kingdoms," by T. S. Beudant, Milne Edwards, and A. de Jussieu, we read: (Geogony, page 217,) "But one theory of the creation of the earth deserves our attention; it is found in the first book of Moses, and proves, after more than three thousand years, to be the clearest application of the best founded theories, as well as the most comprehensive compend of geological facts. Indeed, what is there more rational, and even more consonant to the present state of our knowledge,—whenever men aim at bringing order into the universal confusion of things,—than to produce the vehicle, by means of which the phenomena of light, heat, &c., could manifest themselves, and diffuse light everywhere; than to unite the scattered elements, within certain classes, different from each other;—than to create, here and there, certain points of attraction, around which everything revolves, according to an unchangeable law;" &c.—Now, it is this, that we find exhibited in brief expressions, but intelligible to all, in the first verses of Genesis, of course, with less details, than we now could give by our enlarged attainments, &c.

I. Consider well, kind reader, that, after more than

three thousand years, during which mankind have, with giant's strides, advanced in Astronomy, Physics, Mineralogy, Geology, in short, in all natural sciences, even the greatest naturalists acknowledge the words of Moses to be indisputable truths, however often they may have been misconceived. But how was it possible, that nature presented such correct phenomena to Moses? [2] Where has he listened to her lessons in her laboratory? What mortal could, at that time, have communicated to him, that system of the creation of our globe, as he has communicated it to us? Or, how could he have discovered it himself, at that remote period, when the investigations, inquiries and apparatus of later centuries were unknown? Who could or would demand anything of a man, which is beyond the reach of human faculties? *Hence, the Mosaic accounts, with regard to the creation of our Globe, must be of a Divine origin.*

In order to convince the reader of the truth of this our assertion, we shall, after premising some introductory remarks, endeavor to elucidate the first chapter of Genesis.

The Mosaic cosmogony often was, and still is looked upon, by many learned men, as a mere historical myth, as a philosophical poem, or as an explanation of some hieroglyphic. That this, however, is not the case, but that the Mosaic accounts of the creation are true, and were directly revealed to Moses, by God himself, we shall endeavor to prove, by an explanation of the original text, which is confirmed also by the latest discoveries and investigations in natural sciences.

Gen. i, 1. "In the beginning God created the heavens and the earth."

Throughout the first chapter of Genesis "God" is expressed by the term אלהים (Elohim,) because this term signifies the Divine omnipotence, the Source of all Power, the Power of all Powers, which was alone active in the

[2] It is asserted by Th. Paine, and others, that the History of the Creation is not the work of Moses, but of some other person. Considering, however, that in the institution of the Sabbath, (Exod. xx, 11,) which was promulgated by Moses in the Decalogue, reference is made thereto; — considering, that the six periods of the Creation, constitute the first and real foundation of the institution of the Sabbath; it can not be disputed, that the first chapter of Genesis was written by Moses himself.

creation. Whereas, the term יהוה (Jehovah,) which generally occurs in the Bible, and signifies "Providence," [3] could not have been used in this chapter, since no Providence was required to be active, so long as the earth and its laws were not in existence.

Under השמים (Hash-Shamayim, the heavens,) the "Universe" must be understood in this verse. [4] The Creation of the heavens is mentioned before that of "the earth," because numberless worlds, or constellations were created before our solar system, as, also, evidently appears from Job xxxviii, 7 and 8: "When the stars of morning praised me together, and all the superior beings shouted for joy, who shut up the sea with doors, when it came forth, as out of the womb?" I shall explain farther on, what is to be understood by שמים "Heavens," in a more limited acceptation of the term. Here it is merely said, without any further explications, that the Lord is the Creator of the Universe, whereupon, the periods of the formation of our earth, are at once exhibited before us, in general outlines. The reason why the phrase "in the beginning," is made use of, and no certain date is given, is owing to the fact, that *eternity* preceded the Creation of the Universe, which is a necessary accompaniment of the idea of the existence of God; and the "When," of the eternity or infiniteness can not be given.

Periods might have been stated, referring to another previously created solar system; but as such a statement could have merely gratified our curiosity, without being of any other interest whatsoever, it has been omitted.

2. "And the earth was without form, and void; and darkness was upon the face of the deep; and the spirit of God moved upon the face of the waters."

The truth of the contents of this verse, that the earth originally was in an entirely fluid state, has been confirmed by the latest geological investigations. By immediate measurements of meridians, belonging to the same degree of latitude, taken in different parallel lines, it has been proved, that the earth is somewhat flattened

[3] See Exodus, xxxiii, 18, and the Commentary of Sal. Dubno to Exodus iii, 14.
[4] S. Talmud, Tract. Chagiga. fol. 12.

towards the poles. This discovery of the ellipsoidal form of our earth, confirms the assertion, that the matter particles of our earth must have been, at some period, in such a state of mobility, that they would glide above each other, yielding only to the centrifugal power, which was produced by the daily rotation of the earth.

3. "And the Lord said, Let there be light, and it was light."

Under "light," the "substance of light" must here be understood; for this was created before all other things, because without it, nothing could develope itself, or come to perfection, it being the true source of all life.

4. "And the Lord took care of the light, that it was useful, and he divided the light from the darkness."

The usual translation, "And God saw the light, that it was good," is incorrect. For, should God, the Omniscient, not have already known, beforehand, that the light would be good? Whoever considers, that the term, וירא, signifies "to observe," "to take care," "to mind," and, טוב, not only "good," but "beautiful," "useful," must at once perceive the important meaning, and correctness of this verse. The words, "and God divided the light from the darkness," assert not, that God separated the light from the darkness — for this would be an absurdity; but they mean to say, that a rotation of our solar system around the newly created *light matter* was then begun, and the mutations of day and night thereby produced.

This idea becomes still more apparent to us, when we remember, that day and night now originate, because our earth, while revolving around its axis, is either turned to, or away from the sun, which could not have been the case at that period, since the relation of our earth, to the sun was only established on the fourth day, — especially, also, since the words of the 5th verse, *And it was evening and it was morning the first day*, find their explanation solely in our interpretation, just set forth.

It is impossible, however, to determine, whether the period of the rotation of the earth around its axis, then lasted twenty-four hours, or a hundred, or a thousand, or ten thousand years, (which latter idea is maintained by naturalists;) for the term יום, "day," frequently signifies "period," as we should, at all events, render it in our passage; hence, יום אחד, means not, "the first day," but "the first period," "the first epoch," — יום שני, "the second period," &c., &c.

6. "And God said, There shall be an expansion in the midst of the waters, so that there may be a division between waters and waters."

7. "And God made an expansion, so that it divided between the waters which are under the expansion, and the waters which are above the expansion."

Simple as the History of the Creation of the second epoch is presented to us, its meaning is still very obscure.

Already, the ingenious and clear-thinking *Nachmanides* (רמבן, Ramban,) said, concerning this passage, in his commentary on the Bible: "Expect not from me, that I should tell you anything respecting this; for it belongs to the profound mysteries of the Law, especially since the Scriptures express themselves very briefly on this point."

The explanation of Moses Mendelsohn, that "by the upper waters, the clouds are designated; — by the lower waters, the waters upon the earth, and by רקיע, (*Rakia*,) the clear sky is meant," I can not but declare to be incorrect, however much I admire this world-renowned philosopher; and although he believes his explanation to be quite simple and intelligible. For, as verse 7 says not "he divided between the waters which are on the earth, and between the waters which are above the earth," but "between the waters which are under the expansion, and the waters which are above the expansion," it is clear, that רקיע does not convey the idea of an empty space, free from vapors, which is between the clouds and the earth.

Before, however, I give my own exposition, which is in accordance with the results of the physical sciences, I deem it necessary, to premise a few remarks.

In ancient times the heavens were considered to be a solid vault, in which the stars were fastened; and in order to account for the different movements of the various heavenly bodies, the existence of several celestial globes or spheres, one lying above the other, was assumed; hence the nations of antiquity had three different spaces of the Universe: 1, The heaven, which was looked upon as the habitation of God, the righteous, and the pure spirits; 2, The earth, or the upper world, as the dwelling place of the living; and 3, The netherworld, as the abode of the departed. (Elysium, Earth, and Hades.)

Concerning the idea, which our ancestors entertained of *heaven*, the Rabbins do not agree. Rabbi Yehudah asserts, (Tract. *Chagiga*, sect. ii,) that there are two different heavens; 1, one, in which the constellations are found, and 2, the other, which is elevated above everything that is impure, being filled with the purest light, and constituting the abode of the angels and all the saints. The former is simply designated as שמים, "the heaven," and the other as שמי שמים, "the heaven of heavens."

Resh Lakish, (ibid,) entertained the opinion, that there were seven different heavens, to wit: וילון or גלגל, רקיע, שחקים, זבול, מעון, מכון and ערבות, Vilon or Galgal, Rakia, Shechakim, Zebul, Maon, Machon, and Araboth; the seventh heaven is said to be filled with the sources of life, peace and bliss; the souls of the pious; the spiritual dew, wherewith the dead shall be revived, and the world regenerated; the Seraphim and myriads of angels; and above all, the throne of majesty of the Most High.

These Talmudical views were based neither on tradition, nor on grounds of reason, but upon very arbitrary deductions. It was concluded that, as we find in the Bible, שמים, "heavens," and שמי שמים, "heaven of heavens," (which after all conveys only an idea of "the height and the greatest height,") or because *seven terms are used* to express the idea of "heaven," there must be, therefore, *two*, or even *seven* heavens in existence. How incorrect such a conclusion is, may be perceived from the fact, that the Bible often applies different names to the same thing. Thus for instance, the soul is expressed by five different terms: נפש, רוח, נשמה יחידה, חיה yet we know, that man has not five souls, but only one, which, to say nothing of psychological grounds, is clearly proved by Genesis ii, 7, saying: ויפח באפיו נשמת חיים, "And He breathed in his nostrils a living soul."

However paradoxical such views of the term *heaven* may appear to us, in our day, they were quite plausible at that time, when the system of Aristotle was still venerated and generally believed in: "Space is the utmost quiescent limit of heaven which touches the moving body, or the first immoveable limit of the surrounding ether. Heaven is the most comprehensive perfection, a Divine body, indestructible, subject to no changes or diminution, hence of a more noble nature than sublunary bodies." This Aristotelian system, however, was not countenanced by the greatest number of the Rabbins, as we read in Midrash Bereshith Rabbah: "Rabbi Simeon, son of Yochai, said: We know not whether the stars are fixed on a wheel, (an immoveable, ethereal substance,) or whether they float in space." So, also, we read in *Talmud Pesachim*, fol. 95: "The sages of the Gentiles say, that the heaven, being an ethereal substance, moves, and the planets are fixed therein; but the wise men of Israel assert, that the heaven is an immoveable space, in which the planets move." This system of the Jewish teachers is, according to an assertion of Maimonides in *Moreh Nebuchim*, a tradition, derived from the Prophets. At the present day, we know from incontrovertible evidence, that this most ancient cosmological system of the Jews, which teaches, that the heaven is nothing but *space*, in which innumerable suns and planets, and amongst them also our earth, are moving, is true and correct. For, since astronomers have, through the telescope, observed many stars, calculated their distances from each other, and discovered, among other things, that notwithstanding a ray of light travels seventy thousand leagues in a second, it would, nevertheless, take a thousand years before the light of many stars, which are visible through the telescope, could reach the earth, on account of their immense distance: it is evident that the apparent vault of heaven is but an optical illusion.

And, although, the space which we call heaven, is *blue*, it is not owing to the real existence of such a blue substance, but to the fact, that every ray of light consists of 7, or rather 3 prime-colors, to wit: red, yellow, and blue; and as the light is refracted by the atmosphere, in a manner that, when the sky is free from vapor, the red and yellow colors are absorbed, the blue is reflected. If this were not the case, everything except the sun itself, would appear perfectly dark, even by day-light. When, however, the atmosphere is filled with vapors, all the prime-colors are reflected, hence the whitish color becomes visible. By the expression, *heaven*, we can therefore understand nothing else, than a more blissful and perfect condition in another world, in which the souls of the pious will once obtain their rewards. Whence also the very correct expression of our ancient Rabbins, עולם הבא, "the future world," to designate the blissfulness of the souls, or the paradise. By the expression, "God dwells in heaven," therefore, nothing else is meant, than that God fills the whole space, to all infinity, and that He alone is the Governor and Sustainer of the Universe.

This is, also, strikingly expressed in Psalm LXVIII, 5: [5] "Sing to God, sing praises to His name; extol Him who passeth along through the plains of the ether," that is, through the endless space. The expression ערבות is most happily employed here, not however, as some erroneously supposed, to indicate "pleasantness," "ely-

[5] In the common version v. 4.

sium," or "heavenly dwelling," from ערב, "to be pleasant," but "the immense extent," "the infinite expanse," from ערבה, "the desert." It thus teaches us, that God is the vivifying medium of innumerable worlds, existing in the immeasurable space, and governs all things in their respective courses, as a rider manages his horse.

In order, now, fully to illustrate the verses above quoted, (Gen. i, 6, 7,) I have to add only some few remarks, derived from physical sciences. Vapor consists, as it is well known, of small globules of water, which have in themselves the capacity of rising, not that the atmosphere produces this vaporization, but according to a law of nature prescribed by the Creator; which is evident from the fact, that vaporization proceeds more rapidly in a vacuum. Rain, therefore, is produced, when the vapors, or globules of water, separate themselves, in large numbers, from the atmosphere which has taken them up, touch each other, and flow together; in consequence of which, and owing to their being specifically heavier than the air, they fall in drops.

The air, which flows around our earth, like an ocean, and is likewise called atmosphere, is the scene of manifold changes; it is the laboratory of nature, being a compound of fluids, consisting of vapors, electricity, magnetism, and other imponderabilities. This atmosphere is evidently meant by the term שמים, "heaven," as is indicated also in the Talmud, Tract. Chagiga, Sect. ii, (fol. 12, a,) במתניתא תנא שמים אש ומים מלמד שהביאן הקב"ה ופרבן זה בזה וכו'. "It was taught in the Mishnah, that *heaven*, is called שמים, *Shamayim*, because it consists of *fire*, אש, *Esh*, and *Water*, מים, *Mayim*, which God mingled together, and made the expansion therefrom. The height of heaven, or atmosphere, can not be determined. Although 15,700 feet is the greatest elevation of our earth, where the heat of our atmosphere ceases, and the region commences, where the sun can no more produce any warmth, we can not, nevertheless, determine how far the vapory atmosphere of our earth extends. [6] Astronomers assert and prove, that each planet has an atmosphere like our earth; they, furthermore, maintain, that most of the planets which belong to our solar system, consist of continents and seas. This, for instance, is the case with Mars, which, when viewed through the telescope, presents continents and seas, the former having a reddish, and the latter a greenish appearançe. Besides, it has been incontestably proved, in our day that the tides are produced by the attraction of the moon. Water, therefore, has the greatest tendency to rise, when it lies under the zone of the moon's course. The limit between the atmospheres of the various planets, without encroaching upon each other, is called רקיע השמים, "the expansion of heaven."

By the term, מים מעל לרקיע, "the waters above the expansion," the upper waters, the atmospheres of the other planets are here meant, and by the words, "the waters which are under the expansion," or the lower waters, the atmosphere of our own earth is to be understood.

The meaning conveyed by the verse, "And the Lord divided between the upper and the lower waters," is, therefore, this: That the Lord ordained a law of nature, according to which the various atmospheres might touch each other, without, however, commingling together, kept asunder, as it were by an expansion or a barrier. And, since this law of nature is alike necessary for the existence of our earth and the other planets, the expression, "And the Lord took care, that it was good," is not found here, as in the other epochs, lest it might have been applied to our earth alone, the formation of which is narrated here, whereas it is applicable to all planets. Nor is there any contradiction between the History of Creation of the second, and that of the first period, of which it is said: "In the beginning God

[6] It follows from the phenomena of the twilight, that the atmosphere in a hight of nearly ten geopraphical miles is still dense enough to reflect the light of the sun.

created the heavens and the earth;" for under the term "heavens," שמים, in verse 1, is understood, as I have remarked already, the whole space of the Universe, with its innumerable suns and planets; while שמים, "heavens," as it is used in a more limited sense, in the passage relating to the second period, signifies only the atmosphere and the relation of the earth to the sun.—These ideas seem to be conveyed also in Chagiga, Sect. ii, p. 15 a: מעשה ברבי יהושע בן חנניה שהיה עומד על גב המעלה בהר הבית וראהו בן זומא ולא עמד מפניו אמר לו מאין ולאין בן זומא אמר לו צופה הייתי בין מים העליונים למים התחתונים ואין בין זה לזה אלא שלש אצבעות בלבד.—It is told, that Rabbi Joshua, son of Chananiah, once stood on the top of the temple-mount at Jerusalem, and, perceiving Ben Soma, who sat there, without rising from his seat, to pay him the usual respect, addressed him thus: "Why, Ben Soma, art thou so proud to-day, and what does so engage thy attention, as to disregard me?" To which Ben Soma answered: "I am engaged in an important business: I investigated the distance between the upper and the lower waters, and found, that it is but three fingers wide." רב אחי בר יעקב אומר כמלא נימא Rab Achai, son of Jacob, said: "Only the breadth of a hair." But the Rabbins assert, that there is no distance at all between the upper and the lower waters, but where the one terminates, the other begins.

It appears to me, that the Rabbins meant to convey, in these words, the incontrovertible truth, that the atmospheres of the various planets of our solar system, as I stated above, touch each other without commingling. This will also explain the words, used in the history of the deluge: "And the sluices of heaven were opened;" which means to say, that the upper atmosphere sent water to the lower atmosphere, the separation being then suspended, in consequence of which the whole earth could be covered with water. This hypothesis, I believe, is the key to the Biblical history of the deluge; yet, this is not the place, to expatiate further on this subject.

9. "And the Lord said: Let the waters under the heavens be gathered together unto one place, that the dry land may become visible; and it was so."

The truth of this statement, that the earth existed, from the first period of Creation, in a perfectly fluid state, has been confirmed, by the most recent geological investigations. (See above v. 2.)

10. "God called the dry land Earth, and the gathering together of the waters He called Seas, and God took care that it was good."

All commentators propound the question, why the mass of water, in its great collectiveness, is termed ימים, "Seas," in plural, and not ים, "Sea," in singular, as we find it in Gen. i, 26, Ps. xcv, 5, and in other passages.

Nobody has as yet given a satisfactory explanation on this point.

But, according to my view, the plural form, ימים, "Seas," has been properly used in this passage, both with regard to Grammar and Geology. The grammatical reason is, that fixed magnitudes are often designated, in the Hebrew, by the plural form; viz. שמים, "Heavens," במות, "High places," &c. So also we read in Ezekiel, xxviii, 2: בלב ימים, "in the heart of the *seas*," instead of בלב ים, "in the heart of the *sea*."—The geological ground is this: The various processes of boring, instituted for the purpose of building Artesian wells, have caused the discovery of streams and an immense mass of waters in the depths of the earth. It is, therefore, probable, that under the term ימים, "seas," as used in the third period of the Creation, the subterranean waters must be understood, which are also called in the Scriptures, תהום תהומות, "the deep," "the depths," and תהום רבה, "the immense deep." (Gen. vii, 11.)

11. "And God said: Let the earth bring forth grass, herbs yielding seed, fruit trees yielding fruit after their kind, in which its seed is upon the earth; and it was so."

The attentive reader will, undoubtedly, while reading this verse, be unable to withhold this question: "How could the plants germinate, the warming beams of the sun not having been created before the fourth period?" It is true, we might assume, that the matter of light created already in the first period, and around which the rotation of our earth took place, promoted the growth of the plants; but how could they thrive in light without heat? But, for this, also, the latest geological investigations afford us the solution.

Observations teach us, that in the interior of the earth, the influence of the seasons is perceptible only at a very moderate depth, where the heat begins to increase in the same proportion that we descend farther; and it has been shown, that the heat increases One Degree, (of Reaumur) with every thirty-three metres of depth.

The warmth of the earth, or central heat, which kept the earth in a perfectly fluid state at the period of the Creation, as is still the case in the centre of the earth, and which is proved by the volcanic eruptions, and the existence of warm and hot springs, produced, before the surface of the earth had cooled down to the present degree of temperature, a peculiar temperature, when there were no climates, but when a vapor-atmosphere surrounded our earth, which enabled the vegetation to progress. Thus, vegetable remains of various tropical plants, rooted fast in their original places, have been found in the island of Portland, in England. The same is seen in the collieries of Europe, even in the regions which are at present the coldest. All this proves, that the temperature was at some period alike everywhere; and this time was evidently the third period of the Creation, as it is described in this passage of the Bible, when the plants were kept alive as in a hot house.

14. "And God said: There shall be lights in the expanse of the heaven, to distinguish between day and night, that they may be as signs, for seasons, days, and years."

Under the term מארות, "light," nothing else is to be understood, as I remarked above, than that God now imparted the *matter of light*, which He had created already in the first period, to the sun, in order that its rays may not alone immediately illumine and warm our earth, but that those rays also, which the moon receives, may be reflected upon our globe.

The fourth period does by no means comprise the creation of the stars, but of a luminous fluid around the sun, which reaches us also through the medium of the moon, a fact which is also corroborated by the latest discoveries of astronomers, according to which the sun is a dark body, enveloped in an atmosphere of light. Hence, sun and moon are called lights, not with regard to what they are in themselves, but to what they are for us. The 17th verse should not, therefore, be translated, as it has been erroneously done heretofore, "And the Lord *placed* them in the expanse of the heaven, to give light upon the earth," but: "destined them, in the expanse of heaven, to give light upon the earth," for נתן, (natan,) followed by a ל, means: "to destine something for a particular purpose."

16. "...... and the lesser light to rule by night, and the stars."

Under כוכבים, "stars," only the planets which belong to our solar system must be understood; for as it says: "to rule by night," which evidently refers to every night, it can not possibly mean the innumerable luminous bodies in our firmament, because their light, — although light is the most rapid matter, — can not reach us, in consequence of its immense distance, as astronomers teach us, before three, nay that of the telescopic stars, not before thousand years. And suppose even, that the light of the most distant worlds, has a periodical influence upon our earth, this influence can nevertheless not be so great, as to be meant by the expression, "to rule by night," since, as ALEXANDER VON HUMBOLDT, well observes: "The light of the moon, nay that of the remotest worlds, produces changes in man no less, than in the delicate structure of the flower; but, when a thousand more powerful forces influence us at the same time, the effect of the weaker is set at naught." The correct translation of כוכבים, is, therefore, *planets*.

Verses 20—29 describe the development of animal life, in which sensation, instinct, intelligence and will, are gradually combined, in various proportions with the phenomenon of mere existence. First, we meet with the creeping animals, *Gastrozoa*, שרץ, then with the articulated, *Arthrozoa*, עוף, (as Rashi also properly remarks: "such as flies,") and lastly, with *Osteozoa*, which are denoted 1, as תנינים, *whales*, and *fishes*, in general; 2, as חיה הרמשת, *amphibia;* 3, as עוף כנף, *birds*; and 4, as בהמה וגו׳, *Mammalia*. The highest degree of the fifth and sixth periods of the Creation is embodied in *Man*, he being the immediate work of the Creator, and the image of God. As regards the expression, "in the image of God," Sirach supposes, (xvii, 1—8,) that it designates the power of Man, to rule over all creatures on the earth. This, however, would explain only the expression, "in the image of God," and the words, "in His likeness," would appear to be quite superfluous, a tautology, altogether discordant with the brevity, exhibited in the History of the Creation. Now, it may be asserted, that, notwithstanding this brevity, a *pleonasm* is to be found in almost every line, to wit, that the word, אלהים, "God," occurs thirty-five times in thirty-four verses, which might have been easily avoided; hence, the phraseology used in the History of the Creation should not be so scrupulously scanned. To this, I would reply, that such a refutation is quite superficial; for at a time, when nothing was too low or too high, to be worshipped by mankind as something Divine; at the time, when the whole Universe was supposed to be filled with various Divine beings, it was most imperatively necessary, to counteract this error, by a constant and emphatical repetition of the truth, at every period of the Creation, that there was, and is but *One* Highest Cause, which called every thing into existence. The words in the Book of Wisdom, ii, 23, *Deus enim creaverat hominem ad conditionem incorruptam, et imaginem ipsissimae naturae suae fecerat eum*, seem to convey the idea, that the passage, "in our image, in our likeness," means to say: that man was originally not destined to die; an explanation which is also incorrect. For, man, having become mortal and corruptible, after his so called fall, it was quite improper to use, in Gen. v, 1—3, and ix, 6, the expressions, צלם and דמות אלהים, "the image, the likeness of God," as conveying the idea of incorruptibleness. Besides, this explanation of the Book of Wisdom, militates against the opinion of the Talmud, as *Midrash Rabbah* remarks on Gen. i, 31: "And God took care, that it served the best purpose," טוב מאד, "this is *death*," that is to say, it was God's purpose, that all earthly creatures should be subject to decay. The Talmud, therefore, entertained the opinion, that the first human pair were also created mortal. Should, however, the objection be made, that according to Gen. ii, 17, and iii, 3 and 4, man, originally being created immortal, had rendered himself mortal by his sin, and that, therefore, the opinion of the Talmud must be rejected, I should reply, that Gen. ii, 17, does not mean: "on the day thou eatest thereof thou shalt die,"—but indicates, according to a well-known Hebraism, the early occurrence of a fact; here, therefore, the early occurrence of his death. Hence, the threat means this: "At the time thou eatest of the tree, thou shalt die early;" which was actually the case, since men were no longer permitted to eat of the tree of life, the fruits of which could prolong their lives, if not for ever, at least for many years; for לעלם does not convey the idea of eternity, but of a long time. From Gen. iii, 19, we may especially conclude, that death is not to be looked upon as a punishment, but as a necessary consequence of the nature of the human body. My view, therefore, is this: "in our image" means the psychological, "in our likeness," the moral, and "have dominion," the political freedom, all of which are the offsprings of an all-enlightening reason, given to man as his property here on earth. This pre-eminence makes man the ruler over, and the ideal of perfection of all earthly creatures. The expression, "we will make man," is a *pluralis majestatis*, often used by kings. (Ezra iv, 18, and vii, 24.) This mode of speaking is made use of also in modern languages, in instances of this kind, and no less employed also in addressing single persons, as in German *Sie* and *Ihr*, in French *vous*, in English *you*, &c.

The phrase טוב מאד, "exceedingly suitable," in i, 31, is the Hebrew Superlative, and is applied only in the sixth period of the Creation; for this reason, because it is applicable exclusively to the summing up of the whole Creation on earth, when all things were linked together and followed each other as necessary cause and effect. For, a continual progress from an incomplete to a better state,—from the better to the more perfect,—and from the more to the most perfect, reigning throughout the infinite varieties of creatures: the utmost perfection could have been attained only, in the combination of things, where the highest and the lowest, and the most distant extremes are bound together by one common tie.

Having thus at length shown, that the History of the Creation, whether we view it from an astronomical, physical or geological point, is correct, we add, only, that the "Sabbath," day of rest, constitutes the seventh epoch, teaching us, that God ceased to produce direct creations, and now works only indirectly through the medium of the laws of nature, which He sanctified, that is to say, made immutable for all eternity. This Divine day of rest, therefore, will last as long as our solar system remains unchanged.

I repeat, that a man who, although unacquainted with the theories and facts, the instruments and apparatuses of later centuries, could build a system, which still must be regarded as a perfect one, was utterly unable to do so from mere human suppositions; but solely by means of a particularly wonderful and higher inspiration.

II. In Levit. xi, 4 and 5, and Deut. xiv, 5 and 7, it is said, that there are among all quadrupeds four classes, three of which have one common sign of cleanness, [7] and the fourth class, the other. [8] But, how could Moses know, that there are but these four classes of animals throughout our globe? [9] Might not perhaps a fifth class yet be found, which bears both signs of cleanness? Still, up to our day it has not been discovered.

III. The destinies of Israel have been carried out in history, precisely as they were foretold in the Law.

IV. The Mosaic Law contains such a perfect system of morals and doctrines of civil and political institutions, so thoroughly in accordance with the law of nature, as they could not have been communicated to Moses, [10] in that time of profound darkness, by any man, nor invented by him. It constitutes a harmonious edifice, containing no doctrines whatsoever, which contradict each other. For, although some contradictions may be found with regard to several historical and chronological dates, the *law* of revelation is free from all incongruities; the law may entirely satisfy the moral wants of mankind, for the sake of which, revelation was requisite. I will make mention only of the eternally memorable Ten Com-

[7] Rumination. [8] Cloven feet.

[9] See גַן נעול, Part I, Sect. 7, ch. 7, by Hartwig Wessely; also the Book Siphri Parshat Reeh.

[10] See Herder's "The Spirit of Hebrew Poetry," vol. i, pages 349, and following.

mandments, which have actually been adopted by all civilized nations, and the fundamental doctrines with regard to our duties towards our fellow-men: "And thou shalt love thy neighbor as thyself;" (Levit. xix, 18,) "As the native born shall be the stranger who dwells among you; and thou shalt love him as thyself." (ibid. 19,) "When thou seest the ox or the ass of thine enemy going astray, thou must endeavor to restore it to him; when thou seest the ass of thy enemy lying under his burden, do not withdraw thyself but help him." (Exodus xxiii, 4 and 5.) "In a cause the majority of impartial men must decide," &c. (ibid. 3.) — There were public proceedings in judicial matters, conducted by judges, who were elected by the people. (Deuter. xvi, 18, and xvii, 9.) The Prophet Samuel, filled with the spirit of Moses, inveighed, therefore, against absolute monarchy, representing it as a glittering slavery. (I. Sam. viii, 11, 19.)

V. The Jewish Prophets have proved themselves God-inspired men by this fact, that they did not, like the heathen oracles, foretell future events, in obscure and ambiguous speeches, but predicted coming occurrences, which no human reason could presuppose, with such clear and distinct words, and so recorded them with their own hands in their still well preserved works, as they really took place in later times.

Although the Divinity of these writings, as I have already remarked above, is acknowledged also by all Christendom, they nevertheless call them *The* OLD *Testament*, while they assign to the Gospels, added by the founders of Christianity, the name of *The* NEW *Testament*. Before we enter upon a contemplation of the contents and mutual bearing of both these two religious systems, let us maturely inquire, whether the titles "Old Testament," and "New Testament" are properly applied to these works. The common appellation, "Bible," or "Holy Writ," as assigned to both the Mosaic and Christian doctrines, induces us to conclude, that neither surpasses the other by importance, authority, or significancy. This opinion, however, the Apostle Paul seems not to have entertained. He designates (Hebr. viii, 8 and 15,) the doctrine of his Master with the *New*, and that of Moses and the Prophets with the *Old* Testament, founding it upon Jerem. xxxi, 31, where we read as follows: הנה ימים באים נאם יהוה וכרתי את בית ישראל ואת בית יהודה ברית חדשה, which Paul translates thus: "Behold, the days come, saith the Lord, that I will make a new covenant with the House of Israel, and with the House of Judah." I said, Paul translates ברית, with "Testament," for that he understood by the Greek term *Diatheke*, its original meaning, "last will," and not in the sense as it is used by later Latin writers, for instance *Irenaeus*, is irresistibly evident from Hebr. ix, 16 and 17, where we read: "For where a Testament is, there must also, of necessity, be the death of the testator," &c. To which he says: (ibid. viii, 13,) "By saying a new, he hath made the first old. But that which decayeth and waxeth old is ready to vanish away."

Every one acquainted with the subject, will raise the question: Is the term "New Testament" a correct translation of ברית חדשה? since ברית means only: *foedus*, covenant, contract; whereas the phrase "to make a testament," or "last will," is always expressed by צוה על, or....צוה ל. Nay, the words כרת ברית correspond entirely with the Latin phrase: *foedus icere;* and, as little as these words can be translated with "to make a testament," so contrary is it to the use and spirit of the Hebrew language, to make it the translation of כרת ברית. The apostle, however, made use of this incorrect translation, and desired to attribute to the Hebrew word ברית, the collateral idea of the analogous Greek term *Diatheke*, "contract, covenant, testament," which it never has, for this reason; because he could make use of it for the sake of his system, without exposing himself to a charge of having given a false interpretation. For, whoever does not compare the Hebrew original with the Greek version, is unable to discover the inaccuracy of the Apostle's interpretation. The original name of the Mosaic system is תורה, "Law," (Deut. xxxi, 9 and 24,) or תורת משה, "The Law of Moses," (Joshua viii, 31; Mal. iii, 22, &c.) and Paul's Master himself called the Holy Torah: "The Law." (Matth. v, 17, 18; Luke xvi, 16.) It is called ספר הברית, "The Book of the Covenant," only inasmuch as it contains the Ten Commandments, which comprise the very essence and chief-contents of the covenant. According to Paul's version, therefore, Jeremiah could not have said, וכרתי but וכתבתי or ונתתי nor ברית, but תורהחדשה or ספר ברית חדשה. Besides, Paul's conclusion, that "that which decayeth and waxeth old is ready to vanish away," is likewise entirely incorrect, considering, that this assertion is made with reference to Divine truths. Only earthly things can corrode, and become destroyed by the tooth of time, but the spirit and its productions are eternally young and vigorous.

And should any one say: "This true, Supreme Intelligence revealed the Mosaic Law, as the best possible for a nation of slaves, for a people that still lay in the cradle of infancy, (Gal. iv, 3,) but this law lost its power and had achieved its purpose, when mankind began to enter upon a more mature age, and had, therefore, to yield its place to a better dispensation,"—we would answer: this view, though again and again urged, is repudiated by the following considerations:

1. It was not a nation of slaves, but a free and independent people, grown up under the superintendence of Moses, that were called upon to obey his law; for the generation of slaves, which came from Egypt perished entirely in the desert.

2. The Mosaic dispensation contains the sublimest, purest, and clearest ideas of God and Virtue, which, as we intend to prove by this our work, were not rendered more perfect in the Christian dispensation, but often

even deprived of their lustre. Nay, the latter was not even suitable for the childhood of the heathens, (see No. 4 below,) in the department of Theology.

3. It can be irrefutably proved from the Writings of the Prophets, to whose predictions reference is constantly made in the New Testament, that the Lord will not reject that nation, cherished with so much grace, and prepared to higher knowledge, together with the law given to them. Thus it is said in Is. liv, 10: "Mountains may move, and hills fall down; but my grace shall not depart from thee, and the covenant of my peace shall not be dissolved, saith the Eternal, who hath mercy on thee." Or: (ibid. lix, 21,) "And as regardeth myself, this shall be my covenant with them, saith the Lord: my spirit which resteth upon thee, and my word which I have put in thy mouth, they shall not depart out of thy mouth, and out of the mouth of thy children, nor of the mouth of thy children's children, saith the Lord, from now unto eternity."—Furthermore, in Ps. cxix, 152: "As regardeth Thy testimonies, I have known of old, that Thou hast founded them for ever."

Again, in Jeremiah xxxi, 35 and 36: "Thus saith the Lord, who giveth the Sun for a light by day, and the ordinances of the moon and of the stars for a light by night; who stirreth up the Sea that the waves thereof roar, He whose name is the Lord of hosts: If those ordinances depart from before me, saith the Lord, then the seed of Israel shall cease from being a nation before me for ever."

See also Isaiah lx, 22.

4. Is it the demoralized Greeks, or the effeminate Romans, or the then savage Germans, that were the nations, which constituted the more mature portion of mankind, and for whom the Mosaic law, and the lessons of the Prophets with regard to morals and the knowledge of God, were no longer sufficient? How absurd is it, to assert, that the Israelitish nation which was trained, through forty years, for a higher knowledge of God,

was unable to comprehend that which the most demoralized Roman and the inhabitants of the German forests, could have understood in an instant, as though they had at once become ripe for it. Yet, history teaches us, that, for the most part, violence, the sword, the rudest barbarity on one side, and the most childish simplicity on the other, paved the way for Christianity among the heathens. Thus, for instance, we see that the Emperor Constantinus ordered the heathenish Temples to be closed, and prohibited sacrifices. The Emperor Theodosius banished all heathen scholars from Alexandria. Charles Martel and Charlemagne wore a victorious but gory sword for the conversion of the heathens. What a beautiful maturity!

And should some say, "be this as it may, Christianity has produced the most beneficial results, and caused the re-birth of mankind, all of which no other religion could have effected,"—we would reply, that this assertion was no less a wilful disregard of all historical facts, and a blind submission to preconceived views and opinions. For after being made, in the third century, by the Emperor Constantine, the ruling Religion of the Roman empire, it was not only unable to deliver the Romans from their moral depravity, but checked, on the contrary, by the increased development of its hierarchical power, every real progress in spiritual and moral cultivation, down to the fifteenth century. Or, should the ordeals, the funeral piles, the tortures of inquisition, and whatever other shackles were forged, with the view of pinioning the human mind in darkness and ignorance constitute the truly appropriate institutions for the cultivation of the human race? Or should you call this a progress, that the very Christian Spaniards once butchered, in the most outrageous manner, in this our country, forty millions of men, who had done them no harm whatever, expelled and plundered the rest, and violently took possession of their lands and houses? Surely not!

Although it can not be denied that Christianity exercised, in general, some influence over the civilization in Europe, yet, this advantage has been ten times countervailed by the injuries which it produced during many centuries, through mutual intolerance and religious persecutions—the belief in witches and witchcraft, and the trials resulting from this belief—through the sale of indulgences, through anathemas and excommunications, and a spiritless form of worship, which it imposed upon the nations, although it militates against the outward piety of Pharisees.

Since that time only, when the ancient Greek philosophy revived in Italy, and kindled the light of reason, a new dawn of civilization and enlightenment broke upon Europe; and then only the bold spirit of noble men awoke for the attainment and establishment of freedom of belief and conscience, and a higher moral maturity, and strove, incessantly, for the highest possible civilization.

5. Christ himself declared the Law of Moses to be eternal and unchangeable, even to its most minute tittles. For he teaches: (Matth. v, 19,) "Whosoever, therefore, shall break one of these least commandments, and shall teach men so, he shall be called the least in the kingdom of heaven," &c. By "commandments" he did not only understand the laws of nature and morality, but also the ceremonies; this is satisfactorily shown by the parallel passages in Matthew, as justly observed, in the "Fragments of an Unknown," edited by Lessing. "These ought ye to have done, and not to leave the other undone." (Matth. xxiii, 23.) Here we are shown, beyond all doubt, that not even the least tittle of the Mosaic ceremonial law should be violated.—Again, ib. xxiii. 2 and 3. "The Scribes and the Pharisees sit in Moses' seat. All, therefore, whatsoever they bid you observe, that observe and do; but do not ye after their works; for they say, and do not." Christ, therefore, only rebukes the hypocrisy of his contemporaries, and complains

of this, that they placed the observance of ceremonies above that of the moral laws; but he means not to abrogate, in the least, the Law of Moses, as he himself taught it also by his conduct. He made the pilgrimage to Jerusalem, on the great festivals, according to the injunctions of the Mosaic Law, and fulfilled all the requirement of the Divine worship. He caused the Paschal lamb to be prepared for himself and his disciples, and ate of it amidst the customary thanksgivings and songs of praise; and, lastly, he commanded the leper, (Matthew viii, 2—5,) to show himself to the priest, after he had become healed, and bring the sacrifice ordained by Moses. If the Apostles, therefore, abrogated both the great and smaller precepts, the tittles as well as the larger passages in the Law of Moses, they certainly acted against the command of their Master, and would have exposed themselves to his indignation and severe rebukes, had he been still alive.

As regards the interpretation of the phrase ברית חדשה, however, it is given by the Prophet himself, in the following verse: "For this shall be the covenant, which I will make with the House of Israel after these days, saith the Lord: I will place my law in their inward parts, and upon their heart will I write it. And I will be their God, and they shall be my people." (Jerem. xxxi, 33.) It is here evidently announced only, that the Jews would no longer give themselves up to idolatry; and this prediction has really been accomplished. After their return from Babylon, although they were addicted to many vices, they nevertheless never went so far astray, as to become rebellious to the truly One God.

Having so far shown, in general outlines, that the view of Paul and of modern Christendom, that the New Testament has abrogated the Mosaic Law, is without any foundation whatever, nay even anti-Christian: we shall not only prove this, in detail, by contrasting all the doctrines of the Mosaic and Christian Bible, but show, moreover, that Christianity contains not a single truth, which was not most distinctly and satisfactorily taught, at a far earlier period, in the Mosaic dispensation.

THE GOSPEL OF MATTHEW.

"Already in the most ancient times," says Dr. Bretschneider, [11] doubts were raised, with regard to the genuineness of the first two chapters of Matthew; and these doubts have, as yet, not been so refuted, as to build anything certain, upon their foundation." De Wette, (Biblical Dogmatics, page 270,) Wegscheider, (page 226,) the truth-loving and acute critic David Strauss, (Life of Jesus, vol. I. p. 211,) De Wette, (Brief Explanation of the Gospel of Matth., pages 15 and 20,) and many other theologians, disputed, with good reasons, the genuineness of the genealogy of Christ, as given by Matthew and Luke, and maintained, that it was but a myth. Others observe, that the same myth was known among the Chinese, with regard to the supernatural birth of their *Fohi*, and among the Indians and others, with regard to their *Buddha* or *Sakia muni*. Hence, it might appear to be unnecessary to comment on the first two chapters of Matthew; yet, for sake of completeness, I will add my remarks on these also.

[11] See his Manual of the Dogmatics of the Evangelical-Lutheran Church.

CHAPTER I.

1. The Book of Generation, &c.

25. "And Salmon begot Booz of Rachab; and Booz begot Obed of Ruth; and Obed begot Jesse."

Unlikely as is the combination of the learned Enb Saba or Pethayah, that Joshua should have married Rachab, (Megillah 14, c. 2,) we assert, that equally untrue is the relation of our genealogist, according to which Rachab was the wife of Salmon; since men, like Joshua or Salma, would never have acted against the Mosaic Law, which says: "Thou shalt not intermarry with them; thy daughter shalt thou not give to his son; and his daughter shalt thou not take for thy son." (Deut. vii, 3.)

8. "And Asia begot Josaphat; and Josaphat begot Joram; and Joram begot Ozias."

Three links of the genealogical chain, to wit: Ahaziah, Joas, and Amaziah, are here omitted. (First Kings viii, 25; ib. xiv, 13, and I. Chron. iii, 11.) It is true, that men often find in the genealogies of the old Testament, one or more links left out, for the sake of brevity, or on account of their unimportance, in which case we can not translate the term בן with "filius," "son," but "proles," descendant. For instance, in Ezra vii, 3, we find six links left out between Azariah and Meraioth; and yet, it is said there: בן עזריה, "the *son* of Azariah," and בן מריות, "the son of Meraioth;" and again ib. v, 1: בר עדוא, "the *son* of Iddo," instead of בן ברכיה בן עדו, "the son of Berachiah, the son of Iddo," according to Zech. i, 1.

Even when the term הוליד occurs, it can not always be exclusively translated by "he begot," but conveys, especially when one or more links are omitted, the idea of: "he had for descendant." For instance, I. Chronicle vi, 12: ואחיטוב הוליד את צדוק, can not be rendered by: "And Ahitub begot Zadok," but by: "Ahitub had Zadok for descendant;" for the latter was his grand-son, and son of Meraioth, as may be seen from I. Chron. ix, 11, whose name is left out in our passage for the sake of brevity. So also we see, that (ib. ii, 11—13,) the term הוליד means nothing else than "had for descendant," namely, "Nahshan had for descendant, Salma; Salma, Booz; Booz, Obed, but Obed begot Jesse. For, since, already, in the times of Abraham, it was considered impossible, that a centenarian should have a child, (Gen. xvii, 17,) how can it be at all probable, that at a much later period, when the duration of human life scarcely ever exceeded one hundred years, there should, nevertheless, have been four [12] generations, each of whom begat children at the age of a hundred years? It is evident that some links are omitted here, on account of their unimportance. We can not, therefore, accuse the ancient Bible historian of having made a mistake, since the error lies exclusively in our misunderstanding—in our faulty translation of the word הוליד, by "genuit," "he begat." This, however, can not be urged in defence of our genealogist, since in verse 17, he sums up, as David Strauss correctly observes, and lets us know, unequivocally, that he means to omit not a single link in his genealogy. We are fully justified, therefore, in holding him to a strict accountability.

11. "And Josias begot Jechonias and his brethren, about the time they were carried away to Babylon."

One link is omitted here; for Josiah begot Jehoiakim, whose son was Jechoniah. (See II. Kings xxiii, 34, and xxiv, 6.) It appears, furthermore, clearly, from I. Chronicles iii, 16, that Jechoniah had no brothers. Our author, however, was misled to his error, as also long

[12] The remark of Aben Ezra in his commentary on *Ruth* that there are five links, if we include Nahshan, creates some historical difficulties.

after him, Dr. M. Luther, in his translation of the Bible, and De Wette, in our own time, in his commentary on Matthew, page 11, by taking the term אחיו, (II. Chronicles xxxvi, 10,) in the sense of "Frater," "brother," instead of "cognatus," "relative." But that אחיו in this passage is to be understood as "relative," "uncle," is evident from II. Kings xxiv, 17, where it is said: "And the King of Babel put in the place of Jechoniah, Mathaniah his uncle, as king, and gave him the name Zedekiah."

12. "And after they were brought to Babylon, Jechonias begot Salathiel; and Salathiel begot Zerubabel."

Again a link is wanting; for Salathiel begot Pedaiah whose son was Zerubabel. (I. Chron. iii, 17—19.) And although we read in Haggai i, 1, and Ezra v, 2: זרובבל בן שאלתיאל, Zerubabel son of Shealthiel, it is no support for our author; since, as we have already stated above, to verse 8, בן means often "proles," "descendant," as is the case, also, in this passage, not only according to the opinion of the oldest commentators, but especially as clearly proven from I. Chron. iii, 17—19.

13. "And Zerubabel begot Abiud; and Abiud begot Eliakim, and Eliakim begot Azor."

No mention is made in the Books of Chronicles of an Abiud, hence he is no historical person. On the contrary, it is recorded that Zerubabel begot Meshullam and Hananiah.

17. "So all the generations from Abraham to David are fourteen generations; and from David until the carrying away into Babylon are fourteen generations; and from the carrying away into Babylon unto Christ are fourteen generations."

Although, when resorting to historical records, we can find only fourteen names from Abraham to David, we must, nevertheless, come to the conclusion, as may be seen from our remarks on verse 8, that there must have been more than fourteen links. How much the pen of our historiographer was guided by arbitrary rule, is especially shown by his enumeration of the members of the later lines, where he omits several historical characters, as though they had not existed.

18. "Now the birth of Christ was on this wise: When as his mother Mary was espoused to Joseph, before they came together, she was found with child of the Holy Ghost."

In reading this verse attentively, we find ourselves, even in our time, placed in the situation of Faustus the Manichaean, and can not but ask the question: If it be true, that the Holy Ghost, and not Joseph, was the father of Christ, how could the Apostle prove his descent from David, by the regular descent from David to Joseph, the husband of Mary? Was not Joseph merely his foster-father, without being related to him in any way, whatever? But to judge from this gross contradiction, [13] in which our author happens to be with himself, it appears to us more than probable, that Matthew, ever supposing the first two chapters to be genuine, represented the genealogy of Christ in a most natural way, and not as the text now reads, from verse 18—25. This hypothesis becomes even certainty, when we reflect, that *Cerinthus*, a teacher of the time of the Apostles, who, according to Epiphanius, acknowledged only the Gospel of Matthew, regarded Christ as nothing else than the son of Joseph and Mary, born in the natural way; and that *Carpocrates*, and a party of the Ebionites maintained the same opinion.

22. "Now all this was done, that it might be fulfilled which was spoken of the Lord by the Prophets saying,

23. Behold, a virgin shall be with child, and shall bring forth a son, and they shall call his name Emmanuel, which being interpreted is, God with us."

From the introductory words of the verse quoted: "Therefore, will the Lord Himself give you a sign; behold this young woman is with child," &c., it is

[13] This contradiction is by no means solved by the assertion of some theologians that Mary descended from the House of David; for if this had been the case, Matthew and Luke would have given the genealogy of Mary, and not that of Joseph, who is alleged not to have been the father of Christ; especially Luke, who distinctly records such circumstances; as he, for instance, remarks (—i, 15,—) that Elizabeth was of the daughters of Aaron, would certainly not have passed in silence over the Davidean descent of Mary. The passage in Luke i, 36: "And behold! thy cousin Elizabeth," proves nothing; for Syggenes does not determine, whether the relationship was on the father's or mother's side; and should even the latter be supposed, it would then be an entirely groundless assumption, to assert that Elizabeth's mother was a descendant of David.

evident, that the Prophet, in no-wise, prophesied of Christ, but speaks of and to his contemporaries, and gave a sign to the faltering Ahaz together with the House of David, with the view of confirming the promise of deliverance. This opinion is corroborated also by the fact that the Prophet continues, (Isaiah vii, 16,) "For before yet the child (i. e. Emmanuel) shall know to refuse the evil, and to choose the good, shall the land of which thou hast dread, (Syria, and the land of the ten tribes of Israel,) be forsaken of its two kings," which prophesy can certainly not be applied to the time in which Christ lived. Nor did this prophesy of Isaiah, with reference to the two aforesaid kings, eventuate to the contrary, as Thomas Paine asserts in his examination of the Gospel of Matthew, but was literally fulfilled.

II. Chron. xxviii, 6, informs us of the war, which the King of Israel carried on alone against Judah, and in which Ahaz suffered a terrible defeat.

On the other hand, the prophesy of Isaiah refers to the alliance made at a later time between the Kings of Israel and Syria, who marched as far as the capital of Judah; when it was released through the assistance lent by the King of Assyria to King Ahaz. (See II. Kings xvi, 9.)

CHAPTER II.

2. "Where is he that is born King of the Jews? For we have seen his star in the East, and are come to worship him."

We know at the present day how to value the system of Astrology, and need remark but this, that this fiction, according to which Oriental Astrologers were induced to conclude from the appearance of a star, upon the birth of a Jewish Messiah, is based upon Numbers xxiv, 17. But we are compelled to consign the history of the birth of Christ into the domain of fiction, chiefly for this reason, that it is represented in an entirely varying and contradicting manner, in the Gospels arbitrarily canonized.[14] Without mentioning the manifest contradictions, which any one who compares the genealogies of Christ, according to Matthew and Luke, with each other, will discover, I will merely remark, that Matthew places the birth of Christ in the time of Herod, when Joseph with his wife and newborn child fled to Egypt, and returned only after Herod's death, during the reign of Archelaus, and settled in Nazareth; whereas Luke i, 26 tells us, that Joseph and Mary dwelt in Nazareth, and, in consequence of a taxation ordered by the Emperor Augustus — the first ever imposed on Palestine — went over to Bethlehem, where Mary gave birth to her first son. Now, it is settled by history, [15] that Herod obtained, under the reign of Augustus, a remission of the tribute to be paid to Rome, and that the first taxation mentioned by Luke only took place after the banishment of Archelaus to *Vienne* in Gaul, when Judæa was placed under the government of Procurators, appointed, with the sanction of the Emperor of Rome, by the governors of Syria. Hence, Christ must have been born several years later than stated by Matthew, whose reports, therefore, must be regarded as mere fictions.

Some might rejoin, that Luke was no Apostle; hence, if a contradiction be discovered between his writings and those of Matthew, the statements of the latter must be adopted. To this we answer, that the testimonies of the most ancient Christian Church place both on one level. For *Irenaeus adv. haer.* iii, 1, says: *Et Lucas, sectator Pauli, quod ab illo praedicabatur Evangelium, in libro condidit;* and *Eusebius histor. eccles.* iii, 24, affirms that Paul had read and approved the Gospel of Luke; and tells us in another place, that John, when the elders of

[14] I say: the arbitrarily canonized Gospels; for there were a great many written reports afloat of the birth and life of Christ, which many held to be true, as: *Evangelium de nativitate Mariae; Evangelium infantiae; Evangelium Thomae; Evangelium secundum Hebraeos sive Ebionitas, &c., &c.* But in the second century a collection was made of those writings which were arbitrarily declared to be apostolic, while others were alike arbitrarily rejected as spurious and interpolated.

[15] See "Universe History for Enlightened Readers," by K. H. L. Poelitz, vol. ii., page 29; Leipzig, 1825.—History of the Jews, by P. Beer, pages 4 and 55; Prague, 1831.

Ephesus laid the Gospels of Matthew, Mark and Luke before him, declared them to be deserving confidence, and true. To whom then should we accord credence, with regard to the History of Christ's birth, when the accounts thereof so greatly contradict each other, even with regard to the chief points? Although men who could and should have known all the circumstances of that event, approved those accounts, no rational man can, by such testimony, be convinced of its truth; but is compelled to conclude, that those men did not deem it necessary to establish the truth, but were willing to receive even the most curious and absurd fables, as long as they could thereby win the people over to their system.

5. "And they said unto him, In Bethlehem of Judæa: for thus it is written by the Prophet,

6. And thou Bethlehem, in the Land of Juda, art not the least among the Princes of Juda; for out of thee shall come a Governor, that shall rule my People Israel." (Michah v, 2.)

Reading the following verse in the Prophet cited, we must be convinced that the preceding one also could not have any reference to Christ. For we read: לכן יתנם עד עת יולדה ילדה ויתר אחיו ישובון על בני ישראל, *Idcirco exponet quidem eos usque ad tempus, quo parturiens pepererit; quum residuum fratrum ejus revertentur cum Israelitis.* "Surely, he will surrender them only until the time that she who travaileth hath brought forth; and then shall the remnant of his brethren return with the children of Israel." This prophesy conveys nothing else than, as the whole contest shews, that the ruler who is to spring out of the tribe of Judah, should carry back the Jews, dispersed in foreign countries, especially in Babylon and Assyria. And, granted even, that this prophesy referred to a future Messiah, who was to appear in Israel, the passage quoted can certainly not be applied to Christ. For, it is said in verse 3 and 4, "that" this governor shall rule the children of Israel in a manner as would enable them to dwell securely, &c.; whereas Christ has neither politically nor spiritually procured rest and peace to the Jews; hence Michah can not have meant him.

15. "And was there until the death of Herod; that it might be fulfilled which was spoken of the Lord by the Prophet, saying, Out of Egypt have I called my Son." (Hosea xi, 1.)

The Prophet Hosea relates the benefits which God bestowed upon Israel, hence can not have made even the least reference to Christ, in the verse cited. One needs but read the whole verse, and every unprejudiced person will coincide in my opinion. It reads literally thus: "When Israel was yet young, then I loved him, and out of Egypt did I call my son."

If words so clear are purposely perverted, we easily conceive that a most inventive exegesis is presented to us, which, in its turn, will afford us a measure of comparison to estimate therewith the whole account of the author.

16. "Then Herod, when he saw that he was mocked of the wise men, was exceeding wroth, and sent forth, and slew all the children that were in Bethlehem, and in all the coasts thereof, from two years old and under, according to the time which he had diligently inquired of the wise men."

This narrative is not historical, nor even mentioned by Luke. The desire and anxiety to draw a parallel between Christ and Moses, induced the author to invent for the latter, a fate similar to that of the former. As of all infant boys, whom Pharaoh ordered to be drowned, Moses alone was saved, so does our author represent Christ as being the only one saved of those children, whom his imagination had slain by order of Herod.

17. "Then was fulfilled that which was spoken by Jeremy the Prophet, saying,

18. In Rama was there a voice heard, lamentation and weeping, and great mourning, Rachel weeping for her children, and would not be comforted, for they are not."

It is exceedingly incorrect, on the part of our author, to interpret this verse (Jeremiah xxxi, 15,) with reference to the slaughter of the children of Bethlehem, ordered, as he alleges, by Herod; for the children of Bethlehem were descendants of Leah, whereas it is said in the verse cited: "*Rachel* weeping for her children." Hence, we perceive from this verse, as well as the whole context, that the Prophet speaks of the tribe of Benjamin, which was carried into captivity. (Compare also Jerem. xxxi, 16.)

I repeat again, that we judge from all these points what sort of historians we have before us.

19. "But when Herod was dead, behold, an angel of the Lord appeareth in a dream to Joseph in Egypt,

20. Saying: Arise, and take the young child and his mother, and go into the Land of Israel: for they are dead which sought the young child's life."

This is only an imitation of Exod. iv, 19. "And the Lord said unto Moses in Midian: Go and return into Egypt; for all the men are dead which sought thy life," and contains merely a poetical fiction. This statement, however, I will distinctly substantiate by the illustration of the following verses, which read:

21. "And he arose, and took the young child and his mother, and came into the Land of Israel.

22. But when he heard that Archelaus did reign in Judea, in the room of his father Herod, he was afraid to go thither: notwithstanding, being warned of God in a dream, he turned aside into the parts of Galilee."

The attentive reader will find that the second vision in a dream contradicts the first one. For, as we read in verses 19 and 20: "But when Herod was dead.... Go into the Land of Israel," &c.; the last expression must have reference to the whole Land of Israel, and, consequently, Judea also. Besides it is said verse 20: "For they are all dead," &c., which words be so understood, that Herod and his party had died, and there was none left, who would seek to take the child's life.

Now it is related in verse 22, that Joseph, being warned by a vision in a dream to return thither, retired into the district of Galilee; hence, if according to this narrative it was very dangerous for Joseph and his family to reside in Judea, all those who would seek to take the child's life, were not dead.

How is it possible for any reasonable man to think that God, the eternal providence, having committed an error in the first vision, was, therefore, compelled to appear in a second vision to correct His mistake? We must, therefore, come to the conclusion, that there is not a shadow of historical truth, and that the visions related in these verses happened only in the imagination of our historiographer. Indeed, it seems to me, that the author, having endeavored to find for his narrative some old-biblical grounds, composed facts similar in style and contents to those which are related in the old Bible.

Thus are the two visions and the manner of speaking in them, taken from Genesis xii, 1, "When God called Abraham out of his fatherland, he said to him: Get thee out of thy country.... unto a land that I will show thee," without distinctly telling him whither he should go, and the Lord appeared then again, and gave him the necessary explanation, (Ibid. verse 7,) "Unto thy seed I will give this land."

23. "And he came and dwelt in a city, called Nazareth: that it might be fulfilled which was spoken by the Prophets, He shall be called a Nazarene."

There is no passage to be found in any of the Prophets, which says that the Messiah shall be called a "Nazarene." For the term נזיר, *Nezir*, "the alienated one," in Deuter. xxxiii, 16, which we suppose is here alluded to, refers to Joseph, of whom Moses makes distinct mention in the same verse. Or should Is. xi, 1, perhaps be alluded to? But this verse speaks of a God-fearing and wise hero of the House of David, who would procure internal and external peace for the land, but not of a Messiah. And even admitted that Isaiah referred to the Messiah of the Jews, the poetical term נצר, *Netzer*, "shoot,"—which, moreover, is used, ibid. xiv, 19, to denote "the insignificant," "the common,"—can in no wise have alluded to Christ; since nothing of all that is indicated by the context of the whole chapter, and especially verses 10—12, can be interpreted as applying to his age.

On the contrary, the Messiah shall be called, צמח, "Zemach," according to Zechariah iii, 8; vi, 12, and יהוה צדקנו, "Jehovah Tsidkenoo," according to Jeremiah xxiii, 6; or as tradition tells us: "Shiloh," "Yinnon," "David," "Tsamach," "Tsadek," "Menachem," and "Chaninah." That the Messiah should be called "Jeshuah," or "Jesus," is nowhere said.

CHAPTER III.

1. "In those days came John the Baptist, preaching in the wilderness of Judea,
2. And saying, Repent ye: for the kingdom of heaven is at hand."

This phrase is an imitation of the words of Isaiah lvi, 6, where we read: "Thus hath said the Lord, Keep ye justice, and do equity, for near is my salvation to come, and my righteousness to be revealed." The terms, "Keep ye justice, and do equity," are comprised in the Greek word *Metanoeite*, which is analogous to the Hebrew היטיבו דרכיכם, "Improve your ways." The meaning of this announcement, which is also put into the mouth of Christ, in iv, 17, is, as we may easily deduce from his own and his cousin John's words and teachings, that the people should become completely righteous through the suppression of the evil, and a thorough amendment of the spirit, and thus prepare themselves for the reception of a Messiah who would soon appear, and whose kingdom should speedily commence. Now, we may take this kingdom to have been meant in a worldly or in a spiritual sense; it did not take place in either sense.

For, as a temporal Redeemer, for whom the Jews at that period ardently hoped, Christ ought to have delivered them from the yoke of the Romans, restored joy and peace in the land, governed as a great king, and not have died so miserable a death, to leave his brethren in such deep, political debasement. And as a suffering, spiritual Messiah, he ought not to have despairingly uttered, in the hour of death, the words: (Matth. xxvii, 46,)

Eli, Eli, lama sabachtani! [16] since it is said that he came to this world merely to die in such agonies. Indeed, it would appear from his cry of anguish, that, whatever may have been substantiated by his life and teachings, his sufferings and death were against his will and intention; nay! that he himself, perceived in his last moments, that his intention to rid the Jews of their political oppression and make himself their ruler, had signally failed. But, that the supposition of Christ's spiritual Messiahship is especially erroneous and fictitious, is evident from this fact, that he himself announces in unequivocal terms, (Matth. xxiv, 30—34,) and all the Apostles and first Christians really believed it, (see, besides, other passages, especially I. Thessalonians iv. 17,) that even his contemporaries would live to see him come in all his glory, to his kingdom with the purpose of rewarding the Righteous, whereas, kind reader, mark this well, he has, up to this day, not returned, and all evils and vices, among mankind, remain in their usual course.

In order, however, to arrive at a just appreciation of the alleged deeds of Christ, and the views and ideas of the Jews entertained on the subject, I deem it necessary to give a true and faithful sketch of the doctrine of the kingdom of heaven [17] or that of the Messiah, as it is taught by the Prophets. With regard to the Messianic time we read in Isaiah liv, 8: "In the violence of wrath did I hide my face for a moment; but with everlasting

[16] The entire passage, from which the above is cited, reads thus: "And about the ninth hour Jesus cried with a loud voice saying, "Eli," &c. Now *anaboan fone megale* is analogous to the Hebrew צעק or זעק צעקה גדולה, which phrase is exclusively used to convey the idea of "bewailing," "lamenting," &c., but never that of "praying." Matthew, therefore, when wishing to convey the last idea, uses the term *proseuchestai*, (vi, 5, 6 and 9;—xxvi, 36 and 39.) Hence, the assertion of some theologians, that Christ employed Psalm xxii as prayer, without attaching any particular weight to the words quoted, is against the explicit report of the Evangelist. Moreover, as he cried with such a loud voice, whereas he himself had taught, (chapter vi, 5 and 6,) that this was not the right mode of praying, he could not have prayed, but must have expressed his last feelings from the depth of his heart, which, for this very reason, deserves our respect, in a well known verse from the Psalms.

[17] The term "kingdom of heaven," is derived, as many theologians maintain, from Daniel vii, 17, &c. I opine, it is taken from Obadiah i, 21: והיתה ליהוה המלוכה, "and the kingdom shall be the Lord's;" for, during the second Temple, the term מלכות יהוה was expressed by מלכות שמים as ירא שמים "fear of heaven" was used for ירא יהוה "fear of the Lord."

kindness will I have mercy on thee; saith thy Redeemer, the Lord." Further ibid. lx, 19 and 20: "The sun shall not be unto thee any more for a light by day, and for brightness shall the moon not give light unto thee; but the Lord will be unto thee for a light of everlasting, and ended shall be the days of thy mourning."

We read in the Midrash, on Ps. cvii, verse 2: יאמרו גאולי יהוה וכן ישעיה אמר (ל׳ י׳) ופדויי יהוה ישובון ולא פדויי אליהו ולא פדויי מלך המשיח אלא ופדויי יהוה, &c. "Let those say whom the Lord hath redeemed," and so also says Isaiah: 'And the ransomed of the Lord shall return,' and not: 'The ransomed of Elijah,' nor 'The ransomed of the King Messiah,' but 'The ransomed of the Lord;' which proves, that God will, without any mediator, redeem Israel, and establish the kingdom of heaven on earth." For the same reason do we find in Talmud Sanhedrin, fol. 98, the significant phrase: אין משיח לישראל, "Israel has no Messiah," [18] which means that the Israelites should not expect in the Messiah, a visible ruler, or a man commissioned to make the world happy; but the complete supremacy of godliness on earth; wherefore, we also pray on the Sabbath, which is the symbol of eternal happiness, יום שכלו שבת, "The day which is all rest," as follows: אפס בלתך גואלנו לימות המשיח ומי דומה לך מושיענו לתחית המתים, "There is none beside Thee, O our Redeemer, in the days of the Messiah, and there is none like Thee, O our Savior, at the revival of the dead."

This doctrine is already expounded also in Pesachim,

[18] Even so explained Rashi. He says: שחזקיה. היה משיח ועליו נאמרו כל חנבואות. אצמיח קרן לבני ישראל (יחזקאל כ׳ט כא) ועמד ורעה בעז יהוה מיכה ח׳ ג׳, "For Hezekiah was the Messiah, and to him do all the prophesies refer: 'I shall cause a horn unto the children of Israel,' &c. (Hez. xxix, 21,) 'And he shall stand forward, and feed on the strength of the Lord,' &c. (Michah v, 3.) And adds to the words, "Israel has no Messiah," אלא הק׳ב׳ח ימלך בעצמו ויגאלם לבדו. "For the Holy One, blessed be His name, will govern supremely, and alone redeem them." (Transl.)

fol. 3, where we read: והיה יהוה למלך על כל הארץ ביום ההוא יהיה יהוה אחד ושמו אחד (זכריה י״ד ט׳) אטו האידנא לאו אחד הוא אמר ר׳ יוחנן לא כעולם הזה העולם הבא העולם הזה על בשורות טובות אומר ברוך הטוב והמטיב ועל שמועות רעות אומר ברוך דיין האמת אבל לעולם הבא כל אחד ואחד אומר ברוך הטוב והמטיב, "Then shall the Lord be king over all the earth; on that day shall the Lord be One, and His name One." (Zech. xiv, 9.) "But is He then not now One?" said Rabbi Jochanan: "the future world—that of the Messiah—will not be like the present; in this world we say, for happy events, 'Blessed be He who is good, and doeth good,' and for evil occurrences, 'Blessed be the righteous Judge;' but in the future world every one shall say only this benediction: 'Blessed be He who is good and doeth good;' that is to say, since every thing will be spiritual, and no sin will any more be committed, the מדת הדין, "Judicial Power," will no longer be exercised."

In close connection with this, is the following passage from Talmud Succah, fol. 51, דר״ש ר׳ יהודה בר אלעי לעתיד לבוא מביא הק״בה ליצר הרע ושחטו, "Rabbi Jehudah, son of Elaee, taught: 'At the time of the Messiah, the Holy One, blessed be His name, will bring in the evil inclination, and destroy it;' this means, He will make every thing spiritual."

Again we read in Moed Katon, towards the end: אבל לעתיד לבוא הוא אומר בלע המות לנצח ומחה אדני יהוה דמעה מעל כל פנים וג׳ (ישעיה כ״ה ח׳) "But when the Messiah shall have come, then will be verified the prophecy: 'He will destroy death for ever, and the Lord shall wipe away the tear from every face,' (Isaiah xxv, 8.)" But that by the phrase לעתיד לבוא, "the future," the time of the Messiah is to be understood, may be clearly perceived, besides other passages, from Talmud, Tract. Rosh Hashanah, section i, where we read: ר' יהושע אומר בניסן נגאלו ובניסן עתידין להגאל לילה המשומר לעתיד לבוא, Rabbi Joshua said: "They were redeemed in Nissan, and in Nissan they will be redeemed on some future day, in a night which is preserved *Leathid labo.*" Again, in Tract. Edioth, Sect. ii, Mishnah 10, we read: משפט גוג ומגוג לעתיד לבוא שנים עשר חד'ש, "The judgment over Gog and Magog *Leathid labo* (at the time of the Messiah) will last twelve months."

According to the views presented here, which are derived from the highest and most distinguished Talmudical authorities, all embellishments with regard to the Messianic time, must be taken merely in a figurative sense. Thus it is taught in the Talmud, (see Jalkut, &c.) "All the prayers, all the sacrifices will be abolished at the time of the Messiah; for when all is but of a spiritual character, no law will be any longer applicable; an opinion which was adopted also by Rabbi Jacob Tam, ("Baal Hatosaphot,") the commentator of the Talmud, who says, in his book "Sepher Hayashar," page 28: "There will be a mighty preference for the time of the Messiah to that of the redemption from Egypt. In the time of the Messiah all bodily appetites will have ceased to exist, in consequence of which, and because the means for the preservation of life will no longer be needed, mankind will no more die, but be like angels."

The Messianic time is also called in the Talmud: עולם הבא, "the future world," as we see from Tract. Berachoth, where we read as follows: למען תזכור את יום צאתך מארץ מצרים ימי חייך הימים כל ימי חייך הלילות וחכמים אומרים ימי חייך העולם הזה (כל ימי חייך. להביא לימות המשיח), "In order that thou mayest remember the day on which thou wentest forth from Egypt, all the days of thy life. Our sages say, 'the days of thy life,' refers to the days in this world, whereas the superfluous 'all' alludes to the days of the Messiah." Now, if the time of the Messiah is contrasted with "this world," it can imply only the future world.

The Talmud looks even upon the "Olam Haba," and the "Thecheyath Hametim," (Resurrection of the Dead,) as one and the same thing. This we see from Tract. Chullin, fol. 142, and Kiddushin, fol. 39, where we read: "Rabbi Jacob Ben Eleazar taught: there is no law in the Bible with which reward is mentioned, unless the resurrection of the dead can be deduced therefrom. For instance, the fifth commandment concludes with "In order that their days may be long, and it may go well with thee;" and the law with regard to the taking of birds' nests ends, "In order that it may be well with thee, and thou live long." But how will it be, says he, if a father orders his son to bring him a pair of young pigeons, and the son, in obedience to his father's command, goes, sends away the mother, and takes only the young ones, but in descending from the loft falls and dies: when, then, can he obtain the reward spoken of in the Bible? Why, the meaning is this, that "it will be well with thee," in a world of bliss, "and thou live long," in a world that endureth for ever.—Furthermore, we find in Tract. Baba Kamma, fol. 54, the following explanation: "The long life and all the good promised as a reward for the honoring of parents, are not only confined to this world, but extend to the future." This opinion, that the future world will commence only with the resurrection of the dead, may be clearly deduced from the First Mishnah in Sanhedrin, where we read: "And those will not be partakers of the future world, who say that the Bible does not teach the resurrection of the dead." To this we find in Bereita, fol. 90, the following remark: "He denies the resurrection of the dead, therefore, will he take no part in it; for the Lord pays according to the principle of measure for measure," that is: to return like for like. It is evident that here עולם הבא, "the future world," is identical with תחיית המתים, "the resurrection of the dead." As to the state of the dead during the interval between death and resurrection, our ancient teachers have left but mystical allusions. The pious enter Paradise, גן עדן, and the wicked go to Hell, גיהנם. With regard to the duration of the time of punishment various opinions are advanced in Talmud, Tract. Edioth. According to one, it lasts a twelvemonth, while another limits it to the time between Passover and Pentecost, when they shall be purified.

Let none object, that we read in Tract. Berachoth, fol. 34, 6, and Pesachim, fol. 68; "Samuel asserts, 'there is no other difference between the time of Messiah and this world, than this, that political oppression will cease 'to exist;' and that Maimonides believed in the restoration of the Jewish commonwealth in Palestine, and made it even an article of faith." For these are individual opinions, contradicted, as we have already remarked, by the most ancient teachers and expounders of the Law, and can not, therefore, be taken into account.

The chief reasons then, why Christ was not regarded by the learned of his time, and the Jews of the present day, as the Messiah, are the following:

1. Because no earthly, but only a spiritual redemption of all mankind is expected of the Messiah, so that after his time there will be no more sin, nor any disposition to sin; that is to say, our planetary system will be regenerated, and everything changed to a spiritual state. (Isaiah, lxv, 17.)

2. Because it is hoped, that at the time of the Messiah, not only some dead will rise from their graves, but all that sleep in the dust; and that, since all earthly things will cease to exist, Death itself will exist no more, but heavenly bliss and eternal salvation reign

everywhere; hence, the true heavenly kingdom, מלכות שמים, will commence.

Now, as both these conditions have not been realized, the opinion, that the time of the Messiah has already past, must be rejected.

3. "For this is he that was spoken of by the Prophet Essaias, saying, the voice of one crying in the wilderness, Prepare ye the way of the Lord, make his path straight."

If the version of our Evangelist were correct, that במדבר conveyed a qualification of קול קורא, the words קול קורא במדבר must, according to the principles of accentuation, the most ancient and best commentaries on the Hebrew language, be necessarily accentuated with *Mahpach*, *Pashta* and *Zakef Katon*. But as they are accentuated with *Munach*, *Zakef Katon* and *Zakef Gadol*, and as, according to a well known rule, the first of two distinctive accents, that succeed each other, is separable, the verse must be divided off in this manner: קול קורא | במדבר פנו דרך יהוה | ישרו בערבה מסלה לאלהינו. The word קול is the subject of the sentence, and קורא (the part. pres. standing in the place of the present tense,) is its predicate, and במדבר, the defining object of פנו דרך, and is the parallel of בערבה, in the following part of the verse. Hence we must translate: "A voice calls: 'Prepare ye in the wilderness the way of the Lord, make level in the desert a path to our Lord.'"

This version founded upon traditional accents is supported, also, by the following logical reasons:

1. The word בערבה would be entirely superfluous according to the version of the Evangelist,—indeed, he has left it out;—nor can it be imagined that Isaiah, that exemplary orator, should have introduced such an unmeaning pleonasm into his speech.

2. He continues in verse 6, קול אומר קרא ואמר מה אקרא, "The voice said: Preach! but he said: What shall I preach?" If then the phrase קול קורא in verse 3,

were to be translated, "the voice of a preacher," the word ואמר in verse 6, would either not be explained at all, or only in a very subtle manner.

From all this it is evident, that the verse quoted from Is. xl, 3, is incorrectly cited and translated. The Prophet Isaiah, after predicting, in chapter xxxix, to King Hezekiah the Babylonish captivity, comforts again, in chapter xl, the people, by announcing to them that, when the time shall be completed, and their sins forgiven, even the most impassable roads should be turned into the most lively highways, upon which the people should again go up to Jerusalem, there to worship their God. Not the least allusion is made to a precursor of the Messiah. Let my readers look at the chapter and form their own conclusions.

4. "And the same John had his raiment of camels hair, and a leathern girdle about his loins; and his meat was locusts and wild honey."

It is true, the raiment described here was like that of Elijah; but the garment does not make the man.

5. "Then went out to him Jerusalem and all Judea, and all the region round about Jordan;

6. And were baptized of him in Jordan, confessing their sins."

The immersion or bathing of the whole body, as a means of purification, before the accomplishment of a holy act, or the confession of sins repented of, was customary among the Jews, and in accordance with the Law of Moses, (Levit. viii, 6, &c.,) and was consequently as a holy lustration—no new ceremony introduced by John. But infant-baptism, as introduced through the teachings of Augustine, and which has consisted, since the thirteenth century among the Roman Catholics, and still consists in the Evangelical Church, in a mere sprinkling of the head with water, is, as must appear from what we have just said, a surreptitious ceremony, adopted contrary to the spirit of Christ and his disciples. The Anabaptistes and Mennites have indeed recognized this fact; but their opinion, although it is the correct one, has not been generally assented to.

8. "Bring forth therefore fruits meet for repentance:
9. And think not within yourselves, We have Abraham to our father: for I say unto you, that God is able of these stones to raise up children unto Abraham."

That a mere natural descent does not authorize any one to be proud of the merits of his ancestors, is taught already by Isaiah lxiii, 16: "For Thou alone art our father; for Abraham knoweth nothing of us, and Israel recognizeth us not: Thou, O Lord, art our father; our Redeemer, from everlasting is Thy name." Again in Psalms xxxix, 13: "A stranger am I with Thee, a sojourner, like all my fathers." But, more clearly we see this expressed in Ezekiel xviii, 4, where we read: "Behold! all the souls are mine; as the soul of the father, so also the soul of the son, mine are they: the soul which sinneth that alone shall die." In the very same spirit, the commentators of the Bible remark: (Midrash Tehillim to Ps. xlix, verse 3, &c., גם כספם,) "Let no one say, My father was righteous, and I shall be saved through his merit; my father was pious, and I shall succeed on his account: but let every one remember, that Abraham could not save his son Ishmael, nor Jacob, his brother Esau." "It is this very thing," continues the Midrash, "that the Psalmist means to teach us, saying, (xlix, 8,) A brother can not redeem his brother," &c. So also we find in Tract. Sanhedrin, fol. 38, a: "God created but one pair, and not more at the same time, for this reason, that there should be no pride of ancestry, and that no family should be able to charge another with being of inferior descent."

10. "And now also the axe is laid unto the root of the trees; therefore, every tree which bringeth not forth good fruit is hewn down, and cast into the fire."

This verse is an imitation of Isaiah x, 33 and 34: "Behold the Lord, the Eternal of hosts will lop off the fruitful bough with terrific might: and those of towering growth shall be hewn down, and the high shall be made low. And he will cut down the thickets of the forests with iron," &c. And, ibid. lxv, 8: "Thus saith the Lord, As the new wine is found in the cluster of grapes, and one saith, Destroy it not, for a blessing is in it: so will I do for the sake of my servants, that I will not destroy the whole."

12. "Whose fan is in his hand, and he will thoroughly purge his floor, and gather his wheat into the garner; but he will burn up the chaff with unquenchable fire."

The phrases used here, are taken from Jeremiah xv, 7: "And I winnow them with a fan in the gates of the land;" and Isaiah xlvii, 14: "Behold! they are become as stubble, the fire burneth them; they can not deliver their life from the flame; for there shall not be a coal to warm at," &c.

14. "But John forbade him, saying, I have need to be baptized by thee, and comest thou to me?"

The compliment which John pays here, and continually afterwards, to his cousin, the latter repays him tenfold. He says of him, (Matth. xi, 11,) "Verily I say unto you, Among them that are born of women, there hath not risen a greater than John the Baptist." Both understood well how to raise each other in the estimation of the people.

15. "——— Suffer it to be so now: for thus it becometh us, to fulfil all righteousness. Then he suffered him."

Since Christ now deemed it necessary, for the fulfilment of righteousness, that is for his perfection, to be baptized by John, it is evident that he did not regard himself as immaculate, but as sinful as all other men are.

16. "———and lo! the heavens were opened unto him, and he saw the spirit of God descending like a dove, and lighting upon him:

17. And lo, a voice from heaven, saying, This is my beloved Son, in whom I am well pleased."

This opening of the heavens, which is said to have been made manifest to John, was evidently contrived to give the whole a more imposing effect, and is an imitation of Ezekiel i, 1: "As I was in the midst of the exiles by the river Kebar, that the heavens were opened, and I saw Divine visions." But even the picture of the dove, representing the holy spirit which is said to have descended upon Christ, is by no means the fruit of his own imagination, but taken from Genesis xv, 9 and 10, where it is related, that the Patriarch Abraham did not cut up the doves, which he had sacrificed by the command of God, as he did with the other animals; which, as the Talmud teaches us, meant to show, that the holy spirit, that is, Divine truth and goodness, should remain undivided with his descendants.

This fiction of John originated, as Grotius properly remarks, in Isaiah xlii, 1, whence the phrase בת קול, "heavenly voice," is literally taken. We read there: "Behold, my servant, whom I will uphold, my elect, in whom my soul delighteth: I have put my spirit upon him," &c. Having given the sources whence the vision of John is derived, it is evident that it must be looked upon as a fiction and an assertion of his own, which he could well expect, would find credence with the people, since the Rabbins of that time often referred to the heavenly voice. Thus, we read in many passages of the Talmud: "Let the heavenly voice decide!" whereupon, it is alleged, such a one was really heard. But, how much imagination of this kind may deceive us, every intelligent mind will readily admit.

CHAPTER IV.

1. "Then was Jesus led up of the Spirit into the wilderness, to be tempted of the devil."

The history of temptation is only a myth, as Dr. David Strauss well remarked in his work entitled, "The Life of Jesus," I. book, pages 425—455. For, according to the testimony of Matthew, Mark and Luke, that Jesus was baptized by John, it could, and should, therefore, be best known to John, what was taking place in the life of his Master, after the immersion.

But John contradicts directly the evidence of his witnesses. In the mean time, when Matthew, Mark and Luke immediately after baptism led their Master into the wilderness forty days and forty nights, John (chap. i, 35 and 37,) let, the next day after baptism, two of his disciples follow Jesus, when he was preparing to start into Galilee, and on the third day he let him and his disciples be present at a marriage in Cana of Galilee, (John, chap. ii, 1,) and does not mention with one syllable the story of temptation. This proves evidently, that the narrative of the temptation of Jesus by the devil is a creation of imagination. The ideas of the whole story seem to be borrowed from Gen. xxii, 1: "And it came to pass after these things, that God did tempt Abraham...... and especially from the temptations of Israel in the desert," &c. But, although it is only a fable, it deserves, nevertheless, our attention so far, that it tells us clearly the opinions which three Apostles entertained of the person of Jesus, as I will illustrate in my comment on the following verses.

2. "And when he had fasted forty days and forty nights, he was afterwards a hungered."

This narration of Christ's long fasting is borrowed from Exodus xxxiv, 28, and I. Kings xix, 8, where the same is related of Moses and Elijah.

3. "And when the tempter came to him, he said, If thou be the Son of God, command that these stones be made bread.

4. But he answered and said, It is written: (Deut. viii, 3,) Man shall not live by bread alone, but by every word that proceedeth out of the mouth of God."

From all this it is perceptible that Christ regarded himself simply as man, and wished to be regarded as such by his people. For he did not reply to Satan, that he was a God-man, nor God himself, or an eternal Being that needed no food; but he said, that, however long the Lord might cause him to suffer hunger, he should nevertheless confide in Him, that, as He once fed his sons, the whole people of Israel, from his love for them, in a wonderful manner, so He would feed and preserve Him in a similar way, he also being such a son and favorite of God. This is still more evident from verse 7, where Christ rebukes the tempter with the words taken from Deut. vi, 16: "Thou shalt not tempt the Lord thy God," and himself acknowledges that God was his Master; and again from verse 10, where he replies with the words taken from Deut. vi, 13: "Thou shalt worship the Lord thy God, and Him alone shalt thou serve," and thus regarded himself only as the servant of God.

We may well hope that the idea of God-man, that Sideroxylon which some bold scholars most honestly and frankly refute, as a *contradictio in adjecto*, and which many are still anxious to stamp as a mystery, will soon be consigned to the domain of paradoxes, especially as it is evident from the speeches of Christ that he himself repudiates it,

11. "Then the devil leaveth him, and, behold angels came and ministered unto him."

To the composition of this verse gave rise Ps. xxxiv, 7 or 8 in the common version: "The angel of the Lord encampeth round about them, that fear, and delivereth them."

14. "That it might be fulfiled which was spoken by Esaias, the Prophet saying: (viii, 8,)

15. The land of Zabulon, and Naphtalim, by the way of the sea, beyond Jordan, Galilee of the Gentiles."

The verse cited is given only in part, and reads in the original thus: "For he shall not be weary, he that is to oppress it. As he at first disgraced the land of Zabulon and the land of Nephtali, thus will he at last cause his power to be felt by the way of the sea; this side of the Jordan in Galilee of the Gentiles." As is evident from the context, the Prophet spake only of the political enemies of Israel, and the calamities that they will cause to them. Of course, if we rob the sentence of its subject, change the object into the subject, and give it a predicate *ad libitum*, we may easily prove everything from any thing. Although the not too scrupulous Missionaries no doubt perceived all this, and endeavored in their version of Isaiah to make the proper amendments, by reconciling the whole of verse 23 of chapter viii, with chapter ix, verse 1, they nevertheless succeeded no further, than in subjecting verse 23 to a mediaeval torture. As many states once denied all political and human rights to those denominations which were not Christian, or did not appear Christian enough, so are all un-Christian verses of Holy Writ still treated: they are not yet emancipated. They are tortured, stretched and flaggelated, until they profess Christianity according to modern Christian views.

16. "The people which sat (ought to read: "walked") in darkness, saw great light; and to them which sat in the region and shadow of death, light is sprung up."

By the light which is to spring up for Israel, Christ can by no means be understood, for this reason, because the Prophet speaks of the Deliverer, who is to appear for Israel, in this way: (ibid. verses 5, 6 and 7,) "All the tumult of battle, together with the garment rolled in blood, shall be burnt and become fuel for the fire. For unto us a child is born . . . . . . in order that his government shall increase, and no end unto peace, upon the throne of David, and in his kingdom . . . . . . ;" whereas all this, that is to say, both spiritual and political peace, did not reign in Israel at the time of Christ. Nay, he even maintains the reverse of his mission, saying: (Matthew x, 34,) "Think not that I am come to send peace on earth: I came not to send peace, but a sword." The verse quoted here by Matthew from Isaiah, contains past events, hence can merely be looked upon as a historical narration, and not as a prophecy. Isaiah had not the remotest idea of conveying a prophecy in these words; but depicts, as it is clearly evident from verses 8 and 10, the destruction of the kings of Aram and Israel by the Assyrians, and the miraculous deliverance of Judah at the time of Hezekiah.

17. "From that time Jesus began to preach, and to say, Repent; for the kingdom of heaven is at hand."

Although we have already above observed, (chap. iii, 2,) that the intentions of Christ, as expressed in these words, have been in no wise realized, we shall, nevertheless, also here endeavor to prove, that the Apostles deviated from the doctrines and mode of life of their Teacher, and introduced an entirely new system of their own; of which the anonymous Wolfenbuttel Fragmentist, edited by Lessing, expressed himself thus: (§ 20,) "It is doubtful whether Christ himself ever meant to extend the intention of his heavenly kingdom farther than to the Jewish nation. For the words with which he sent his Apostles upon the mission of proclaiming the heavenly kingdom are explicit enough, saying: 'Go not into the way of the Gentiles, and into any city of the Samaritans enter ye not, but go rather to the lost sheep of the house of Israel.' (Matth. x, 5 and 6.) And Christ, moreover, says of himself: 'I am not sent but unto the lost sheep of the house of Israel.' (Matth. xv, 24.) I confess, that I am unable to reconcile with these and similar speeches, the order which he is said to have given afterwards: 'Go and teach all Gentiles,' &c. If the Apostles, when they shortly before started upon preaching the Gospel, had received the order to convert all Gentiles, why should the Apostle Peter have hesitated to go to Captain Cornelius to convert him, as though he would render himself unclean thereby? Why had he first to be informed by a special vision, that the Lord wished also the Gentiles to be made Christians? Why should the Apostle and his brethren, when he came to Jerusalem, have contended with him because he went to a Gentile? And why should Peter, with the view of justifying his course, have referred to this, that their Teacher had told them: 'ye (of course the Apostles) shall be baptized with the Holy Ghost?' (Acts xi, 16.) Forasmuch as God gave them the like gift as he did unto us, who believed on the Lord Jesus Christ, what was I, that I could withstand God? (Acts xi, 17.) Why should he not have referred rather to the explicit order of Christ, and his mission to all Gentiles? If Christ had given him such an order, he could have simply said: you know, my dear brethren, that our Master ordered us to go and baptize all Gentiles, and preach the Gospel unto all creatures; such is the will of our Master, and such is our mission. But the Apostle says not a word like it Our opinion is still more forcibly confirmed by this, that the Apostles, also after the death of Christ, did not express themselves about his plan and design in any other way, than that he intended and strove to save Israel alone, as we read in Luke xxiv, 21 : 'But we trusted that it had been he which should have redeemed Israel.' It is evident that they hoped for the redemption of the Jewish nation, and not that of the human race in general. It was a redemption that, as they hoped, should be accomplished, but was not fulfiled. Besides," continues our Fragmentist, (§ 20,) "the first Christians, who had originally been Jews, were so much convinced of Christ's intention to see the whole of Judaism exist in Christianity, that they, notwithstanding they had embraced Christianity, nevertheless preserved all Jewish ceremonies, nay were very zealous followers of the law." So also we read the confession of Paul, in Acts xxiv, 14: "But this I confess unto thee, that after the way which they call heresy, so worship I the Lord of my fathers, believing all things which are written in the law and in the Prophets." According to Christ's teachings, no other change should be made in the religion of the Jews than this, that they should henceforth believe that the redeemer had come, instead of believing that he had yet to appear. Now, when the Apostles, seeing themselves disappointed, after the death of their Teacher, in their hope for the redemption of Israel, established an entirely new system, we can not regard it as a system of Christianity, but of the Apostles, which, conflicting as it does with the lessons and life of Christ, must be put down as unfounded and incorrect.

18. "And Jesus, walking by the sea of Galilee, saw two brethren, Simon called Peter, and Andrew his brother, casting a net into the sea: for they were fishers."

The report given in this verse as well as in Mark i, 16, and Luke v, 1—10, is in every respect in contradiction with that of John, chap. i, 37—43. I refer now to the judgment of the kind reader, whether we can rely upon any depositions of such witnesses, who are guilty of counter statements.

19. "And he saith unto them: Follow me, and I will make you fishers of men."

The figure presented here is borrowed from Jeremiah xvi, 16, where we read thus: "Behold, I will send for many fishers, saith the Lord, and they shall fish them," &c. Now, the question arises: Were Peter and Andrew commissioned to bring spiritual life, or death unto the people? A fisher who takes the fishes out of their element, consigns them to destruction, in which sense alone the inspired Prophet employs the above figure. The Evangelist, therefore, failed here in copying the words of the Prophet; for the symbol of preservation, which the former means to convey here, can never represent that of destruction. Compare also Habakkuk i, 14 and 15.

24. "And his fame went throughout all Syria . . . . . . and healing all manner of sickness, and all manner of diseases among the people."

Why Christ wished to be regarded as a worker of miracles by the people, we shall explain in our remarks on chapter xi, verse 5.

CHAPTER V.

Although Christ's Sermon on the mount abounds with important lessons for all conditions of life, yet it is unjustly called the new legislation. For, mark well, dear reader, it contains nothing more than what the Prophets had, long before, many times said and taught, as we shall now show.

3. "Blessed are the poor in the spirit."

"I dwell in the high and holy place, *with him also that is of a contrite and humble spirit*, to quicken the spirit of the humble, and to revive the heart of the contrite ones." (Isaiah lxvii, 15.) "To this man will I look, *even to him that is poor and of a contrite spirit*, and feareth my word." (ibid. lxvi, 2.) "The Lord is nigh unto them that are of a broken heart; and saveth such as are of a contrite spirit." (Ps. xxxiv, 19.) The Lord protects the poor in spirit. (ibid. cxvi, 6.) So also we find in Talmud Sanhedrin 43, the following sentence: "Come and learn, how highly regarded the contrite of spirit are by God," &c.

4. "Blessed are those that mourn; for they shall be comforted."

"I, even I, am he who comforteth ye: who art thou that thou shouldest be afraid of a man," &c. (Is. li, 12.)

"I have seen his ways, and will heal him; I will lead him also, and restore comforts unto him, and to his mourners." (ibid. lvii, 18.)

"Thy sun shall no more go down, neither shall thy moon withdraw itself; for the Lord shall be thine everlasting light, and the days of thy mourning shall be ended." (ibid. lx, 20.)

5. "Blessed are the meek; for they shall inherit the earth."

"The meek shall inherit the earth; and shall delight themselves in abundance of peace." (Is. xxxvii, 11.)

6. "Blessed are they which do hunger and thirst after righteousness: for they shall be filled."

"Ho, every one that thirsteth, come ye to the waters; and he that hath no money: come ye, buy, and eat; yea, come, buy wine and milk without money and without price .... hearken diligently unto me, and eat ye that which is good, and let your soul delight itself with pleasure." (Isaiah lv, 1 and 2.)

7. "Blessed are the merciful; for they shall obtain mercy."

"He that followeth after righteousness and mercy, will find life, mercy and honor." (Prov. xxi, 21.)

"Whoso stoppeth his ear unto the cry of the poor, he also will cry himself, but shall not be heard." (ibid. verse 13.)

"He that hath pity upon the poor, lendeth unto the Lord; and that which he hath given, will He pay him again." (ibid. xix, 17.)

"Blessed is he who considereth the poor; the Lord

will deliver him in time of need." (Ps. xli, 2.) See also Psalm cxii, 5.

8. "Blessed are the pure in heart, for they shall see God."

"Who shall ascend into the hill of the Lord? and who shall stand in his holy place? He that hath clean hands, and a pure heart;" &c. (Ps. xxiv, 3, 4.)

9. "Blessed are the peace-makers: for they shall be called the children of God."

"As a father pitieth his children, so the Lord pitieth those who fear Him." (Ps. ciii, 13.) Who, however, may render himself worthy of the above name, may be seen from Zechariah viii, 19, where we read: "love truth and peace," and verse 16: "these are the things which ye shall do: speak ye every man the truth to his neighbor; execute the judgment of truth and peace in your gates."

10. "Blessed are they which are persecuted for righteousness' sake: for theirs is the kingdom of heaven."

"The mouth of the righteous speaketh wisdom, and his tongue teacheth wisdom. The law of his God is in his heart; none of his steps shall slide. The wicked watcheth the righteous, and seeketh to slay him. But the Lord will not leave him in his hand," &c. (Ps. xxxvii, verse 30—34.)

11. "Blessed are ye when men shall revile you, and persecute you," &c., &c.

This is an imitation of Ps. xlii, 10; Jerem. xx, 7—11; Isaiah l, 6—11, and lastly, Isaiah li, 7—9, where we read as follows: "Hearken unto me, ye who know righteousness, the people in whose heart is my law. Fear ye not the reproach of men, neither be ye afraid of their revilings. For the moth shall eat them up like a garment, and the worm shall eat them like wool: but my righteousness shall be for ever, and my salvation from generation unto generation."

In reading the exhortations contained in the Sermon on the mount, we are involuntarily reminded of the blessings pronounced upon the mount Gerizim, and the curses held forth on Ebal, (Deut. xxvii, 11.) Aside from the fact, that the form and substance of the Sermon on the mount are borrowed from the Law and the Prophets, the Jewish Bible has this advantage, that it contains many other most beautiful and profound sentences of benedictions, of which we will here exhibit some in a systematic order.

THE PSALMS.

I, 1. "Blessed is the man who walketh not in the counsel of the ungodly, nor standeth in the way of sinners, nor sitteth in the seat of the scornful," &c. This sentence is followed by a most beautiful, though simple figure, representing the same sublime truth.

Xxxii, 1, 2. "Blessed is he whose transgression is forgiven, whose sin is covered. Blessed is the man unto whom the Lord imputeth not iniquity, and in whose spirit there is no guile."

Xl, 5. "Blessed is that man who maketh the Lord his trust, and respecteth not the proud, nor such as turn aside to lies."

Xli, 2 and 3. "Blessed is he that considereth the poor; the Lord will deliver him in time of trouble. The Lord will protect him, and keep him alive; and he shall be blessed upon the land," &c.

Lxv, 5. "Blessed is the man whom Thou choosest, and causest to approach unto Thee, that he may dwell in Thy courts; we shall be satisfied with the goodness of Thy house, even of Thy holy temple."

Lxxxiv, 5—7. "Blessed are they that dwell in Thy house, they will praise Thee without ceasing. Blessed is the man whose strength is in Thee, and follows Thy ways with his heart. Who passing through the valley of tears, makes it a fount," &c.

Ibid. 13. "O Lord of hosts! blessed is the man who trusteth in Thee!"

Lxxxix, 16 and 17. "Blessed is the people that knoweth the sound; they shall walk, O Lord! in the light of Thy countenance. In Thy name shall they rejoice every day, and in Thy righteousness shall they be exalted."

Cvi, 3. "Blessed are they who keep judgment, and he who doeth righteousness at all times."

Cxii, 1. "Blessed is the man who feareth the Lord, and delighteth greatly in His commandments. His seed shall be mighty upon earth," &c.

Cxix, 1 and 2. "Blessed are those whose way is perfect, who walk in the Law of the Lord. Blessed are they that keep His testimonies, that seek Him with their whole heart."

Cxxviii, 1. "Blessed is every one that feareth the Lord, that walketh in His ways."

Cxliv, 15. "Blessed is that people, whose God is the Lord."

Cxlvi, 5 and 6. "Blessed is he who hath the God of Jacob for his help, whose hope is in the Lord his God: who made heaven, and earth, the sea, and all that therein is."

THE PROVERBS.

Iii, 13. "Blessed is the man who findeth wisdom; and the man who getteth understanding."

Xiv, 21. "He that hath mercy upon the poor, blessed is He."

Xxviii, 14. "Blessed is the man who feareth always,"&c.

ISAIAH.

Lvi, 2. "Blessed is the man that doeth this, and the son of man that layeth hold on it; that keepeth the Sabbath from polluting it, and keepeth his hand from doing evil."

JOB.

V, 17 and 18. "Behold! happy is the man whom God correcteth; therefore despise not thou the chastening of the Almighty; for He woundeth, and bindeth up, He lacerateth, and His hand healeth."

SIRACH.

Xiv, 20. "Blessed is the man who doeth wise things, and reasoneth of holy things by his understanding."

Xvii, 41. "Blessed is he who trusteth in the grace of God, and receives His chastenings with patience."

Xxv, 12, 13 and 14. "Happy is he that doth not create his own misfortune with his tongue, and the respectable, who can not be subjected to the wicked. Blessed he who findeth a true friend, &c. Blessed he that is not bent by poverty, and doth not lose his courage in his trouble."

Xxxi, 13. "Blessed is the rich that is without blemish, and hath not been blinded by great treasures."

Xxxiv, 15. "Blessed is he that worshippeth God, great is his deliverer, powerful his protector."

13. "Ye are the salt of the earth."

This metaphor is borrowed from Job vi, 6, where the godly life is compared, symbolically, to meat savored with salt, and the ungodly life is called unsavory food.

14. "Ye are the light of the world. A city that is set on a hill, can not be hid."

These phrases are imitations of several passages in Isaiah. "It is an easy thing that thou art my servant.... I will also give thee for a light unto the Gentiles, that thou mayest be my salvation unto the end of the earth." (Is. xlix, 6.) "I have not spoken in secret, in a dark place of the earth," &c. (Is. xlv, 19.)

15. "Neither do men light a candle and put it under a bushel, but on a candlestick, and it giveth light unto all that are in the house."

The figures contained in this verse are taken from Proverbs vi, 23, where we read: "For the commandment is a lamp, and the law is light," &c.; and Ps. cxix, 105: "Thy word is a lamp unto my feet, and a light unto my path."

16. "Let your light so shine before men, that they may see your good works, and glorify your Father which is in heaven."

This exhortation is taken from Ps. xl, 9—12: "I delight to do Thy will, O God! Thy law is within my heart. I have preached righteousness in the great congregation: behold! I have not refrained my lips, O Lord! Thou knowest."

(We should compare the above verse of the Evangelist with Deut. iv, 5—6.—Tr.)

17. "Think not that I am come to destroy the law, or the Prophets. I am not come to destroy, but to fulfil."

Christ here exhibits his whole mission as consisting in this, that he should complete the Mosaic Law and the teachings of the Prophets, which completion he terms a higher *Dikaiosyne*, "righteousness." But this completion had long before been begun by the Prophets and other inspired men, and had reached such a degree of maturity, that we read in Ethics of the Fathers, Sect. ii, 4: "Make God's will thine own, that He may make thine His own;" that is to say, if thou be just, righteous and virtuous, thou livest entirely in God.

18. "For verily I say unto you: Till heaven and earth pass, one jot or one tittle shall in no wise pass from the law till all be fulfilled.

19. Whosoever, therefore, shall break one of these least commandments, and shall teach men so, he shall be called the least in the kingdom of heaven: but whosoever shall do and teach them, the same shall be called great in the kingdom of heaven."

Whatever general remarks I could make here, may be found above, page 25, &c. I add only, that the phraseology of verse 18 is an imitation of Is. li, 6: "The heavens shall vanish away like smoke and the earth shall wax old like a garment.... but my salvation shall be for ever, and my righteousness shall not be abolished;" while its contents are distinctly proclaimed in Is. xl, 8: "The grass withereth, the flower fadeth: but the word of our God shall stand for ever."

The doctrine held forth in verse 19, may be found in Ethics of our Fathers, Sect. ii, 1: "Observe a slight commandment as the more important one, since thou knowest not the reward for the observance."

20. "For I say unto you, That except your righteousness shall exceed that of the Scribes and Pharisees, ye shall in no case enter into the kingdom of heaven."

The reform plan of Christ is but a dim shadow of Isaiah's, who with glowing imagination, yet clear perception and correct judgment, begins (chap. i, 11—17,) to develope and exhibit the means for imitating Divine mercy, joy and peace, love and grace, benevolence and goodness; breaks down, with fiery zeal, the barrier between the Divine and the Human, (see besides many other passages, chap. lvi, 1, and lviii, 1—11;) desires that the Universe should be permeated by the light of genuine justice, (chap. lx, 18—20,) and concludes his admonitions with the same doctrine, chapter lxvi, 1—3.

But the Rabbins also most urgently taught the holiness and purification of the heart. In Treatise Berachoth, Sect. i, fol. 5, we find the following sentence: "It matters not, whether the good ye do be much, or little, as long as you do it for God's sake;" which means, that every thing which we undertake, should be done from pure motives.

As we meet here with an invective against the Scribes and Pharisees, which is found on almost every page of the New Testament, and directed not only against their character, but often their doctrines, we deem it proper, with the view of enabling our readers to form a correct judgment, to communicate some historical facts with regard to the designs and aims of the authors of these sects, their views and mode of thinking, and the influence which they exercised over the moral character of the Jewish nation.

When, in consequence of the Babylonish captivity, the schools of Prophets which had been founded by Samuel, and produced, especially in the time of David, men of exalted wisdom, did no longer exist, and no one appeared, who was willing and able further to effect the spiritual and moral development of his people, the learned and talented priest Ezra went to Palestine, in the seventh year of the reign of Artachshast, (Darius Hystaspis) to accomplish the work of reforming the religious affairs of the Jews, to arrange them according to Mosaic principles, and to appoint or dismiss teachers and judges; for which he was most fit, as he had so much ingratiated himself with the king and his seven counsellors, that the jurisdiction of Judea was exclusively placed in his hand. (Ezra vii, 25—27.) Wisely availing himself of the power thus given to him, he endeavored to awaken the spiritual culture of his people by the following institutions:

He called the most talented and learned men, (see Nehemiah viii, 13,) according to Tradition [19] to the number of 120, to his aid, (Megillah, ¶ 17, p. 2,) endeavored together with them, the Great Assembly, אנשי כנסת הגדולה, to accommodate the Mosaic Law to local circumstances, and the new, changed religious views of the people, and founded Synagogues and religious schools, in which the Scriptures were read, and their contents explained to the people, in order that morality, virtue and justice, these principal pillars of a state, and human society in general, might be diffused and promoted. The men educated in these schools were called סופרים, Scribes, learned in the Scriptures, after the name of their Founder, עזרא הסופר, Ezra the Scribe.

But the continual reading and study of the Holy Writ by degrees awakened a general desire for investigation, and the Synagogue was thus soon converted into an Academy of Theology, Philosophy and Politics, where doctrines were taught, in which original, personal views were mixed up with Indian, Egyptian, and afterwards also Grecian elements and ideas; and this combination applied to the development, interpretation, extension and authentication of Biblical doctrines. And as Grecian philosophy began with single sentences and proverbs of the so-called Seven Sages, so must we regard the profound maxims and ascetic doctrines of the first Teachers, which are contained in the "Ethics of the Fathers," and the "Aboth of Rabbi Nathan," as the beginning and origin of philosophical studies among the Jews. Among

[19] This traditional assertion is supported by a strong historical probability; for, as the directors were called "chiefs of the fathers," ראשי האבות, (Ezra iv, 2 and 3,) it is evident that the most talented, the purest and most respectable member of every family was, according to ancient, patriarchichal custom, named chief; and as the families, together with the most prominent men who went to Judea with Zerubabel, numbered 119, (Ezra ii, 2—61,) there were 119 chiefs, so that, when Ezra was added to them, their number was increased to 120.

the noble men who, from the time of Ezra, taught the principles of morality and virtue, we meet also with *Antigonus of Socho*, who flourished in the third century before the Christian era, and, probably acquainted with the doctrines of Socrates, (Xenophon, Mem. I, 1, § 2, 3; III, 9, § 15,) [20] pronounced the sentence, that doing right, even because it is right, and without regard to future reward, was worshipping God, was Religion. But in consequence of the conciseness of the language, used in this sentence, his disciples Zadok and Baithos misunderstood its meaning, drew false conclusions from it, and adopted the system of the Stoics, then flourishing in Greece.

Since, however, the Bible was and remained the centre and guide of all their investigations, it was but natural that their new philosophical system produced a new mode of interpreting the Bible, and with it a new religious sect.

The maxim of Antigonus referred to above, runs literally thus: "Be not like servants who serve their master with the view of receiving reward; but be like servants who serve their master without the view of being rewarded; and then only, ye will be truly God-fearing." (Ethics of the Fathers, I, 3.) This principle was propagated by the disciples of Zadok and Baithos in the obscure phraseology of Antigonus. Allured, probably by Grecian Stoicism, some teachers strove to vindicate this system for Antigonus. They remarked: "From what motives was this principle advanced? And why has it been upheld by later teachers? Is it to be imagined, that a laborer should work the whole day without receiving due reward in the evening? If our Fathers had acknowledged a life to come and the resurrection of the Dead, they would never have adopted this principle of Antigonus. (Aboth of Rabbi Nathan, Sect. v.)

By these and similar reflections they gained many vo-

[20] It is not only historically certain, that, in consequence of the invasion of Alexander the Great in Asia, Grecian language and culture were transplanted to Palestine, but the very name "Antigonus" leads us to suppose that the Chaldaic and Hebrew languages had to yield their places to the Grecian.

taries, established a school of their own, and assumed, after the names of Zadok and Baithos, the appellations *Sadducees* and *Baithosians*. The former term, however, remained preponderant. [21]

They assumed, like the Stoics, two eternal principles of all things, a passive one, (*Hyle*, תהו ובהו,) and an active principle, God; hence their system is the *Dualistic System*. It was for this reason that they were designated by their opponents as heretics, as we read in Talmud Horioth, fol. 11: "Who is a Sadducee? Every idolater" (Compare also Talmud Sanhedrin, fol. 38, a and b, and Midrash Rabba Genesis, chap. viii.) Although they regarded the soul as a part of the Deity, they nevertheless held it to be perishable, like every other material being; for they professed the conviction, that it was absurd to believe in the existence of immaterial things; and it was this conviction that dictated the ironical question, with regard to the resurrection of the dead, which they addressed to Christ. (Matthew xxii, 23—29.)

The opponents of this system, led by the principle, to enjoy the substance, but to cast away the shell, seem to have made an eclectic use of the Grecian philosophy, assigning as they did high authority to the Socratic, Platonic and Aristotelian school.

As votaries of Supernaturalism they entertained the following opinions:

God is an infinite, (Midrash Rabba Genesis, chapter lxviii,) unique, spiritual, (Treatise Chagigah, fol. 15,) eternal, necessary, providential Being, (Midrash Rabba Exodus, chap. iii, and Treat. Berachoth, fol. 9,) which can not be conceived by human understanding, (Treat. Berachoth, fol. 31.)

He does not exist in the world, but the whole Universe exists in Him, (Midrash Rabba, chap. lxviii,) wherefore God is called also the "Infinite Space," מקום. He can

[21] That the Sadducees and Baithosians were regarded by the Rabbins as one and the same sect, see Jost's History of the Israelites, (larger work, in 12 vol.) Vol. I, page 66, and appendix No. 31; Universal History of the Israelites, (smaller work, in 2 vol.) Vol. I, p. 519.

be perceived only through His works, (ibid. chap. i.) As regards the Creation, they teach, that out of the many systems of worlds, which were present to His wisdom, He created the best possible one, and instituted the best order— *Optimism,* (ibid. Gen., chap. iii.) Hence the principle: "Whatever God does, is well done," (ibid. Gen., chap. iii, and Treat. Berachoth, fol. 60.) As a consequence of this principle, which is applicable to both physical and moral evils, they taught, that we should thank God also for evil events, (Treat. Berachoth, 34.)

There is no chance on earth, but all that happens is so ordained by God, (Treat. Chullin, fol. 7, b,) except virtue and piety, which are entirely left to man's free choice, (Treat. Berachoth, fol. 16.) He, however, who pursues, or endeavors to pursue the path of virtue, receives the support of God; whereas the designs of him, who chooses the way of wickedness, are not fixed from above, but entirely the fruits of his own choice, (Treat. Yomah, fol. 38.) These principles are based upon Ps. xxxvii, 23 and Proverbs xx, 23.

The soul is a spiritual, (Midrash Rabba Genesis, chapter 12, and Levit. 4,) unique, simple, everlasting, (ibid. Gen. 14, and Levit. 4,) self-acting being, (ibid. Levit. 4,) which is called upon to perfect itself in this world, the antechamber of that to come, (Ethics of the Fathers, iv, 21,) that it may be admitted into the Palace, the realm of the Saints, where it will immediately partake of God's majesty; that is to say, where it will increase in moral and intellectual strength in such an extraordinary degree, as to fill it with unspeakable delight, surpassing all joys that this earth can afford, (ibid. iv, 22.) They believe in the doctrine of a separate creation of the soul, hence maintain its pre-existence, (Midrash Rabba, chap. 24, and other passages.) Like Plato, (Tim. vol. ix, p. 338, and Theaet. ii, 176,) they teach, that virtue consisted in imitating God; as the Mechilta observes: "We must strive to become like God. As God is gracious and merciful, so be thou gracious and merciful," &c. Or as Moses teaches;

(Levit. xix, 2,) "Ye shall be holy, for I the Lord your God am holy." This injunction is furthermore held forth as the highest principle of all virtue and piety. In former times, thus it is related in Maccoth, fol. 24, they enumerated six hundred and thirteen laws, affirmative and prohibitory, which had been delivered to Moses on Mount Sinai. But already David taught that all these Mosaic Laws could be comprised in eleven principles: "to walk uprightly; to work righteousness; to speak the truth; to abstain from slander; to abstain from doing evil unto one's neighbor; not to bring any reproach upon one's fellowman; to condemn vile persons; to honor the God-fearing; to swear to one's own injury and keep the oath; to lend out money without usury, ("even to the heathens," add the Rabbins,) and to protect the innocent disinterestedly." (Psalm xv.) The Prophet Michah again reduced them to three, to wit: "to exercise justice, to be benevolent towards every one, and to humbly walk before God." (Michah vi, 8.) Isaiah, in his turn, reduced them to two principles: (lvi, 1,) "justice and benevolence;" and Habakkuk, lastly, established *one* highest principle: "The Righteous liveth in his belief," meaning that God desires the holiness of our sentiments and actions. This holiness, however, we can reach only, when we elevate ourselves above all that attracts our senses, and obey the dictates of reason alone, as it is expressed in these few words: "Let all thy actions be directed to what is Divine, sublime," (Ethics of the Fathers, Sect. ii, § 17,) yet in a manner as admits not of the principle, "the aim sanctifies the means." (Midrash Rabba, Levit. 30, and Tract. Succah, in several places.) Similar to the Aristotelian doctrine, that Virtue is manifested in seven cardinal characteristics, namely: *Andria*, (fortitude,) *Sofosyne*, (temperance,) *Eleuteriotes*, (liberality,) *Megaloprepeia*, (magnificence,) *Megalopsychia*, (magnanimity,) &c., the opponents of the Sadducees teach seven cardinal virtues: Wisdom, Justice, Righteousness, Probity, Mercy or Meekness, Sincerity and Peace, (Aboth of Rabbi Nathan,

Sect. 37,) but regard, like Aristotle, the virtue of "righteousness," *Dikaiosyne*, צדקה, since it consists in the observance of all Divine and civil laws, as the complex of all virtue. This virtue of righteousness balances all virtues. (Tr. Baba Bathra, fol. 9, a.) The Aristotelian doctrine of *Autarkeia*, (self-contentedness,) is taught as a duty towards one's self, (as Moses Landau most ingeniously interpreted,) in the following proverbs: "If I am not satisfied with myself, who could be; but if I think of myself also, what do I accomplish? and if I do not work now, when should I." (Ethics of the Fathers, I, 14)

The categorical Imperative is thus expressed by R. Hillel: (100 B. C. E.) "Do not unto others, as thou wishest not to be done to." (Tr. Sabbath 31, a.) As an enlargement upon this highest principle, the same sage teaches: "Judge not of thy neighbor, until thou be in his situation." (Ethics of the Fathers, ii, 5.)

With this also Leibnitz, (in his Nouv. Essai 48,) agrees, saying: "*Le veritable sens de la Regle est, que la place d'autrui est le vrai point de vue pour juger equitablement lorsqu'on s'y met.*"

The Scotch philosopher, Adam Smith, who at first studied Theology, has made this Rabbinical doctrine the basis of morals, in his "Theory of Moral Sentiments."

They furthermore teach, like Socrates, (Xenophon Mem. iii, 9, § 5,) that wisdom consists in practical knowledge. Thus we read: (Berachoth 17,) "The aim of wisdom is improvement, and the achievement of good deeds." Again in Ethics of the Fathers i, 17: "Not Study, but the practice thereof is the principal thing." [22] Practice is Man's destination. "However much thou mayest have studied, do not boast of it, for thou hast been created for this purpose." (ibid, ii, 9.) This alone will enable man to procure Salvation: "He who hath acquired wisdom, hath acquired for himself eternal life." (ibid. ii, 8.)

[22] See Maimonides' Commentary on this passage.

With regard to Church government and theologic Orthodoxy they establish, among other beautiful rules, the following: "Do not pass any laws, by which the majority can not exist," (Tr. Baba Bathra, 60,) which conveys the idea, that due regard must be paid to local, temporary and political conditions and circumstances, whenever religious institutions and ordinances are intended to be established. "The Biblical laws should not be multiplied from too great love for the Law." (Hierosol. Talmud, Tr. Nedarim, Sect. 9.)

The votaries of this system, in order to distinguish themselves from the Sadducees, who had likewise their origin in the midst of the "Scribes," סופרים, adopted the name of "Therapeutae or Essenees." Philo calls them *Hosioi*, "the holy ones," while their Hebrew name is פרושים, the Pharisees; either because this Sect of Communists, which grew into existence several decennia before that of the Sadducees more closely connected themselves with them, when they had established themselves, than with their adversaries, and were absorbed by them; or because the Therapeutae were truly pious men, and respected as such by the People.

In later times, however, they exclusively called themselves חכמים, "the Sages," or, in Chaldee, רבנן, "the Learned."

The independent investigation, and the beautiful development and establishment of a Mosaic-religious Philosophy, through the Academies of the Pharisees, soon degenerated into sophistic subtilities and braggart mock-erudition, because every one was admitted, even without being first examined as to his abilities, and indispensable preparatory accomplishments, and thus way was made for false learning and education. (Tr. Sotah, 22, b; Sanhedrin, 98, b.) And as Sophistry in Greece, by its dialectical artifices, perverted all truth and knowledge, undermined the foundations of political life, and largely contributed to the corruption of morals, so did the puffed-up-mock-sages of Judea, exercise the most destructive influence upon the character of the nation at large. Being but spiritless imitators of others, without having arrived, by rational conviction, at the knowledge of the highest things and of God, they sank to the low level of hypocrites, vaingloriously strove to gain notoriety by meaningless, outward observances, and neglecting all higher duties, diffused a childish-religious disposition for trifles, by means of which they often fanaticized the multitudes, and used them for their own political purposes, as may be seen from Josephus' "History of the Wars of the Jews."

This course of action soon became known to the intelligent Teachers. Although they perceived the danger that threatened to disturb the moral purity of the people, and gradually to deaden the awakened speculative spirit, they knew, nor had any other means at their disposal whereby to avert the danger, than urgent admonitions to shun these seducing teachers, and a distinct portraiture of the true Scholar and Sage, whose highest aim of life consisted in attaining to the most sublime traits of moral and spiritual perfection. (Tr. Derech Erez Sutta; Ethics of the Fathers v, 10, and iv, 7:) "Make not the knowledge of the Law a crown to render thyself great thereby; nor make a spade thereof to dig therewith." (See further ibid. iii, 4, 12, and 22.) This is most generally expressed thus: (Tr. Yomah, 72, b,) "A learned man, whose inner being does not correspond with his outward appearance, can not be looked upon as a learned man." Besides, they enjoined upon every theologian, to teach theology, to those only, who are properly prepared for speculative and demonstrative thinking, and strive to lead a pure life. They say therefore: "Theological aphorisms can then only be communicated even to the President of Sanhedrin, if he connect the highest moral state of mind, with that scientific education, which his position required." Again: "Theological mysteries should be imparted only to him, who is known to be of a practical turn of mind, knows the world, is endowed with oratorical talents, and well able to express himself in appropriate and figurative language." "The Sages communicate the quadliteral name of God but once a week to their children and disciples." (Tr. Kid. 71.) This means, says Maimonides: (Moreh Nebuchim Lib. I, Sect. 34,) "They taught them the significance of this name, so that they perceived, that it was not derived from some Divine action, had nothing in common with any other name, but signified, in a peculiar manner, the nature of the Deity." In the same manner it is explained in Midrash Rabba, saying: "The name that truly signifies my Divine being, is even my peculiar name."

"In olden times, the knowledge of the duodecim-literal name of God, was imparted to every man; when, however, the number of presumptuous, immoral men more and more increased, it was made known only to the most pious of the Priesthood." (ibid.)

"The scientific name of God, consisting of forty-two letters, must be regarded as awful and holy. It can be communicated only to him, who is pious, has reached the age of mature manhood, is of a calm, cool temperament," &c. (ibid., and Tr. Chagigah, fol. 12.)

Besides this strict, and timely discipline, which was introduced in the Academies of the Scribes, they intended radically to remedy the evil by a throughgoing classification of all Pharisean parties, in order that the people might be the better enabled to guard themselves against the stigmatized ones. The Pharisees were divided into seven classes, five of whom were scouted on account of their immoral life, and two—according to some authorities, even but one—were held forth as good and God-pleasing, because they taught the principle, that the knowledge of God should be acquired and diffused only from pure love of God and Virtue. (Tr. Sotah, fol. 22, b.)

From all this it is evident that, however necessary it was, to discriminate between local, temporary, and political, and generally valid laws, and of the latter, to separate again those which were of judicial significance, all those principles which contain doctrines foreign to the normal system of the Pharisees, and diffused by men of the repudiated parties, must be discarded.

The attacks made upon the doctrines and life of the Scribes and Pharisees in the New Testament, are not directed against the first Teachers of the Jewish nation, but exclusively the degenerated factions, the mock Pharisees, as it can be proven by historical arguments.

With the view of consoling and advising his wife, the dying King Jannaius addressed her thus: "Fear not the Sadducees, for they are my friends; nor yet the Pharisees, for they are not cruel; but beware of the *Zeboongion*, (the dyed—the Chameleons,) who commit deeds like Zimri, and yet covet the reward of Phinehas." (Numbers xxv, 6, 14; Tr. Sotah 22, and Josephus.) Judea did not lose her political existence in consequence of a general corruption of morals, and extinction of true religion, but because the Law was too strictly observed and executed, as we learn from Tr. Baba Mezia 30: "Jerusalem was destroyed for this reason alone, because no one was willing to sacrifice even the least tittle of his right." This naturally led to inhuman severity, pertinacity and discord, and at last to the destruction of the national power; all of which was hastened on also by the Priests, who, from untimely patriotic zeal, and in spite of the admonitions and resistance of the prudent portion of the leaders, (Tr. Gittin 56,) stirred up the people to a rebellion against the all-conquering and irresistibly victorious power of the Romans. (Josephus.) It can not be doubted that the spiritual culture of the Jews in Palestine, and their ever faithful allies, the Helenists, would have reached the highest degree of maturity by the assiduous study of the Greek and Roman Classics—these chief sources also of our modern civilization—if their political life had not received its death-blow at the hands of the Romans.

21. "Ye have heard that it was said by them of old time, Thou shalt not kill; and whosoever kills, shall be in danger of the judgment:

22. But I say unto you, That whosoever is angry with his brother without a cause, shall be in danger of the judgment: and whosoever

shall say to his brother, Raca, shall be in danger of the council: but whosoever shall say, *Thou* fool, shall be in danger of hell-fire."

The charge made here upon the Scribes and Pharisees, that they had taken the Commandment, "Thou shalt not kill," only in the literal sense of the phrase, and declared the crime of real murder alone to be sinful, is highly unjust. They, too, cautioned against internal evil affections, and held them to be as vicious and punishable, as the bodily injuries inflicted upon persons; with this difference, however, that they adopted a more strictly logical classification than Christ. Under the Commandment, "Thou shalt not kill," they comprised all kinds of real personal injuries; both physical, and moral violence, the murder of both the body and character or reputation of a man. Thus they teach: (Tr. Baba Kamma 59,) "He who publicly puts his neighbor to shame, is to be reckoned like him who sheds man's blood." On the other hand they maintain, that the law, "Thou shalt have no other Gods besides me," contains, also, an admonition to guard one's self against the vices of impetuousity and anger. "He who is given to anger is like him who worships idols." (Tr. Sabbat, fol. 105, b.) For, even the holiest things are violated, when anger has destroyed the soberness of mind, and rendered it thoughtless. "He who is in anger, disregards even the Deity." (Tr. Ned. 22.) In fine, they teach, that every passion which man suffers to find a domicil within his bosom, such as envy, hatred, avarice, ambition, lust, &c., is an idol which he worships, and to which the words of the Psalmist are to be applied, saying: (lxxxi, 10,) "There shall no strange God be in thee; neither shalt thou worship any strange God."

23. "Therefore, if thou bring thy gift to the altar, and there rememberest that thy brother hath aught against thee,

24. Leave there thy gift before the altar, and go thy way; first be reconciled to thy brother, and then come and offer thy gift."

In Leviticus vi, 2—5, and Numbers v, 6 and 7, it is distinctly enough commanded, that a real reconciliation with an injured brother must be effected, before the trespass-offering could be brought. So also it is taught in

Proverbs xxviii, 13: "He that covereth his sins shall not prosper: but whoso confesseth, and forsaketh them, shall have mercy." To which our Sages remark, (Tr. Yom. 87,) "he who has offended his brother even with the least word, must first endeavor to conciliate him."

25. "Agree with thine adversary quickly, while thou art in the way with him; lest at any time the adversary deliver thee to the judge, and the judge deliver thee to the officer, and thou be cast into prison."

The contents of this verse are borrowed from Sirach xxviii, 2—6: "Forgive thy neighbor the hurt that he hath done unto thee, so shall thy sins also be forgiven when thou prayest. One man beareth hatred against another, and doth he seek pardon from the Lord? He sheweth no mercy to a man that is like himself; and, doth he ask forgiveness of his own sins? If he that is but flesh nourish hatred, who will entreat for pardon of his sins? Remember thy end, and let enmity cease!"

The Scribes (Tr. Rosh hashanah 17,) substantiated the same principles by reference to Michah vii, 18, and supply: "The Lord will forgive only the sins of him, who has forgiven offences done to him. See also Ethics of the Fathers v, 14, "The characteristic of a pious man is, not easily to be provoked, and easily to be appeased."

26. "Verily I say unto thee, Thou shalt by no means come out thence, till thou hast paid the uttermost farthing."

To the same effect we read in Ethics of the Fathers iv, 29: "Do not suffer thyself to be assured by thy evil inclinations, that the grave shall be for thee a place of refuge. For by compulsion thou hast been created, by compulsion thou hast entered the life, by compulsion thou doth live, by compulsion thou shalt die, and by compulsion thou shalt render account before the King of kings, the holy One, blessed be He."

27. "Ye have heard that it was said by them of old time, Thou shalt not commit adultery:

28. But I say unto you, That whosoever looketh on a woman to lust after her, hath committed adultery with her already in his heart."

According to Luther's interpretation, Christ here charges the Scribes with having maintained that the Commandment, "Thou shalt not commit adultery," forbade only that adultery which is consummated by illegal cohabitation, whereas impure thoughts, (lust,) were not forbidden. This charge is false. For they all agree (Tr. Sanhedrin 100 b,) with Sirach, (ix, 10,) that "a man should turn away his eye from a beautiful woman, and not look upon another's beauty," &c. How greatly they condemned such sensual thoughts may be seen from Sanhedrin 75 a, where we are told, that a man, who became enamored with a maiden, and not being able to marry her, was taken dangerously ill, as not permitted to speak to her, not even through a lattice, although he could have been cured thereby of his mental sufferings.

29. "And if thy right eye offend thee, pluck it out, and cast it from thee; for it is profitable for thee, that one of thy members should perish, and not that thy whole body should be cast into hell.

30. And if thy right hand offend thee, cut it off, and cast it from thee; for it is profitable for thee, that one of thy members should perish, and not thy whole body should be cast into hell."

How sinful desires may be hushed in their very birth, we shall more clearly explain below, in our commentary on xviii, 8 and 9. The above verses are evidently an imitation of Numbers xv, 39: "that ye seek not after the inclinations of your hearts, and the delight of your eyes." The phrase "inclinations of your hearts," is circumscribed by the symbolical application of the terms, "eye" and "hand," as in Mark ix, 43, 45 and 47, by that of "hand," "eye," and "foot."

Yet, the metaphor of the "foot" limps, and that of the "hand" is not quite handy; for hand and foot are, as it were, the blind messengers of desire, whose seat is in the heart. These can not, therefore, offend us. If we cast them off, we have not yet removed the offence, because it had not originated in them, but they had blindly obeyed their master. Job, therefore, very properly exclaims: (xxxi, 21 and 22,) "If I have lifted up my hand against the fatherless, when I saw my help in the gate: then let mine arm fall from my shoulter-blade, and mine arm be broken from the bone." He would not cast off his hand because it offended *him*, but because *he* offended others with it.

31. "It hath been said, Whosoever shall put away his wife, let him give her writing of divorcement: (Numb. xxiv, 1.)

32. But I say unto you, That whosoever shall put away his wife, saving for the cause of fornication, causeth her to commit adultery: and whosoever shall marry her that is divorced, committeth adultery."

Our ancient Sages are unjustly reproached with having taught, that a man could obtain a divorce even for trifling causes. The few lax opinions found in the Talmud with regard to this point, are by no means authoritative; since it is said: (Tr. Gittin 20,) "No one can divorce his wife, unless he have proven that she violated her chastity."

But how scrupulous our Sages were with regard to the violation of woman's dignity, and how greatly they disapproved of careless divorcements, is clearly shown in Tr. Sanhedrin 22 a: "Over him, who carelessly puts away his wife, the altar of God itself sheds tears;" which means, that even this pure, unstained spot, which in olden times was the asylum of every unfortunate person, would receive such a man, on account of his unjustifiable deed, with grief and reproach.

Besides, Malachi (ii, 13, 14 and 15,) had long before the time of Christ, powerfully inveighed against reckless divorcements.

33. "Again, you have heard, that it hath been said by them of old time, Thou shalt not forswear thyself, but shalt perform unto the Lord thine oaths:

34. But I say unto you, Swear not at all: neither by heaven, for it is God's throne;

35. Nor by the earth, for it is his foot-stool: neither by Jerusalem, for it is the city of the great King;

36. Neither shalt thou swear by thy head, because thou canst not make one hair white or black;

37. But let your communication be, Yea, yea; Nay, nay: for whatever is more than these cometh of evil."

Already the third Commandment (Exodus xx, 7,) is directed against reckless swearing, saying: "Thou shalt not take the name of the Lord thy God in vain." Sirach also (xxiii, 9—12,) gives the following admonition: "Accustom not thy mouth to swearing; neither use thyself to the naming of the Holy One. For as a servant that is continually beaten, shall not be without a blue mark, so he that sweareth, and nameth God continually shall not be faultless. He that useth much swearing, shall be filled with iniquity and the plague shall never depart from his house," &c.

Hence, Christ merely repeated what had often been taught before him, and the Therapeutae [23] had established, according to the reports of Philo and Josephus, as one of the principles of their system. The Scribes knew full well, from Isaiah lxvi, 1, that the heaven was the throne of God, and the earth His foot-stool, wherefore they established this principle: (Tr. Nedarim 10, b,) that every man who should declare anything to be holy to him as Jerusalem, as heaven or earth, was bound to perform the vow made in this manner. But an oath pronounced merely by the heaven or earth was by them declared to be invalid. (Tr. Shebuoth 31, a.) Mark well! They did not teach that we could easily swear by God's creatures, but that that oath alone was binding, which was taken by God's holy name; and probably for this reason, because He alone is eternally true and unchangeable, whereas all His creatures are subject to change, decay and final destruction, and can not therefore attest an eternal truth.

38. "Ye have heard, that it hath been said: An eye for an eye, and a tooth for a tooth."

The verse cited from Exodus xxi, 24, contains a simple law for worldly government, such as it existed also in Thurium in Italy, (Diodorus Bibl. Histor. l. xii, chap. 17,) and is not applicable, therefore, to the civil and domestic life of the individual, affording but a rule to magistrates. This view was entertained also by our ancient Sages, so that the assertion, that they had made the judicial rule,

[23] The learned Orientalist Bellermann maintains, in his "Historical Reports about the Essenes," (Berlin 1821,) p. 7, that the Greek term *Therapeuo*, is a translation of the Syriac term אסא, *assa*, "to cure," "to heal," and that Sect was called *Therapeutae*, *Assaim*, *Essenes*, because they cured the soul by the strict practice of virtue.

"Measure for measure," also a moral principle for private life, is without foundation whatever. On the contrary, they teach: (Tr. Rosh Hashanah 17,) He who forgives his friend for injuries done by him, will receive forgiveness for his tresspasses at the hand of God." The Scribes, in pronouncing this doctrine, probably remembered the words of Solomon: (Proverbs xxiv, 29,) "Say not, I will so do to him, as he hath done to me: I will render to the man according to his work."

39. "But I say unto you, That ye resist not evil; but whosoever shall smite thee on the right cheek, turn to him the other also;

40. And if any man sue thee at the law, and take away thy coat, let him have thy cloak also.

41. And whosoever shall compel thee to go a mile, go with him twain."

These verses contain rules that tend to teach us an absolute passiveness to every injury, insult and offence, which, if it were strictly adhered to, would produce but this result, (See M. Paley's "Principles of Morals and Politics,") that the good would be given into the power of the wicked, and one portion of mankind exposed to the robberies and extortions of the other. And yet, the above words should contain truths of life, Divine doctrines? How? Precepts, the strict observance of which would not promote the happiness, but the misery of the better portion of the human race, should have proceeded from the justest and most beneficent Being? No! they are not Divine, but human lessons, which is incontrovertibly proved by this also, *that Christ himself violated them*. In the Gospel of St. John, (xviii, 22 and 23,) we read that, when one of the officers of the high-priest struck him, saying: "Answerest thou the high-priest so?" he answered, "If I have spoken evil, bear witness of the evil: but if well, why smitest thou me?" but did not, as he himself had taught, offer also his other cheek; that is to say, he did not quietly bear the insult, but from serious indignation rebuked the high-priests' officer for it.

42. "Give to him that asketh thee, and from him that would borrow of thee, turn not thou away."

Of the numberless parallel passages which may be found both in the Old Testament and the writings of the Rabbins, we will quote here but a few. Lev. xxv, 35 and 36: "If thy brother be waxen poor, and fallen in decay with thee: then thou shalt relieve him: yea though he be a stranger, or a sojourner; that he may live with thee. Take thou no usury of him, or increase, but fear thy God. [24] Deuteronomy xv, 7 and 8: "If there be among you a poor man of one of thy brethren, ... thou shalt open thy hand wide unto him, and shalt surely lend him sufficient for his need, in that which he wanteth." Proverbs xxviii, 27: "He that giveth unto the poor, shall not lack; but he that hideth his eyes shall have many a curse." Ethics of the Fathers, i. 5: "Let thy house be open to the needy, and let the poor be the inmates of thy house." In Tr. Sabbath 63, a, we read: "It is far more praiseworthy to lend the Poor without usury, than to give him alms; but the best is, to make him advances, and thus enable him to carry on some trade or business." Compare also Sirach xix, 1 and 2, &c.

43. "Ye have heard that it hath been said, Thou shalt love thy neighbor, and hate thy enemy.

44. But I say unto you, Love your enemies, bless them that curse you, do good to them that hate you, and pray for them that despitefully use you, and persecute you."

The passage quoted in the above verse 43 from Leviticus xix, 18, runs literally thus: "Thou shalt not avenge, nor bear any grudge against the children of thy people, but thou shalt love thy neighbor as thyself: I am the Lord." Both the phrase לא תטור, "thou shalt not bear any grudge," and the whole context, clearly show that, whenever an opportunity is presented to us, to let our enemy feel our hatred, we should not do so; since he has not ceased, in consequence of our enmity, to be

[24] Can there be a more sublime principle of practical charity and brotherly love, than the above, which knows no distinction of creed or country? Indeed! that principle bears the impress of Divinity upon its very face, and is alone apt, to fill every Jew with the justest pride, affording at the same time the best refutation of every attack upon him and his holy Religion! A Religion that teaches such a doctrine, can proceed from God alone, and can never be surpassed!—(Translator.)

our neighbor, towards whom we have to fulfil all the duties which we owe to our fellow-men. Thus we are told: (Exodus xxiii, 4 and 5,) "If thou meet thine enemy's ox, or his ass going astray, thou shalt surely bring it back to him again; if thou see the ass of him that hateth thee lying under his burden, and wouldest forbear to help him, thou shalt surely help with him."

The phrase "and hate thy enemy," is not only not to be found in the Law of Moses, but stands in diametrical contradiction to both its spirit and doctrines. [25] Nothing less was intended by this barefaced misrepresentation than to cry down and disgrace Mosaism in the eyes of the Gentiles, who were unacquainted with the Hebrew Bible.

Some, however, may say, that the addition "and hate thy enemy," is a doctrine of the Pharisees, against whom Christ inveighs here. To this we would answer, that the Scribes endorsed and taught, unchanged, the Biblical doctrine: that it is God-pleasing to help and love an enemy. (Baba Metsia 32.)

That the same doctrine was taught also by the Prophets, is proved by a historical fact, narrated in II. Kings vi, 21 and 22: "And the King of Israel said unto Elisha, when he saw them, (the Syrians,) My father, shall I smite them? shall I smite them? And he answered, Thou shalt not smite them: wouldst thou smite those whom thou hast taken captive, with thy sword and with thy bow? set bread and water before them, that they may eat and drink, and go to their master," &c. Compare also the words of Solomon: (Prov. xxv, 21,) "If thine enemy be hungry, give him bread to eat; and if he be thirsty, give him water to drink." Nay! we are not even permitted to rejoice at our enemy's misfortune; as we read: "Rejoice not when thine enemy falleth," &c. (Prov. xxiv, 17.) "Have I rejoiced at the destruction of him that hated

[25] It is indeed! strange, how Christ could have made the above assertion. Can there be a higher, more sublime doctrine of love for our enemy, than that contained in Deuteronomy xxiii, 7: "Thou shalt not abhor an EGYPTIAN, for thou wast a stranger in his land?" This passage alone covers the whole question.—(Translator.)

me, or lifted up myself when evil found him?" &c.—(Job xxxi, 29.) "But as for me, when they (my adversaries) were sick, my clothing was sackcloth; I humbled my soul with fasting; and my prayer returned into my own bosom. I behaved myself as though he had been my friend or brother," &c. (Psalm xxxv, 13 and 14.)

In the same spirit our Sages composed the following prayer, to be offered up every day: "I am ready to fulfil the Law," thou shalt love thy neighbor as thyself "with all my heart. Mayest Thou, O God! forgive also all mine enemies!"

The doctrine, therefore, that we should love also our enemy, is not a new, Christian one, but as old as Mosaism itself. Nay, it was clearly and convincingly taught even among the heathens, before Christianity was known.

"But," says Plutarch, in his Moral Writings, "it proves a noble soul, not to take revenge on an enemy, when opportunity presents itself. But whoever does not love a man for the sake of his kind-heartedness, and praises him for his righteousness, when he sympathizes with his distressed enemy, takes care of his children and substance, zealously and readily, bears within him a black soul, made of stone, or iron." And Cicero teaches: (De officiis, lib. i, chap. 25,) "*Nec vero audiendi graviter qui inimicis irascendum putabunt, idque magnanimi et fortis viri esse censebunt. Nihil enim laudabilius, nihil magno et praeclaro viro dignius placabilitate atque clementia.*" (Nor, indeed, are those to be listened to who consider that we ought to cherish a bitter resentment against our enemies, and this is characteristic of a high-minded and brave man. For nothing is more noble, nothing more worthy of a great and a good man, than placability and clemency.)

45. "That ye may be the children of your Father which is in heaven: for He maketh His sun to rise on the evil and on the good, and sendeth rain on the just and on the unjust."

To base the doctrine of love for our enemy upon the fact, that God loves His adversaries, the evil and unrighteous, nor deprives them of rain and sun-shine, or, in a wider sense of the phrase, of general benefits, is logically incorrect. For it is inconceivable, that the Supreme justice and love, which are equitably bestowed upon all, should directly or indirectly afford benevolent assistance to injustice. God loves not his adversaries, as Sirach says: (3, 5 and 6,) "Think not, His (the Lord's) mercy is great; he will be pacified for the multitude of my sins; for mercy and wrath (punishment) come from Him, and His indignation resteth upon sinners."

If God bestows general benefits upon the wicked, He does so not from love for them, but for this reason, because He would not, on their account, change the beautiful order of the Universe. If He were to punish the foolish aberrations of men by changes in nature, indeed! He should be soon compelled to destroy the whole Universe! This was long ago expressed by the Jewish Elders in Rome. Being asked by some Philosophers, why God, if He really abhorred idolatry, did not destroy the idols, they replied: If such things alone were worshipped whose existence could be dispensed with without endangering the universal order, the Lord should long ago have destroyed them; but Sun, Moon, and Stars, nay, even animals and human beings being worshipped as Gods,—should the Supreme Being destroy the Universe on account of fools? No; Nature retains her ordinary course, and the stiff-necked fools who do not listen to better instruction will have to give account thereof on some future day. (Treat. Abodoh Sarah, 54, b.)

And when we take the above verse 45 in its more limited and real meaning, we shall find that it is incorrect also with regard to facts. When we consider that Christ, according to Matthew x, 29 and 30, adhered to the true opinion, that nothing on earth happens by chance, not even the falling of a sparrow, but is worked out by the will of our heavenly Father; he must consequently concede this also, that when too dry or too rainy a season destroys the crop, and thus causes famine and a host of miseries in many countries, this does not happen by chance, or is to be ascribed to blind fate, but is so ordained, as already Moses and the Prophets taught, by God Himself, as a punishment for the sinners. Hence, God deprives the unrighteous of sun-shine and rain, since it can be, and is done without the least perceptible change of nature.

Regarding the true motive for the love of our enemy, I refer to my remarks made above on verses 43 and 44, which I have partially derived from Malachi ii, 10, where we read: "Have we not all one Father? Hath not one God created us? Why then do we deal treacherously every man against his brother, by profaning the covenant of our fathers?"

46. "For if ye love them which love you, what reward have ye? do not even the publicans the same?

47. And if ye salute your brethren only, what do ye more than others? do not even the publicans so?"

The same doctrine is taught by the Scribes: (Ethics of the Fathers v, 13,) "Four qualities are found with man; one says whatever is mine, *is* mine; and whatever is thine, *is* thine; this is the character of the ordinary men, or as others assert, was the custom of Sodom. Another says, whatever is thine is mine, and whatever is mine is thine, this is the custom of the Vulgar. Another again says, what is mine is thine, and what is thine is thine; this constitutes the character of the Pious. Another, lastly, says, what is mine is mine, and what is thine is mine also; this is the character of the wicked."

That we have to fulfil the duties of brotherly love towards every one, whether or not he be one of our acquaintance, whether or not he belong to our creed and country, is most urgently enjoined upon us in many passages of the Old Biblical Scriptures, but especially in Lev. xix, 33 and 34: "And if a stranger sojourn with thee, in your land, ye shall not vex him. But the stranger that dwelleth with you shall be unto you as one born among you, and thou shalt love him as thyself: for ye were strangers in the land of Egypt, I am the Lord your God."

48. "Be ye therefore perfect, even as your Father in heaven is perfect."

In whatever way we may interpret this verse, it is entirely incorrect. If it means to convey the idea, that we should attain on earth to the perfection of God Himself, we ask, is this possible? How can poor mortal man exhaust the fathomless fount of virtue? Man can never, even by the most strenuous exertions, reach Divine perfection, as it is said (I. Kings viii, 46,) and confirmed by sound reason: "There is no man that sinneth not;" or (Ecclesiastes vii, 20,) "For there is not a just man upon earth, that doeth good and sinneth not." Again: If we assume, that the above verse enjoins upon us the duty of imitating God, who loves the sinners though they are his adversaries, it is but a repetition of what verse 45 contains; and if this be really so, it contains the same incorrect reasonings on the love for our enemies, as that verse.

We believe, on the contrary, that it is but an imitation of Leviticus xix, 2, where we read: "Speak unto the Congregation of the Children of Israel, and enjoin upon them, Ye shall be holy, for I the Lord your God am holy." Yet the changed phraseology of Matthew has in a high degree missed the original. If we assume that the term קדוש, "holy" must be taken in a moral sense, expressing, as Kant has it, "the highest concord between the Divine will and the law of nature;" that, therefore, the phrase "and ye shall be holy" enjoins upon us the precept to do and learn but what is true and salutary, no objection whatever can be made, especially as the precept contains also an excellent rule of life which every man can most faithfully observe. On the other hand, if we take the term "holy" in this acceptation: "separated from the vulgar," "consecrated," "pure," "stainless," this precept contains again nothing that would surpass human power, and may, therefore, be well followed as our guide in all our actions.

CHAPTER VI.

1. "Take heed that ye do not your alms before men, to be seen of them: otherwise ye have no reward of your Father which is in heaven.

2. Therefore when thou dost thine alms, do not sound a trumpet before thee, as the hypocrites do in the Synagogues and in the streets, that they may have glory of men. Verily I say unto you, They have their reward.

3. But when thou doest alms, let not thy left hand know what thy right hand doeth:

4. That thine alms may be in secret: and thy Father which seeth in secret, himself shall reward thee openly."

As regards the proper mode of giving alms, we are taught already in Deuteronomy xv, 10: "Thy heart shall not be grieved when thou givest." Sirach (xviii, 15—17,) says: "My son, blemish not thy good deeds, neither use uncomfortable words when thou givest any thing. Shall not the dew assuage the heat? so is a word better than a gift. Lo! is not a word better than a gift? but both are with a gracious man." Our Rabbins, also, treat upon the same subject in extent. "Alms-giving will be rewarded hereafter only with regard to the kindness of feeling with which it was practised." (Tr. Succah 49.) "Whoever giveth publicly to the poor is a sinner." (Tr. Chagigah 4.)

5. "And when thou prayest, thou shalt not be as the hypocrites are: for they love to pray standing in the Synagogues and in the corners of the streets, that they may be seen of men. Verily I say unto you, they have their reward."

Already the Prophets inveighed against the loud praying of the hypocrites. Amos v, 23: "Take thou away from me the noise of thy song; for I will not hear the melody of thy viols." Isaiah xxix, 13: "Wherefore the Lord said, Forasmuch as the people draw near me with their mouths, and with their lips do honor me, but have removed their heart far from me," &c. The Psalmist also urgently recommends silent and solitary prayer. "At midnight I will rise to give thanks unto Thee, because of Thy righteous judgment." (Ps. cxix, 62.) "The Lord will commend his loving-kindness in the day-time, and in the night his song shall be with me, and my prayer unto the God of my life." (Ps. xlii, 9.) "Stand in awe and sin not, commune with your own heart upon your bed, and be still." (Ps. iv, 5.) Compare, also, the words of the Rabbins: "Whenever ye pray, follow the example of the pious Hannah, of whom it is said: (I. Samuel i, 13,) she spake in her heart, only her lips moved, but her voice was not heard."

6. "But thou, when thou prayest, enter into thy closet, and, when thou hast shut thy door, pray to thy Father in secret; and thy Father which seeth in secret shall reward thee."

The lesson taught here, is borrowed from II. Kings iv, 33: "He—Elisha—went in therefore, and shut the door upon them twain and prayed unto the Lord."

The form of the above verse is taken from Isaiah xxvi, 20, where we read: "Come my people, enter thou into thy chambers, and shut thy door about thee," &c. The words "and thy father which seeth in secret," &c., are far more forcibly expressed in Jeremiah xvi, 17: "For mine eyes are upon all their ways, they are not hid from my face," &c; and ibid. xxxii, 19: "Great in counsel, and mighty in work; for Thine eyes are open upon all the ways of the sons of men, to give everyone according to his ways, and according to the fruit of his doings." The same lesson we learn also from Sirach xvii, 14 and 15.

7. "But when ye pray, use not vain repetitions, as the heathens do for they think that they shall be heard for their much speaking."

Already Solomon taught: (Ecclesiastes v, 2,) "Be not rash with the mouth, and let not thy heart be hasty to utter anything before God; for God is in heaven, and thou upon earth: therefore, let thy words be few." The same lesson is taught by Sirach vii, 14: "Use not many words in a multitude of elders, and make not much babbling when thou prayest." The Rabbins especially refer to the concise prayers in the Bible, as examples; for instance, the prayer of Moses, offered up in behalf of his diseased sister, and consisting only of five monosyllables: "O Lord! do heal her!"

8. "Be not ye therefore like unto them: for your Father knoweth what things ye have need of before ye ask him."

The same was already said by David, Psalm cxxxix, 5: "There is not a word on my tongue, but lo! O Lord! thou knowest it altogether."

9. "After this manner, therefore, pray ye: Our Father which art in heaven, hallowed be thy name."

The first part is taken from Isaiah lxiii, 15 and 16: "Look down from heaven...... thou, O Lord! art our Father!" The second part is an imitation of Ezekiel xxxviii, 23: "Thus will I magnify myself, and sanctify myself," &c., or of ibid xxxvi, 23: "And I will sanctify my great name," &c.

10. "Thy kingdom come. Thy will be done in earth, as it is in heaven."

The first part of this verse is based upon Obadiah i, 21: "And saviors shall come upon Mount Zion to judge the Mount of Esau; and the kingdom shall be the Lord's;" or, Zechariah xiv, 9: "And the Lord shall be king over all the earth—in that day shall the Lord be One, and His name One." The latter part is taken from I. Samuel iii, 18: "He is the Lord: let him do whatever seemeth good to Him;" II. Samuel xv, 26: "Behold, here am I, let the Lord do to me, as it seemeth good to Him."

11. "Give us this day our daily bread!"

This verse is borrowed from the excellent prayer of Agur, (Proverbs xxx, 8,) "....Give me neither poverty nor riches, but give me my daily bread."

12. "And forgive us our debts, as we forgive our debtors."

This passage contains verse 2 of chap. xxviii, from Sirach in reverse order: "Forgive thy neighbor the hurt that he hath done unto thee, so shall thy sins also be forgiven when thou prayest."

13. "And lead us not into temptation."

Although many theologians are pleased to call this prayer "a model of prayers," it, however, contains a great absurdity.

If we reflect on human life in this world, we find, that it is in all its ages in a state of temptation. In the prime of life, when the world, with all its pleasure, is opening to us, when our heart is shining with golden treasures of innocence, and glowing for all that is good and noble; when our imagination, filled with ethereal forms pure as angels, and when the equilibrium of our qualities is not yet interrupted, then it is the lightness which leads us, like a *ignis fatuus*, on unbeaten ways and paths, where we are exposed to all the great dangers of the labyrinths of all ignoble feelings and follies, and our virtue has to endure a fiery trial.

In the meridian of our days, when our faculties are completely developed, and they should manifest themselves by noble deeds, then, like the waves of the sea, roar in us the passions and evil propensities, and we have again to fight a violent battle to gain the ever-blooming crown of virtue. And in the winter of our earthly existence, in old age, when stormy blood rolls no more in the veins, even then the temptations do not cease. Like a frightful tempest, coldness, peevishness, distrust, severity, censoriousness, and dissatisfaction with God and men, and, especially, natural weakness and despondency, are collecting over our heads, and incite us to many evil actions.

Indeed, there is not a man upon earth, who can boast of himself, that he was never in a difficulty, was never overtaken by distress, never involved in any battle, and has never been afflicted with any trouble.

The changeable state of human life is, therefore, nothing else than a chain of temptation, and it is entirely left to us, whether we will act with firmness and dignity, observing with circumspection that which duty and virtue command, or prohibit.

According to this, it is highly necessary to be tried by temptations; for only in the hour of trial can our consistency be manifested, sacrifices be made to our holy principles; and without this there is no virtue conceivable. Convinced of these truisms the Scribes laid down the principle: (Treat. Berachoth, fol. 16,) "Everything happens by especial dispensation of the heavenly Father, with exception of the moral conduct of men, which is left to their free will."

As little as a warrior can claim the attribute of heroism, who never went to war, even so little we would have a right of claiming the merit of a noble deed, when there was no occasion to do the reverse of it. From all these it follows, that verse 13 is incorrect for the following reasons:

1. If God would grant us such a desire as is expressed in this verse, he would have to remove all human nature from the whole human race.

2. He had to esteem virtue very highly, as such, without exertion and sacrifice, and had also to consider one as a victor, and acknowledge the merits of him who never fought any battle.

Nay! every unbiased mind would admit, that one can not act more foolishly than to lay extraordinary claims to the providence, asking, that it shall change for our sake the system of the world.

We find, however, a very true and correct form of prayer in the name of Moses, Psalm xc, 12: "So teach us to number our days, that we may apply our hearts unto wisdom." We ought in this land of temptation to wish and ask for true knowledge alone, which is the mother of all firm principles. If we are in possession of this, life with all its charms and death with all its terrors have lost their domineering power over us. For then is our highest treasure the ideal world, where we ascend the scale of gradation of the most noble and sublime ideas to the throne of the Most High.

These ideas probably inspired Agur to compose his beautiful prayer, (Prov. xxx, 8—10,) which commences: "Remove from me vanity and deception," &c., that is, in other words: "give me a true understanding;" but Jesus, by his disposition to extravagant ideas, (see my remarks chapter v, 39—41,) deviated from the original, (Prov. xxx, 8—10,) which he has imitated, and composed this very unreasonable passage, as I have stated above.

"But deliver us from evil;"

This phrase is borrowed from Psalm cxix, 133: "Secure my steps through thy words, and let iniquity have no dominion over me."

"For thine is the kingdom, and the power, and the glory, for ever, Amen."

This last part of the verse is taken literally from I. Chronicles xxix, 11: "Thine, O Lord, is the greatness and the power, and the glory, and the victory, and the majesty: for all that is in heaven is thine, thine is the kingdom, O Lord, and thou art exalted as head above all." The omission of the term "majesty," and the substitution of "kingdom," which is mentioned at the end, are evidently intended to give the prayer of Christ the appearance of originality.

However little originality there is in this formulary of prayer and its wording, as Mr. Wetzstein already observed, (*tota haec oratio ex formulis Hebraeorum concinnata est*,) it clearly proves at least this much, that Christ never meant to be regarded as God's son, or that God should be addressed in the name of the Son, or, lastly, that we should pray to God Father, God Son, and God Holy Ghost; but that we should address our adoration to God alone; the heavenly Father of all men, the Sole King of the Universe, and pray exclusively to Him.

14. "For if ye forgive men their trespasses, your heavenly Father will also forgive you.

15. For if ye forgive not men their trespasses, neither will your Father forgive your trespasses."

The substance of these two verses is taken from Sirach xxviii, 2—5: "Forgive thy neighbor the hurt that he hath done unto thee, so shall thy sins also be forgiven when thou prayest," &c. (The same doctrine is taught already in the precepts about the trespass-offerings, saying, that they should be brought, only after a full reparation had been made to our brother, for any injury or offence we may have committed against him. (Leviticus vi, 1—6.) The Rabbins mean to teach the same lesson by saying that "sins between man and his neighbor, the Day of Atonement will not expiate, unless he have satisfied his neighbor." Treatise Yomah lxxxv, b. —*Translator*.)

16. "Moreover, when ye fast, be not as the hypocrites, of a sad countenance; for they disfigure their faces, that they may appear unto men to fast. Verily I say unto you, They have their reward."

The right manner of fasting is taught already by Isaiah: (lviii, 5—7,) "Is it such a fast that I have chosen? a day for a man to afflict his soul?" &c. "Is not this the fast that I have chosen? to loose the bands of wickedness?" &c. The same is taught also by the Talmud, saying: (Treat. Taanith, fol. 16,) "Neither sackcloth nor fasting, but repentance and good deeds alone are acceptable before God."

17. "But thou, when thou fastest, annoint thy head, and wash thy face;

18. That thou appear not unto men to fast, but unto the Father which is in secret: and thy Father, which seeth in secret, shall reward thee openly."

The contents of these verses are the same as those of the preceding one, on which we have already expatiated, with the exception of the concluding part, "that the Lord sees all secret doings, but rewards publicly," which is borrowed partly from Sirach xvii, 14, 15, and 29, and partly from Psalms xxxi, 20. The passage from Sirach, alluded to here, has been mentioned already in our commentary on verse 6 of this chapter, and runs thus: "He gave every man commandment concerning his neighbor. Their ways are ever before Him, and shall not be hid from his eyes. How great is the loving kindness of the Lord our God, and His compassion unto such as turn unto Him in holiness.

19. "Lay not up for yourselves treasures upon earth, where moth and rust doth corrupt, and where thieves break through and steal:

20. But lay up for yourselves treasures in heaven, where neither moth nor rust doth corrupt, and where thieves do not break through nor steal:

21. For where your treasure is, there will your heart be also."

The same lesson is already taught by Sirach xxix, 11—13: "Lay up thy treasure according to the commandments of the Most High, and it shall bring thee more profit than gold. Shut up alms in thy store-houses: and it shall deliver thee from all affliction. It shall fight for thee against thine enemies, better than a mighty shield and strong spear." The same moral doctrine we find contained in the following Talmudical legend: (Treat. Baba Batra, fol. 11, a,) "When King Munebos, who lived at the times of the Maccabees, distributed, in years of famine, his own treasures and those which he had inherited from his ancestors, his friends and relatives rebuked him, saying, 'Thy ancestors filled the stores of thy treasury and thou wastest them!' To which the king replied: 'My ancestors accumulated treasures on this earth, but I lay them up in heaven; they placed all their substance where any one may steal them, but I keep them in such places to which none can have access; they gathered barren things, but I, such as will bring profit; they amassed gold, but I adorn my treasuries with souls delivered from death and sufferings; they strove to gather riches only for their descendants, but I wish to gather something for myself; and lastly, they gathered only for this world, but I gather also for the world to come, as it is said: (Isaiah lviii, 8,) thy righteousness shall go before thee, the glory of the Lord shall be thy reward.'"

22. "The light of the body is the eye: if, therefore, thine eye be single, thy whole body shall be full of light.

23. But if thine eye be evil, thy whole body shall be full of darkness. If, therefore, the light that is in thee be darkness, how great is that darkness."

Sin is symbolically termed "darkness," in Prov. ii, 13, whereas virtue and wisdom are called "light" by Isaiah (xlix, 6, and xlii, 6, and 7.) The form of these verses is an imitation of Ecclesiastes ii, 14: "The wise man's eyes are in his head, but the fool walketh in darkness." The moral lesson, that we should not allow ourselves to be led astray by the desires of our eye and heart, is taught already in Numbers xv, 39: "Seek not after your own heart and your own eyes, by which you have been wont to go astray."

24. "No man can serve two masters; for either he will hate the one,

and love the other; or else he will hold to the one and despise the other. Ye can not serve God and Mammon."

That we should not serve the all-alluring Lord, enticing gold, is taught in Job xxxi, 24 and 25: "If I have set my trust in gold, or have said to the fine gold, Thou art my confidence; If I rejoiced because my wealth was great, and because my hand had gotten much;" &c. "This also were an iniquity, to be punished by the Judge, for I should have denied the God that is above." (ibid. verse 28.) The same we read in Psalms lii, 8 and 9: "Lo, this is the man that made not God his strength; but trusted in the abundance of his riches, and strengthened himself in his mammon;" [26] ibid. lxii, 11: "if your riches increase, set not your heart upon them."

25. "Therefore, I say unto you, Take no thought for your life, what ye shall eat, or what ye shall drink; nor yet for your body, what ye shall put on. Is not the life more than meat, and the body than raiment?"

The Psalmist, led by the conviction that He who gave life would attend also to its preservation, often and most urgently enjoins confidence in Divine Providence, upon us. "Commit unto the Lord thy ways, trust also in Him, and He will bring it to pass," (Ps. xxxvii, 5.) "All wait upon Thee, that Thou mayest give them their food in due season. Thou givest, they gather; Thou openest Thy hand, they are filled with good." (ibid. civ, 27 and 28.) "Who giveth food unto all flesh; for His mercy endureth for ever," (ibid. cxxxvi, 25.) "The eyes of all wait upon Thee, and Thou giveth them their food in due season. Thou openest Thy hand, and satisfiest the desire of every living thing," (ibid. cxlv, 15 and 16.)

26. "Behold the fowls of the air: for they sow not, neither do they reap, nor gather into barns; yet your heavenly Father feedeth them. Are ye not much better than they."

This verse contains an imitation of Psalms cxlvii, 9—11: "He giveth to the beast his food, to the young ravens which cry. He delighteth not in the strength of the horse,

[26] The term הוה, corresponds with the expression "Mammon," "worldly treasure;" for only with this signification can it constitute the parallel to עשר, "wealth," "riches." Thus the Chaldean translator renders והות רשעים, (Prov. x, 2,) by וקניני דרשיע.

He taketh not pleasure in the begs of a man. The Lord taketh pleasure in them that fear Him, in those that hope in His mercy."

The form of our verse is taken from the Mishnah, Treat. Kiddushin, fol. 82, a, where we read: "Rabbi Simeon, son of Eliezar, used to say: Hast thou ever seen that a beast, or any bird carried on a trade for it's life's maintenance? and yet, they get their food without trouble, although most of them are created for my own benefit. How much more will I find my sustenance, whom the Most High has made to worship and adore Him."

27. "Which of you by taking thought can add one cubit unto his stature?"

The contrast between man's frailty and weakness, and the Supreme power of God, is far more beautifully described in Job xl, 4, 5, &c., where we read: (verse 9,) "Hast thou an arm like God? or canst thou thunder with a voice like Him?" &c.

The lesson, however, that it is an idle thing to build up, by cares and anxieties, our happiness and peace, is taught already by King Solomon: "And also that every man should eat and drink, and enjoy the good of all his labor; it is the gift of God. I know that, whatsoever God doeth, it shall be for ever: nothing can be put to it, nor anything taken from it: and God doeth it, that men should fear before Him." (Ecclesiastes iii, 13 and 14.) "Therefore I commended mirth, for man hath no better thing under the sun, than to eat, and to drink, and to be merry," (that is to say, to abstain from unnecessary anxieties:) "for that shall abide with him, of his labor the days of his life, which God giveth him under the sun." (ibid. viii, 15.)

28. "And why take ye thought for raiment? Consider the lilies of the field how they grow; they toil not, neither do they spin;

29. And yet I say unto you, That even Solomon in all his glory was not arrayed like one of these."

The figure contained in these verses is taken from Solomon's Song ii, 1, where he says of himself: "I am the rose of Sharon, and the lily of the valleys."

30. "Wherefore, if God so clothe the grass of the field, which to-day is, and to-morrow is cast into the oven, shall he not much more clothe you, O ye of little faith?"

That we should not give ourselves up to great anxieties about our food and raiment, is taught in Deut. x. 18: "He doth execute the judgment of the fatherless and widow, and loveth the stranger, in giving him food and raiment." The Psalmist tells us the same thing, in more concise language: "O! fear the Lord, ye His saints; for there is no want to them that fear Him;" (Psalm xxxiv, 10,) "Cast thy burden upon the Lord, and He will sustain thee: He will never suffer the righteous to be moved." (Ibid. lv, 23.)

31. "Therefore, take no thought, saying, What shall we eat? or, What shall we drink? or, Wherewithal shall we be clothed?

32. (For after all these things do the Gentiles seek,) for your heavenly Father knoweth that ye have need of all these things.

33. But seek ye first the kingdom of God, and His righteousness, and all these things shall be added unto you."

All this is contained in one verse of the Psalm: (xxxvii, 4,) "Delight thyself in the Lord, and He will give thee the desires of thy heart."

34. "Take, therefore, no thought for the morrow: for the morrow shall take thought for the things of itself. Sufficient unto the day is the evil thereof."

This verse is literally taken from Sirach xxx, 23, or from Proverbs xxvii, 1. In like manner the Psalmist exclaims: (lxviii, 20,) "Blessed be the Lord, who daily loadeth us with benefits, even the Lord of our salvation."

CHAPTER VII.

1. "Judge not, that ye be not judged."

The same is taught by Sirach xviii, 21: "Examine thyself before thou judgest others, and thou wilt find mercy, when others are punished." (Has the great Hielel, who lived almost half a century before the birth of Christ, not taught the same, when he says: "Judge not thy neighbor until thou be placed in his position?—*Translator.*)

2. "For with what judgment ye judge, ye shall be judged: and with what measure ye mete, it shall be measured to you again."

We find the same idea conveyed in Proverbs xii, 14: "A man shall be satisfied with good by the fruit of his mouth; and the recompense of a man's hands shall be rendered unto him;" that is, as he judged, and did to others, so will he be judged and done to by them. Thus, also, we read in Psalm lxii, 13: "Also unto thee, O Lord, belongeth mercy; for Thou renderest to every man according to his work." Furthermore, we find in the Talmud, (Treat. Sanhedrin, fol. 100, a,) the following: "With whatever measure man meteth, it will be meted to him; for Divine rewards and punishments are meted out according to the actions of man." To authenticate this assertion, the passage, II. Kings vii, 2 and 20, is referred to. In the same sense the principle is laid down in Ethics of the Fathers, I, § 6: "Judge every man from a favorable point of view!"

3. "And why beholdest thou the mote that is in thy brother's eye, but considerest not the beam in thine own eye?"

In Treat. Baba Bathra, fol. 15, b, we find the translation of the first verse of chapter i, of the Book of Ruth, "In the days when the Judges were ruled," with the following commentary: "For they were then so wicked that, when they should have admonished any one to remove the mote from his eyes, they could be answered, to take the beam from their own." From this we may learn that the figure used by Christ was not originally used by him, but lived as a proverb in the mouth of the people.

4. "Or how wilt thou say to thy brother, Let me pull out the mote out of thine eye; and, behold, a beam is in thine own eye?

5. Thou hypocrite, first cast out the beam out of thine own eye: and then shalt thou see clearly to cast out the mote out of thy brother's eye."

The same is taught already by Sirach xviii, 20: "Before thou judgest others, examine thyself." Nay, this admonition was, according to the Rabbins, (Treat. Sanhedrin, fol. 18, a,) given already by the Prophet Zephaniah: (ii, 1,) "Gather yourselves together, yea, gather yourselves together, O nation not desired!" For from this verse they deduced the general lesson: "Examine thyself, and then others!"

6. "Give not that which is holy unto the dogs, neither cast ye your pearls before swines, lest they trample them under their feet, and turn again, and rend you."

The metaphor which occurs in this verse is an imitation of Proverbs xi, 22: "As a jewel of gold in a swine's snout, so is a fair woman which is without discretion." That we should not teach Divine truths to reckless scorners, we are told by King Solomon, saying: (Proverbs ix, 7 and 8,) "He that reproveth a scorner, getteth to himself shame; and he that rebuketh a wicked man, getteth himself a blot. Reprove not a scorner, lest he hate thee; rebuke a wise man, and he will love thee."

7. "Ask, and it shall be given you; seek, and ye shall find; knock, and it shall be opened unto you;

8. For every one that asketh, receiveth; and he that seeketh, findeth; and to him that knocketh, it shall be opened."

In I. Chronicles xxviii, 9, and II. Chronicles xv, 2, we read the following: "If thou seek Him, He will be found of thee;" in Sirach xi, 12, we find: "My son, if thou doest not run, thou wilt obtain nothing; if thou seekest not, thou wilt find nothing;" and in Proverbs viii, 17: "I love them that love me, and those who seek me early, shall find me."

9. "Or what man is there of you, whom if his son ask bread, will he give him a stone?

10. Or if he ask a fish, will he give him a serpent?

11. If ye, then, being evil, know how to give good gifts unto your children; how much more shall your Father which is in heaven give good things to them that ask Him?"

The contents of these verses are taken from Ps. ciii, 13: "Like as a father pitieth his children, so the Lord pitieth them that fear Him."

12. "Therefore all things whatsoever ye would that men should do to you, do ye even so to them: for this is the Law and the Prophets."

The same is said by Tobit iv, 15: "Do that to no man which thou hatest." And Hillel the Sage, gave the same lesson to a heathen who wished to be converted to Judaism: "Whatever is not pleasing unto thee, do not unto thy brother; this is the substance of the Law and the Prophets; all the rest is but the commentary thereon." (Talmud, Treat. Sabbath, fol. 31, b.)

13. "Enter ye in at the strait gate; for wide is the gate, and broad the way, that leadeth to destruction, and many there be which go in thereat:

14. Because, strait is the gate, and narrow is the way, which leadeth unto life, and few there be that find it."

All this is borrowed from Proverbs iv, 18 and 19: "But the path of the Just is as the shining light, that shineth more and more unto the perfect day. The way of the wicked is as darkness: they know not, at what they stumble." Isaiah xxvi, 2: "Open ye the gates, that the righteous nation which keepeth the truth may enter it." Psalms cxviii, 19 and 20: "Open to me the gates of righteousness; I will go into them, and I will praise the Lord. This is the gate of the Lord, into which the righteous shall enter."

15. "Beware of false Prophets, which come to you in sheep's clothing, but inwardly they are ravening wolves."

Here we have an imitation of Jeremiah xiv, 14, 23; xxvii, 14, and Ezekiel xxii, 25 and 27, where false Prophets are compared to "a roaring lion ravening the prey," and avaricious princes to rapacious wolves. The phrase, "which come to you in sheep's clothing," seems to be borrowed from Zechariah xiii, 4.

16. "Ye shall know them by their fruits: do men gather grapes of thorns, or figs of thistles?

17. Even so every good tree bringeth forth good fruit; but a corrupt tree bringeth forth evil fruit.

18. A good tree can not bring forth evil fruit, neither can a corrupt tree bring forth good fruit.

19. Every tree that bringeth not forth good fruit, is hewn down, and cast into the fire.

20. Wherefore, by their fruits ye shall know them."

Here we have but an extension of what is said, in a few words, in Sirach xxvii, 6: "The fruit declareth, if the tree have been dressed, so is the utterance of a conceit in the heart of man." In the writings of the Prophets, we find man frequently compared with a tree; for instance, Isaiah ii, 13; lxi, 3; Jeremiah xi, 16, 19; xvii, 8;

Ezekiel xxi, 3; &c. See also, Psalms i, 3; lii, 10; xcii, 13.

21. "Not every one that saith unto me, Lord, Lord, shall enter into the kingdom of heaven; but he that doeth the will of my father which is in heaven."

The lesson that man should not act hypocritically, hence not bear God only upon his lips, but keep His commandments, is taught in Jeremiah xii, 2: "Thou art near in their mouth, and far from their reins;" Isaiah xxix, 13: "Wherefore the Lord said, Forasmuch as this people draw near me with their mouth, and with their lips do honor me, but have removed their heart far from me," &c.

I forbear expatiating upon the twenty second and twenty-third verses, because they contain merely self-praising remarks of Christ.

24. "Therefore, whosoever heareth these sayings of mine, and doeth them, I will liken him unto a wise man, which built his house upon a rock."

The figure contained in this verse, is borrowed from Numbers xxiv, 21: "And he looked on the Kenites, and took up his parable, and said, strong is thy dwelling-place, and thou puttest thy nest in a rock;" or from Isaiah xxxiii, 16, where it is said that the virtuous man dwells on high, and "his place of defence shall be the munitions of rocks."

25. "And the rain descended, and the floods came, and the winds blew, and beat upon the house; and it fell not: for it was founded upon a rock.

26. And every one that heareth these sayings of mine and doeth them not, shall be likened unto a foolish man, which built his house upon the sand:

27. And the rain descended, and the floods came, and the wind blew, and beat upon the house; and it fell: and great was the fall of it."

The contents and diction of these verses are borrowed from Ezekiel xiii, 8—16, with this difference, however, that the term "house," has been substituted for "wall," as the Prophet has it.

28. "And it came to pass when Jesus had ended these sayings, the people were astonished at his doctrine.

29. For he taught them as one having authority, and not as the Scribes."

We think we have already satisfactorily proven, that, even aside from the omissions and errors, the moral lessons held forth in the Seven Chapters upon which we have commented, contain in no wise any improvements of the doctrines taught by Moses and the Prophets. How, then, can it be possible, that the people were astonished at the sayings of Christ, well acquainted, as they were with almost all phrases and figures employed by him? But should they have admired his doctrine, we are justified in concluding that the multitude which he addressed, consisted of such people as had never read the Law and the Prophets, nor ever listened to, and understood the Scribes; hence could be very easily, and were really imposed upon.

CHAPTER VIII.

In this, and the following chapters, miracles are narrated which are said to have been wrought by Christ; but it is preposterous to attempt to establish thereby the authenticity of his Divine mission, or even his own Divine nature.

1. As there were many Thaumaturgi among the Scribes, of whom history relates as true facts, that they exorcised devils, healed sick persons by prayer, and resuscitated the dead; and that the Sea, storm and rain obeyed their commands: it is evident that the founder of the Christian Religion, trained as he was in the school of the Sopherim, (see Luke ii, 46,) did that only for the authentication of his purported Divine mission, which the Scribes had done, or pretended to have done for other purposes; hence, he was not endowed with any supernatural power, but employed those thaumaturgic arts, which he had learned from the Sopherim for the accomplishment of his object.

2. There is no reason why those men, whom the heathens deified, should not have deserved adoration. They, too, are said, according to supposed authentic reports, to have wrought miracles before assembled multi-

tudes, as no man could accomplish them without special assistance of the Deity. I leave it, therefore, to the sound understanding of my readers, to form their own judgment with regard to the stories about miracle-workers, and shall relate some miracles of the Sopherim, to be compared with those of Christ.

In Treat. Meilah, Sect. Kodshay Hamizbeach, we read the following story: "A Roman emperor once forbade the Israelites the celebration of the Sabbath, circumcision, &c., whereupon the Jews elected the Thaumaturgi Rabbi Simeon, son of Jochai, and Rabbi Eliezar, son of Joshua, deputies to the imperial court, to effect the repeal of the awful decree. On their voyage they were met by the spirit of Ben Themalyon, who said to them, 'if ye have no objection, I will precede you and enter the soul of the princess, so that she shall be seized with such madness as no physician is able to cure. When ye arrive, command unto me: withdraw Ben Themalyon, and I shall leave her. By means of this aid ye shall find favor in the eyes of the emperor. And as a sign that I shall really have left her, all glass-ware in the palace shall be broken.' And so it happened."

In Treat. Baba Meziah, fol. 59, we read the following story: "Rabbi Eliezar once solved all casuistic questions proposed to him, but seeing that his colleagues would not acknowledge his interpretations as legally valid, he said: 'as a proof that ye may decide according to my interpretations, I tell you that even the tree which stands before the gate will move from its place in obedience to my command.' And behold! the tree soon moved four-hundred feet from its former place. But his colleagues answered: 'this is no authentication as yet;' whereupon the Rabbi said: 'may the current of yon brook prove it then!' And the brook soon flooded towards its source. And the former said again: 'Even this can not convince us.' 'May then,' said the Rabbi, 'heaven show you that ye should follow my opinion, by causing the walls of this house to fall.' And the walls already bent over to fall, when Rabbi Joshua addressed them thus: 'What is it to you when the learned dispute about the Law?' And the walls neither fell in honor of Rabbi Eliezar, nor rose again in favor of Rabbi Joshua, but stand to this day bent over, as though they were ready to fall. Hereupon Rabbi Eliezar exclaimed: 'May heaven decide!' And a voice immediately came from heaven, saying: 'Why do you thus treat Rabbi Eliezar? let his decision be everywhere followed!' Then Rabbi Joshua sprang from his seat, and said: 'The Law is no more in heaven; we are to be guided by the Bible already received, in which we read, that the majority has to decide wherever a doubt existed.'"

"On the same day," thus it is related in the same passage, "the spiritual superiority of Rabbi Eliezar was revealed also by this, that every one on whom he cast his eye in anger, stood as struck by lightning.

"The ship on which was Rabbi Gamaliel was about to founder, when he said: 'this certainly happens because I opposed Rabbi Eliezar.' He prayed to God: 'Lord of the Universe!' &c. and the Ocean immediately ceased to be stormy."

See also: Treat. Taanith, fol. 20, a, fol. 24, a; Treat. Sanhedrin, fol. 100, a; Treat. Baba Metsiah, fol. 85, b; Treat. Sabbath, fol. 33, b; Treat. Berachoth, fol. 33, &c.

The *Anonymous Fragmentist* also makes the following excellent remarks, with regard to the miracles related in the New Testament: "May Jesus, may his Apostles have cured ever so many blind and lame persons, or exorcised many legions of devils, they can not thereby remedy the contradiction between their system of the Messiah, and their self-conflicting testimonies with regard to his resurrection and re-appearance: contradiction is a devil and author of untruths, that can not be exorcised, either by fasting or prayer. May these men have done whatever they wished to do, they can not thereby effect this, that things were carried out which never occurred; that Christ had reappeared in clouds of heaven, ere all those who, before his death, stood by him had tasted death. No miracle can prove that the phrase, 'from Egypt I have called my son,' alluded to Christ, or that there is a prophetical passage saying: 'he shall be called Nazarene.'" (See the above quoted "Fragmentist," &c., page 138.)

4. "—but go thy way, shew thyself to the priest, and offer the gift that Moses commanded, for a testimony unto them."

It is evident from these words, that Christ meant not to reject the Ceremonial Law of Moses; otherwise he would not have told the leper to bring the usual sacrifice.

11. "And I say unto you, That many shall come from the east and west, and shall sit down with Abraham, and Isaac, and Jacob, in the kingdom of heaven."

Christ clearly teaches here that every man, though he do not profess the Christian Religion, may become a partaker of the kingdom of heaven, by leading a pious and virtuous life. For if eternal salvation indeed depended upon the profession of Christianity, how could he have announced to the people, that the Jewish Patriarchs who certainly knew nothing of his religious system, were sitting foremost in the kingdom of heaven?

12. "But the children of the kingdom shall be cast out into outer darkness: there shall be weeping and gnashing of teeth."

The punishment held out here to hypocrites was before repeatedly and powerfully pointed to, both by Jeremiah, (iv, 2—5,) and the other Prophets.

The phrase "shall be cast out into outer darkness," is taken from Jeremiah xiii, 16: "Give glory to the Lord, your God, before he cause darkness, and before your feet stumble upon the dark mountains, and while ye look for light, he turn it into the shadow of death, and make it gross darkness."

17. "That it might be fulfilled which was spoken by Esaias the Prophet, saying, Himself took our infirmities, and bear our sicknesses."

It is evident from the context of the verse as well, as the whole chapter of Isaiah, that the Prophet does not speak of a redemption from bodily, but merely spiritual diseases. Hence, the Apostle has misinterpreted the clear words of the Prophet with the view of corroborating his own system. And however great the effect may be with which his interpretation is sought to be justified, it is incontrovertibly certain, that Isaiah never alluded to the Christ either in chap. lii, 13—15, or throughout the fifty-third chapter; since he says in the last named chapter: (verse 10—12,) "he shall see his seed, he shall prolong his days," &c., all of which is inapplicable to Christ.

19. "And a certain Scribe came, and said unto him, Master, I will follow thee whithersoever thou goest.

20. And Jesus saith unto him, The foxes have holes, and the birds of the air have nests; but the Son of man hath not where to lay his head."

Thus Christ says not, that he co-operated in the creation of heaven and earth, but confesses to be a son of man, a weak, miserable being, that is so poor, that he can not call even the least piece of land his own, and openly contradicts, therefore, the paradox doctrine which means to declare him a world-creating Godhead.

21. "And another of his disciples said unto him, Lord, suffer me first to go and bury my father.

22. But Jesus said unto him, Follow me; and let the dead bury their dead."

A mere play upon words does not yet constitute a sufficient reason why Christ should have prohibited his disciple from paying the last tribute of love to his recently departed parent. Such a doctrine of wilful violation of our duties towards our parents is utterly irreconcilable with sound morals. Eliah acted in a far worthier manner, when he was called upon to consecrate Elisha as Prophet. (I. Kings, xix, 20.) Indeed! Christ who took great pains to imitate Eliah in every thing, even in his food and clothing, ought to have followed him also in the last point, instead of establishing the originality of his system by some false moral doctrine.

CHAPTER IX.

6. "But that ye may know that the son of man hath power on earth to forgive sins, (then saith he to the sick of the palsy,) Arise, take up thy bed, and go into thy house.

7. And he arose, and departed to his house.

8. But when the multitude saw it, they marvelled, and glorified God, which had given such power unto men."

Aside from the fact, that this story belongs to the domain of fiction, its contents are highly absurd. For, having announced himself, as we have proved from chapter iv, and other passages, as a frail being that needeth the mercy of the Lord, how can he assume, or have the power to forgive the transgressions of men against the Supreme Being. For the Almighty One who foreseeth all effects, can alone execute or remit punishment for transgressions committed, according as he thinks most to correspond with His love for perfection. Should any one say: be this as it may, Christ at least proved by the miracle here narrated, that he possessed the power of forgiving sins: we can refute this objection by simply pointing to the fact, that Moses, Elijah, Elisha and others are likewise said to have wrought similar, and even more miraculous deeds, while, at the same time, these men, whom Christ himself acknowledged to have been sent and inspired by God, distinctly assert, as it may be seen also from their doctrines and lives—that no one can forgive sins in the place of God. (See Exod. xxiii, 21; Psalm cxxx, 4, 7 and 8, &c.)

9. "And as Jesus passed forth from thence, he saw a man, named Matthew, sitting at the receipt of custom: and he saith unto him, Follow me. And he arose, and followed him.

10. And it came to pass as Jesus sat at meat in the house, behold, many publicans and sinners came and sat down with him and his disciples.

11. And when the Pharisees saw it, they said unto his disciples, Why eateth your Master with publicans and sinners?"

This report of the vocation of Matthew, belongs to the province of fables and poetry, as Dr. Strauss justly remarks, in his work, (The Life of Jesus, I, pages 568—576,) and has proved it by the following reasons:

1. The Evangelists in Mark ii, 14, and Luke v, 27, mention the name of Levi, the son of Alpheus, instead of the name of Matthew. If an occurrence which should have happened only to one person is reported of two different persons, one of them must confessedly be invented.

2. If Levi was the original name of the Evangelist, who assumed afterwards the name Matthew, and, under the latter appellation, should be understood Levi, this double name would undoubtedly have been mentioned, as those of the other Apostles.

Nay, Mark and Luke having omitted the epithet, "the publican," which occurs Matthew x, 3, prove that they hold as a settled opinion that Matthew was not called by Jesus from the publicans. And I would add that the epithet, "publican," (Matth. x, 3,) shows that our historiographer was of the opinion that none but Matthew had been called from the publicans. For, if there another publican also had been called, such a surname was of no significance whatever, and contradicts therefore directly the statement of Mark and Luke.

But even the report of the latter, says Dr. Strauss, is an anecdote; because if the disciples of Christ shared in the repast which took place in the house of the publicans, how could they be reproached by the Pharisees during it, without the latter defiling themselves by entering such a house of sinners, as they should have strongly reprimanded Jesus for it. (Luke xix, 7.) The rebuke made by the Pharisees, therefore, only existed in the imagination of the historiographer.

To this, however, I must add, that the unhistorical contents of these verses can be proved, also, by the fact, that it is impossible that the Pharisees should have objected to the endeavors of Jesus to improve the publicans and sinners.

For the Sopherim (Pharisees) laid down the principle (Ethics of the Fathers v, 21,) "One, who leads and accustoms others to virtue, no sin will be caused by him, &c. Moses was virtuous and taught others to be so, therefore, the merits of others are ascribed to him," &c.

12. "But when Jesus heard that, he said unto them, They that be whole need not a physician, but they that are sick."

Psalm xli, 6; Jerem. iii, 22; Hosea xiv, 4, gave rise to the contents of this verse.

13. "But ye go and learn what that meaneth, I will have mercy, and not sacrifice: for I am not come to call the righteous, but sinners to repentance."

This verse contains an untrue statement, because the principles laid down by the Sophrim show clearly, that they entered truly into the spirit of the words of the Prophet Hosea, (vi, 6,) which are quoted here literally. Thus it reads, for instance, Treat. Rosh Hashanah, fol. 18, a, "It is said: I. Samuel iii, 14, that the iniquity of Eli's house shall not be purged with sacrifice or offering for ever The meaning of this verse is, that the sins shall not be forgiven by sacrifices, but by gaining a true knowledge of the Divine Laws and by a noble eagerness to serve his fellow-men." Again, Treat. Succah, 49, b, "charity and noble actions are more meritorious than sacrifices."

14. "Then came to him the disciples of John, saying, Why do we and the Pharisees fast oft, but thy disciples fast not?"

The report, that the Pharisees fast very often is unhistorical. They taught explicitly, Treat. Tanith, fol. 11; Nedarim, fol. 4; Nasir, fol. 19, &c., "that every one who fasts voluntarily is called a sinner." Again they had a traditional apothegm: "If the pious would enjoy the happiness of this world and that to come, who will be displeased by it?" [27] (Treat. Horioth, page 10, b.)

15. "And Jesus said unto them: Can the children of the bride-chamber mourn, as long as the bride-groom is with them! but the days will come, when the bride-groom shall be taken from them, and then shall they fast."

The parabolical expression is borrowed from the Song of Solomon, or it is an imitation of the Book of Wisdom viii, 2, where it reads: "This (the wisdom) I loved and

[27] אטו צדיקי אי אכלי תרי עלמא מי סנו להו. הוריות דף י

sought it out from my youthful days. I searched for it to gain her as my bride, and I became the bride-groom of its beauty."

17. "Neither do men put new wine into old bottles: else the bottles break, and the wine runneth out, and the bottles perish: but they put new wine into new bottles, and both are preserved."

We know the old bottles; but, as yet, we have not been able to discover the new wine. Or should the indignation manifested by Christ at the hypocritical fasting constitute that very new wine? Well, that wine had long before his time been offered to the people of Israel by their Prophets. (See Zechariah vii, 5, 8; Isaiah lviii, 3, 4.)

33. "And when the devil was cast out, the dumb spake: and the multitudes marvelled, saying, It was never so seen in Israel."

That the people should have expressed themselves in this way, is highly improbable. For, were not far greater miracles of more ancient time related to the people, and believed by them? Thus, for instance, we read that the Prophet Elisha cured the captain of the King of Aram by simply telling him: "Go and wash in Jordan seven times, and thy flesh shall come again to thee, and thou shalt be clean;" that he called the dead to life again; caused iron to float on the water: smote an Aramaic army with blindness, and cured them again, &c. How, then, can we believe, that the Jews regarded the stories of Christ's miraculous deeds as extraordinary and unprecedented?

34. "But the Pharisees said, He casteth out devils, through the prince of the devils."

This casting out devils, can in no wise prove and substantiate the supernatural powers of Christ, since he himself asserts (chap. vii, 22 and 23,) that there were many who exorcised devils, and performed many miracles, yet were hypocrites and impostors. How, then, can this be done otherwise, if there are devils, than by the prince of the devil himself? (See about this point, my remarks on chapter xii, verse 26, below.)

36. "But when he saw the multitudes, he was moved with compassion on them, because they fainted, and were scattered abroad, as sheep having no shepherd."

This verse is taken from Ezekiel xxxiv, 5: "And my

sheep were scattered, because there is no shepherd." But at the time of Christ, when so many Sects existed in Israel, there were too many shepherds, so that he could have with more propriety borrowed the third verse of the thirteenth chapter from the same Prophet, saying: "Thus saith the Lord God: Woe unto the foolish Prophets, that follow their own spirit, and have seen nothing!"

CHAPTER X.

With regard to the fifth, sixth and seventh verses, see my remarks on chapter xv, verse 24, below. [28]

15. "Verily I say unto you, It shall be more tolerable for the land of Sodom and Gomorrah, in the day of judgment, than for that city."

This verse is an imitation of Isaiah xiii, 19: "And Babylon . . . . shall be as when God overthrew Sodom and Gomorrah;" or Jeremiah xx, 16.

16. "Behold, I send you forth as sheep in the midst of wolves: be ye, therefore, wise as serpents, and harmless as doves."

The phrase "I send you forth as sheep," is taken either from Ezekiel xxii, 27, or Zephaniah iii, 3: "Her princes within her, are roaring lions; her judges are evening wolves, they leave not even a bone for the morrow." The second part of the above verse, "be ye, therefore," &c. contains a lesson borrowed from Jeremiah iv, 42, where he says by way of rebuke: "they are wise to do evil, but to do good they have no knowledge."

19. "But when they deliver you up, take no thought how or what ye shall speak, for it shall be given you in that same hour what ye shall speak.

20. For it is not ye that speak, but the Spirit of your Father which speaketh in you."

It is evident that we have here an imitation of Exodus iv, 10—12: "O my Lord, I am not eloquent . . . . . .

[28] However many hypotheses have been proposed by the learned with regard to the term "Iscariot," in the fourth verse, they are all too artificial and improbable. We opine that this surname "Iscariot," *Ho Iscariotes*, was given to Judas, because he suffered himself to be hired for the betrayal of his master. The term is derived from the Hebrew שכיר, "Sachir," "hireling;" as Simon was surnamed "the Cananite," *Zelotes*, which is derived from the Hebrew קנא, "Kannah," "to be jealous," "to be zealous."

Now, therefore, go and I will be with thy mouth, and teach thee what thou shalt say."

21. "And the brother shall deliver up the brother to death, and the father, the child: and the children shall rise up against their parents, and cause them to be put to death."

This verse is an imitation of Michah vii, 6, which verse we shall literally transcribe below, in our remark on verses 35 and 36.

23. "But when they persecute you in this city, flee ye into another: for verily I say unto you, Ye shall not have gone over the cities of Israel till the son of man be come."

History has shown that these words have not been fulfilled.

28. "And fear not them which kill the body, but are not able to kill the soul: but rather fear him which is able to destroy both soul and body in hell."

This doctrine of obedience to the will of God, for the sake of the eternal salvation of our soul, is held out by most theologians as a special virtue of Christianity, because, as they opine, the Old Testament speaks only of earthly reward and punishment, nowhere makes mention of the continuation and salvation of the soul after the dissolution of the body, and represents it merely as something corporeal.

Now, as we learn from Herodotus, L. ii, chap. 123, that the Egyptians were the first, [29] who expressed the opinion that the soul was immortal and after the dissolution of the body, migrated from one creature to another, and thus connected with this doctrine of the immortality of the soul, the idea of reward and punishment, it is highly improbable that Moses, who was undoubtedly initiated into the Egyptian religious system should have remained ignorant of all this. Hence, an assertion to this effect must rest upon errors, as a closer investigation of the matter will show.

[29] I could prove that the doctrine of the immortality of the soul, and that the Lord, according to our deeds on earth, either admitted it into the land of bliss, or consigned it for some time to hell, was known in the Orient, and especially in India, two thousand years before the Christian era, and that Zoroaster, — about 680 B. C. E. — taught the same doctrine in the Zend-books, which exercised an undeniable influence over the nations of Asia; all of which would at once confute the opinion of the great superiority of the Christian Religion with regard to this doctrine. But I shall expatiate only upon the moral doctrine of the Egyptians, which Moses undoubtedly knew, because we have to speak of the views of Moses and the Prophets with regard to the nature of the human soul.

Granted even that Moses has not distinctly taught the doctrine of the Immortality of the soul, we must nevertheless acknowledge, unless we read the Pentateuch with preconceived opinions, that he has exhibited it clearly enough, *Kata Ten Dianoian*, that is to say, that the Pentateuch contains passages, the contents of which must lead us to the conclusion, that he did not regard body and soul as one material whole, but knew well how to discriminate between them.

Of the many passages of this kind, I will adduce but a few.

Genesis ii, 7: "And the Lord formed man of the dust of the ground, and breathed into his nostrils the breath of life; and man became a living soul."

The "breath of life," נפש, that made man a living soul, is thus represented, before it entered his body, a נשמת חיים, a self-acting, living breath; and this too, as an immediate emanation of the Deity; so that this animation of man is consequently expressed by "He breathed into his nostrils," that is to say, God immediately created the soul out of Himself; whereas the creation of the animals is expressed by "and the earth," or, "the water brought forth," (Gen. i, 20, 24,) to show distinctly that the animals were created indirectly, that is, of earthly elements, and thus placed in one category with the plants, at the creation of which we read the same phrase, "the earth brought forth." Finiteness could produce only finite things.

Now, as Moses represents the soul as an emanation from God Himself, he must necessarily have held it to be simple, hence indestructible, and, therefore, also immortal. And this higher nature and origin he endeavored to show also by the peculiar signification of the human soul by the term נשמה, which he nowhere attributes to animals. [30] Nor is the רוח, or נפש, which he attributes alike to man and animals, homogeneous with the נשמה, but must be compared with the *Thymos*, or *Thymoeides*, of Plato that

[30] See Kimchi's Commentary on Genesis ii, 7.

constitutes the connecting link between soul (נשמה) and body (גוף.) The *Neshamah* is otherwise called also כבוד, "honor," (Gen. xlix, 6,) because it alone constitutes man's true dignity and majesty.

In Genesis ix, 5, we read: "And surely your blood of your lives will I require; at the hand of every beast will I require it, and at the hand of man; at the hand of every man's brother, (that is of him who kills himself or others,) will I require the life of man."

The idea expressed in this verse, is according to our opinion the following: After the prohibition to shed man's blood had been pronounced in general terms, all possible special cases, on account of the great importance of the subject, are enumerated, and the prohibition repeated at every instance. According to the commentary of Rabbi Jitzchaki on Genesis ix, 5, and the explanation of Professor Levison, in his Tochachot Megillah, chap. iv, 18, (ed. Hamburg, 1784,) this verse would read thus: "But the blood which you shed on yourselves will I require of you," &c., an interpretation to which I can not agree, because the phrase "at the hand of man, and at the hand of every man's brother," would contain nothing but a tautology, which would be out of place in the text of so important a Law. But most important is the remark of Professor Levison: (in the above named work, page 26, col. b,) "Had Moses regarded the soul as mortal, how could he have taught this, that God would visit the sin of suicide upon the perpetrator, since his existence would utterly cease with his last breath?" Moses certainly presupposed the belief in the Immortality of the soul, and Reward and Punishment beyond the grave as something known, otherwise he could not have spoken of the punishment which a suicide had to expect after his death.

In Leviticus xx, 2 and 3, we read again: "Thou shalt say to the children of Israel, Whosoever he be of the children of Israel, or of the strangers that sojourn in Israel, that giveth any of his seed unto Moloch, he shall surely be put to death; the people of the land shall stone him with stones. And I will set my face against that man, and will cut him off from among his people; because he hath given of his seed unto Moloch, to defile my sanctuary, and to profane my holy name."

How could the worshipper of Moloch have been cautioned by the threat that, after he had been stoned to death by the people, the Lord would set His face against him, and cut him off from his people, that is to say, deprive him of eternal salvation, if the doctrine of eternal life had not been known then?

Should it be said, that verse 3 meant to convey this idea, that God would Himself punish this sin, if it were otherwise to go unpunished, I should remark, 1, that in this case too much would be read between the lines, and 2, that this was distinctly mentioned in the fourth verse.

Again. In Leviticus xviii, 5, we are told: "Ye shall, therefore, keep my statutes and my judgments: which if a man do, he shall live in them," that is to say, obtain eternal life.

That I have not given an arbitrary version of this verse, I shall prove by the best commentators.

Onkelos interprets the words וחי בהם, "he shall live by them," by: "he shall live by them in eternal life."

Jitzchaki (Rashi) says: "the words, 'he shall live by them,' relate to eternal life; it would be incorrect to refer them only to this world, since every man must die on some day."

Moses Mendelssohn: "for which man, if he do them, will be rewarded with eternal life."

Johannes Gerhardus adds: (in his glosses to Luther's Bible version, edited Jena, 1640,) "he will be happy in this, and eternal life." [31]

[31] Note by the Translator.—That Moses indeed knew and taught the doctrine of the Immortality of the soul, is most distinctly and conclusively perceptible from the third verse of *his* prayer, (Psalm xc,) which must be translated thus: "Thou turnest man unto dust, and sayest, Return, ye children of man." The term דכא, for which the common English version has "destruction,"—how can anything return again, that has once been destroyed? דַכָּא, is derived from דוך, "to be crushed," "to be beaten in small pieces," and has reference to the body, which dissolves into dust after death. This is the more forcibly expressed by its connection with the term אֱנוש, which signifies "frail," "mortal," "finite." man. (Compare Psalm viii, 5; Job xxv, 6.) The second part of this verse,

After having shown that these commentators agree with regard to the doctrine of Immortality as distinctly taught by Moses, I must call the attention of my readers to the words of Hezekiel, relating to this passage. (Lev. xviii, 5.) In rebuking his people, in the name of God, he says: (xx, 21,) "But the children rebelled against me: they walked not in my statutes, neither kept my judgments to do them, which if a man do, he shall even live in them." After having spoken of the Lord's long-suffering and beneficence toward the people of Israel, and announced to them their punishment, he continues: "Wherefore I gave them also statutes that were not good, and judgments whereby they should not live."

Now, as the Prophet understands by the phrase לא יחיו, as Dr. Martin Luther properly remarks, "the darkness of the soul, and spiritual death," he analogically connected with the words וחי בהם, the idea of "eternal life in God," but not of "worldly happiness," in the physical sense of the term.

The Psalmist also seems to allude to the passage under consideration, when he says: (Psalm xix, 10 and 11,) "The judgments of the Lord are true and righteous altogether; more to be desired are they than gold, yea, than much of fine gold: sweeter also than honey...... and in keeping of them there is great reward." Now, as the Psalmist prized this reward higher than all earthly happiness, he can have alluded only,—under the impression wrought upon him by the passage under consideration—to heavenly reward, that is to say, eternal salvation. And under this impression only he could exclaim: "There is none upon earth that I desire beside Thee; my flesh and my heart faileth: but God is the

when speaking of "return," does not address the "Enosh," the "frail," "mortal," man, but the "Son of *Adam*," that noble being, which constitutes the master-piece of Creation, even on account of its being created in the image of God, of having a "breath of His breath," an *immortal soul* implanted in its inner parts. The term "return," therefore, is addressed to man, with regard to his immortal soul, so that the whole verse contains this idea: While man's finite part is turned unto dust, his immortal part returns to its Source, the Eternal Lord. Thus we have in the above verse a complete parallel to Ecclesiastes xii, 12: "And the dust shall return unto dust, as it was, and the spirit returneth unto God, who gave it." This interpretation of the above verse, which, in our humble opinion, alone corresponds with the whole tenor of the Psalm, gives us a clear insight into the belief of Moses, as including also that in the Immortality of the soul.

strength of my heart, and my portion for ever." (Psalm lxxiii, 25 and 26.) "My soul is continually in my hand: yet I do not forget Thy law;" though the wicked lay snares for me: yet I will not err from Thy precepts." (ibid, cxix, 109.) "Thy loving kindness is better than life." (ibid. lxiii, 4.)

But how thoroughly the people were acquainted with the doctrine of the Immortality of the soul, may be seen from the speech of the wise woman of Tekoah addressed to King David: "For we must needs die, and are as water spilt on the ground, which can not be gathered up again; neither doeth God take away life, but deviseth means, that the banished be not banished from Him for ever." (II. Samuel xiv, 14.) The idea conveyed here, is this: time and opportunity should be granted to the sinner, even during this life, for his improvement and reconciliation with God. For sincere repentance and atonement are of avail only in this life, which we have to pass but once, if we wish to receive forgiveness at the hand of our Heavenly Father; whereas, after death, only reward or punishment, but not forgiveness can be expected of God's supreme justice.

Thus also says Elihu: (Job xxxiv, 13—15,) "Who hath given him a charge over the earth? or who hath disposed the whole world? If He set His heart upon man, if He gather unto Himself His spirit and His breath; All flesh shall perish together, and man shall turn again unto dust." [32]

Furthermore, we clearly see from I. Kings xvii, 21 and 22, as Mr. Kaemph, (Orient, No. 26, 1842,) properly remarks, that the ancients had a true knowledge of the relation between soul and body. For how could a *return*

[32] Had the *Anonymous Fragmentist*, (edited by Lessing, page 328,) instead of asserting that especially the chapters 7 and 14 of Job prove, that every thing ceases with death, maturely reflected upon the form and contents of this book, he would never have arrived at such an erroneous conclusion. For how can we attach any importance to the remarks of Job with regard to the finiteness and evanescence of human existence, uttered in his conversations with his friends,—e. g. in chap. vii and xiv,—when we see, that they are afterwards refuted by Elihu, or retracted by Job himself, (chap. xl, 3 and 4.) who acknowledges that the Lord's governance on earth is a problem that human understanding will never solve?

of the soul to the body — תשב־נא נפש — be otherwise spoken of?

King Solomon also distinctly speaks of the continuation of the soul after death. "And [33] the dust returneth unto dust, whence it came, and the spirit returneth unto the Lord, who gave it." (Ecclesiastes xii, 7.)

The Psalmist also unequivocally expresses himself with regard to eternal life, saying: (Psalm xvii, 14 and 15,) "...... who have their portion in this life...... As for me, I will behold Thy face in righteousness: I shall be satisfied, when I awake, with Thy likeness." Alike clearly Isaiah speaks of reward and punishment beyond the grave, saying: (xxii, 14,) "And it was revealed in mine ears by the Lord of hosts, Surely this iniquity shall not be purged from you even after your death. [34] saith the Lord God of hosts." Or chapter lxvi, 24: "And they shall go forth, and look upon the carcasses of the men that have transgressed against me: for their worm shall not die, neither shall their fire be quenched; and they shall be an abhorrence to all flesh."

That the doctrine of the Immortality of the soul was generally known to the Jews, is clearly perceptible from the history of the martyrs, contained in chap. vii, of the Second Book of the Maccabees. When Antiochus raged against the Jews in Jerusalem, and attempted to force all of them to heathenism, a mother with her seven sons was brought before him. The king endeavored to induce them to apostacy by various flatteries and promises; but they all answered with one accord: "We shall never forsake the only true and living God, to

[33] The objections to the above, which the *Fragmentist* (page 313,) derives from what Solomon immediately afterwards says, "Vanity of vanities, says the Preacher; all is vanity," are removed by the consideration that these words can have reference only to earthly things; as we clearly see from the very last verses of the book: "The conclusion that contains the whole is: Fear God, and keep His commandments! For this is man's destination. For God shall bring every work into judgment, with every secret thing, whether it be good, or whether it be evil. Now, had Solomon not been convinced of the Immortality of the soul, and had he, therefore, looked upon all spiritual concerns also as vanities, how and for what purpose should he have recommended spiritual occupations to man, as the highest mission of his life?

[34] I understand the phrase עד תמתון, according to the well known rule עד ועד בכלל

Jonathan, probably, for the same reason, translates our phrase, by: "he dies a second death in the future world."

worship an idol that is but the work of man; ...... Thou like a fury takest us out of this present life, but the King of the world shall raise us up, who have died for His laws, unto everlasting life." (II. Maccabees vii, 9.) "For our brethren, who now have suffered a short pain, are dead under God's covenant of everlasting life." (ibid. verse 36.)

Still more distinctly, that is beyond all cavil, this doctrine of Immortality is taught in the Book of Wisdom: (chapter i, 15,) "Righteousness is immortal;" ibid. iv, 10—14—17; v, 15 and 16; and iii, 1—5: "But the souls of the righteous are in the hand of God, and there shall no torment touch them. In the sight of the unwise they seemed to die: and their departure is taken for misery. And their going from us to be utter destruction: but they are in peace. For though they be punished in the sight of men, yet is their hope full of immortality. And having been a little chastised, they shall be greatly rewarded: for God proved them and found them worthy for Himself."

That the Pharisees, and later Rabbins believed in the Immortality of the soul, and reward and punishment hereafter, I have shown already above, in my remarks on chap. v, verse 20.

Thus, then, we have proved, that Christianity has no advantage over Judaism by teaching the Immortality of the soul, which was taught by the latter, at a much earlier period.

29. "Are not too sparrows sold for a farthing? and one of them shall not fall on the ground without your Father.

30. But the very hairs of your head are all numbered.

31. Fear ye not, therefore, ye are of more value than many sparrows."

These verses are occasioned by Psalm xxxvi, 7 and 8: "Thy righteousness is like the great mountains; Thy judgments are a great deep: O Lord! Thou preservest man and beast. How excellent is Thy loving kindness, O God! therefore the children of men put their trust under the shadow of Thy wings."

The doctrine contained in these verses, that there is no blind chance cruelly sporting with man, but that the hand of Providence directs everything, and as higher Intelligence, therefore, governs All, is, aside from many other passages, taught in Psalm ciii, 19: "The Lord hath prepared His throne in the heavens; and His kingdom ruleth over all." Ibid. xxxiii, 13—20: "The Lord looketh from heaven; he beholdeth all the sons of men. From the place of His habitation He looketh upon all the inhabitants of the earth. He that fashioneth the hearts of all, considereth all their works," &c. Ibid. xciv, 9: "He that planted the ear, shall He not hear? He that formed the eye, shall He not see?"

In the same manner we are taught by the Talmud, (Treat. Chullin, fol. 7, b,) that, "as far as man's destiny is concerned, not even a finger is injured without Divine predestination." According to the doctrines of our Biblical books, physical life alone with all its vicissitudes, but not that of the spirit with all its manifestations and creations, is subject to the predestination of Divine Providence. For thus we read in Deuteronomy xxx, 15—19: "See, I have set before thee, this day, life and good, and death and evil; . . . . . . thou mayest choose life." It is evident from this passage, that the power of independent self-determination, free agency, is accorded to man. When, therefore, Divine prescience of man's actions seems to cancel—as taught in Jeremiah xvii, 9 and 10,—his moral freedom, we must consider—to solve this seeming difficulty—that time is but a subjective idea, which is inapplicable to God; that there is no prescience with God, but that He sees everything without regard to time, and at the same moment. Hence, the pre-supposition that man's actions must be accomplished, because God foreknows them, rests upon a mode of thinking peculiar to man, but inapplicable to God. In this wise it is that Rabbi Akiba endeavors to solve the apparent contradiction between human free agency, and the belief in Divine Providence and Omniscience, saying: (Ethics of the Fathers iii, 19,)

"All is seen," that is to say, what we, in our limited faculties, divide into three periods, Past, Present and Future, is seen by God, in one and the same moment; there is no succession of perceptions in God; "and freedom of will is given," that is: the voice of reason which admonishes us to do the good and shun the evil, reminds us at the same time of this, that as rational beings, we are free and independent.

[The most striking proof that Biblical Judaism repudiates the idea and doctrine of blind chance, and teaches us that the Lord regulates all things, I find in Exodus xxi, 12 and 13: "He that smiteth a man, so that he die, shall be surely put to death. And if a man lie not in wait, BUT GOD DELIVER HIM INTO HIS HAND," &C. Here we distinctly see that unpremeditated homicide is not attributed to mere chance, but to the ordination of God.—*Translator.*]

32. "Whosoever, therefore, shall confess me before men, him will I confess, also, before my Father which is in heaven.

33. But whosoever shall deny me before men, him will I also deny before my Father which is in heaven."

From the parallel passage in Mark viii, 39, it is clearly perceptible, that I. Samuel ii, 30, has been imitated here; "for them that honor me, I will honor; and they that despise me, shall be lightly esteemed."

34. "Think not that I am come to send peace on earth; I came not to send peace, but a sword."

Christ, who endeavored to refer all Messianic passages in the Prophets to himself, undoubtedly forgot here, that all their prophecies agree in this, that the Messiah was destined to establish an eternal, political and spiritual peace in the world. Thus we read in Isaiah ii, 4: "And he shall judge among the nations, and shall rebuke many people: and they shall beat their swords into ploughshares, and their spears into pruning-hooks; nation shall not lift up sword against nation, neither shall they learn war any more." Nay, the entire abolition of war, and the establishment of an universal, spiritual peace, is to be effected by the precursor of the Messiah, (Malachi iii,

23 and 24,) as an introduction to the work of Salvation which the latter will accomplish by the indestructible fraternization of all mankind.

35. "For I am come to set a man at variance against his father, and the daughter against her mother, and the daughter-in-law against her mother-in-law.

36. And a man's foes shall be they of his own household."

The Prophet Michah, from whom these two verses are borrowed, (vii, 6,) complains therein of the moral corruption of his time, rebukes the wicked for their rebellious deeds, and pronounces his reproofs in flaming words. Christ, who finds his mission occasioned by such a perverse age, maintains also, (Math. xi, 10 and 14,) that John the Baptist was the precursor of whom the Prophet Malachi speaks, in chap. iv, verse 5. But as such a precursor was destined, according to the prophecies of the same Prophet, (iv, 6,) "to turn the heart of the fathers unto the children, and the heart of the children to their fathers," that is to say, worthily to prepare, as it were, the world for his reception, it is rather unnatural to suppose, that he who announces himself as the Messiah, and is destined to complete the work of his harbinger, should act against him and thus again destroy the universal peace established by him with so much care and many troubles. Hence, as little John, who accomplished nothing, represented Elijah, whose coming our Prophet predicted, so little can we look upon Christ as the desired Messiah, as his intentions were rather un-Messianic, nay even diametrically opposed to the true acts of the predicted Messiah.

37. "He that loveth father or mother more than me, is not worthy of me: and he that loveth son or daughter more than me, is not worthy of me."

This is taken from Deuteronomy xxxiii, 9: "Whoso says to his father and to his mother, I do not see them; nor does acknowledge his brethren; nor knows his own children: they observe thy word, and keep thy covenant."

38. "He that taketh not his cross, and followeth after me, is not worthy of me."

This verse is an imitation of Psalm cxix, 143: "Though trouble and anguish take hold of me, yet Thy commandments are my delight."

39. "He that findeth his life shall lose it: and he that loses his life for my sake, shall find it."

This is taken from Proverbs viii, 35 and 36: "For whoso findeth me, findeth life, and shall obtain favor of the Lord. But he that sinneth against me wrongeth his own soul: all they that hate me, love death."

40. "He that receiveth you receiveth me; and he that receiveth me receiveth him that sent me."

This verse is imitated after Proverbs xix, 17: "He that hath pity upon the poor, lendeth unto the Lord; and that which he hath given will He pay him again."

41. "He that receiveth a Prophet in the name of a Prophet, shall receive a Prophet's reward; and he that receiveth a righteous man in the name of a righteous man, shall receive a righteous man's reward."

The doctrine conveyed in this verse, is borrowed from the narrative of the preservation of the Prophet Elijah through the widow of Zarephath. (I. Kings xvii, 10.)

CHAPTER XI.

2. "Now when John had heard in the prison the words of Christ, he sent two of his disciples,

3. And said unto him, Art thou he that should come?"

From these verses it is evident, that the first chapter of Luke contains a mere fiction. For had the important occurrence related by Luke really happened to the mothers of the two cousins, John and Jesus, how is it to be imagined that they should not have communicated it to them? And if they did communicate it, why did the cousins act the strangers toward each other, so that John had to ask: "Art thou he that should come?"

For the same reason we are justified in asserting that both the testimony of John, (John i, 32—34,) and the reports given by Matthew, (ii, 16 and 17,) are mere inventions. For had John really received such an infallible sign from heaven, that Jesus was *the* Messiah, how could he have asked: "Art thou he that should come?"

We see, then, that all these narratives are, as I have had frequent occasion to remark, mere fictions.

4. "Jesus answered and said unto them, Go and show John again those things which ye do hear and see;

5. The blind receive their sight, and the lame walk, the lepers are cleansed, and the deaf hear, and the dead are raised up, and the poor have the Gospel preached to them."

Christ, alluding, as he does, to Isaiah xxxv, 5, 6, &c., takes the phrases: "then the eyes of the blind shall be opened, and the ears of the deaf shall be unstopped," in their literal sense, whereas the Prophet himself declares, (xlii, 16,) that by the terms, "blind," and "deaf," he meant to refer to spiritual diseases, saying: "And I will bring the blind by a way they knew not; I will lead them in paths that they have not known: I will make darkness light before them, and crooked things straight," &c., and: (ibid. 18 and 19,) "Hear ye deaf; and look ye blind, that ye may see. Who is blind but my servant? or deaf as my messenger that I sent? who is blind," &c.

Besides, all Messianic prophecies of the Prophets tell us that the wonderful power of the Messiah and his golden age does not consist in the performance of supernatural deeds, but solely in this, that morality and wisdom will be spread among all mankind; nay! that the Messiah is after all nothing but the victory of truth over falsehood, the sincere fraternity of all nations and denominations: ALL MANKIND WILL CONSTITUTE BUT ONE NATION, AND PROFESS ONE RELIGION. Thus it is said,—besides other passages—in Isaiah ii, 2 and 3: "And it shall come to pass in later days that the mountain of the Lord's house shall be established in the top of the mountains, and shall be exalted above the hills, and all nations shall flow unto it. And many people shall go and say, Come ye, and let us go up to the mountain of the Lord, to the house of the God of Jacob; and He will teach us of His ways, and we will walk in His paths;" &c. Zechariah xiv, 9: "And the Lord shall be King over all the earth: in that day the Lord will be One, and His name One."

The phrase, "and the poor have the Gospel preached to them," is taken from Isaiah lxi, 1: "He hath annointed me to preach good tidings unto the meek."

10. "For this is he of whom it is written, Behold I send my messenger before Thy face, which shall prepare thy way before thee."

This verse taken from Malachi iii, 1, can by no means be applied to John, since he accomplished nothing of all that the angel (messenger) was to have performed.

11. "Verily I say unto you: Among them that are born of women there hath not risen a greater than John the Baptist: notwithstanding he that is least in the kingdom of heaven is greater than he."

Although John authenticated his greatness of mind, so highly praised here, neither through the teaching of extraordinary truths never before known, nor by the performance of wonderful deeds, it may nevertheless easily be imagined, why his cousin Jesus lauded him so much.

14. "And if ye will receive it, this is Elias which was for to come."

This assertion is contradicted by John himself: (i, 21,) "Art thou Elias? And he saith: I am not. Art thou that Prophet? And he answered, No." And should it be remarked, that this verse meant to convey the idea, that John was equal to Elijah in power and mind, we would answer: the comparison between the life of the latter, and that of the preacher in the desert, is a sufficient refutation.

19. "The son of man came eating and drinking, and they say, Behold, a man gluttonous, and a wine-bibber, a friend of publicans and sinners. But wisdom is justified of her children."

Here we can not forbear asking: Whereby has the son of man manifested himself as Wisdom?

21. "Wo unto thee, Chorazin! wo unto thee, Bethsaida! for if the mighty works which were done in you had been done in Tyre and Sidon, they would have repented long ago in sackcloth and ashes."

This verse is an imitation of Ezekiel xxvii, 30 and 31, where it is prophecied that the Tyrians would "cast up dust upon their heads," and "wallow themselves in ashes," on account of the destruction of their city."

23. "And thou, Capernaum, which art exalted unto heaven, shalt be brought down to hell: for if the mighty works which have been done in thee, had been done in Sodom, it would have remained until this day.

24. But I say unto you, that it shall be more tolerable for the land of Sodom, in the day of judgment than for thee."

The phrase, "which art exalted unto heaven," is taken from Isaiah xiv, 12; the balance of verses 23 and 24, is borrowed from Ezekiel xvi, 47 and 48. Such imitations were intended to give the New Testament a prophetic coloring. But honest as we are, we wish to return whatever was borrowed and see what may remain as real, original property.

25. "At that time, Jesus answered and said, I thank Thee, O Father, Lord of heaven and earth, because Thou hast hid these things from the wise and prudent, and hast revealed them unto babes."

This verse is imitated after Psalm viii, 3: "Out of the mouths of babes and sucklings hast thou established thy power," &c., and proves, at the same time, that Christ acknowledged but One, unique, and eternal Source; otherwise he should have been compelled to employ the formula with the Trinity.

27. "All things are delivered unto me of my Father; and no man knoweth the Son, but the Father; neither knoweth any man the Father, save the Son, and he to whomsoever the Son will reveal him."

What Christ here asserts of himself exclusively, King David says of every man, namely: "that the Lord made man a little lower than the angels, and crowned him with glory and honor; made him to have dominion over the works of His hands, and put all things under his feet." (Psalm viii, 6, 7.) The phrase, "and no man knoweth the Father, save the Son," is nothing but an empty speech; for Christ taught those no more perceptible and distinct knowledge of our heavenly Father, to whom he intended to reveal Him, than Moses and the Prophets had already done before him.

28. "Come unto me, all ye that labor, and are heavy laden, and I will give you rest."

Christ here employs the same words that Jeremiah addresses to the Israelites in the name of God: "For I will satiate the weary soul, and replenish every sorrowful soul." (Jeremiah xxxi, 25.)

The thinking reader can not, in this connection, suppress the questions: How could Christ, who in the hour of his death was unable to alleviate his own sufferings, but proved so weak and powerless, that he despairingly exclaimed: "My God! My God! why hast Thou forsaken me?" (Matth. xxvii, 46,) how could Christ pretend to bring consolation unto the whole world from his own power?

29. "Take my yoke upon you, and learn of me: for I am meek and lowly of heart; and ye shall find rest unto your souls."

The contents of this verse are borrowed from Michah vi, 8: "It hath been told thee, O man! what is good, and what the Lord requireth of thee: nothing but to exercise justice, and to love mercy, and to walk humbly with thy God." The phrase, "and ye shall find rest," &c., is taken from Jeremiah vi, 16. Thus also it is taught in Treat. Sanhedrin, fol. 43: "Come, and convince thyself, how greatly the meek are respected before God."

30. "For my yoke is easy, and my burden is light."

The representation of the Law by the figure of "yoke," is borrowed from Jeremiah v, 5: "......but these have altogether broken the yoke," &c. The metaphor, that the yoke is easy and light, is but a dim reflection of the words of the Psalmist xix, 8, 9, &c.: "The Law of the Lord is perfect, quickening the soul," &c.

CHAPTER XII.

1. "At that time, Jesus went on the Sabbath-day through the corn, and his disciples were hungered, and began to pluck the ears of corn, and to eat.

2. But when the Pharisees saw it, they said unto him, Behold thy disciples do that which is not lawful to do upon the Sabbath-day.

3—7. But he said unto them,......but if ye had known what this meaneth, I will have mercy and not sacrifice, ye would not have condemned the guiltless."

When we consider that the Scribes have, among other

principles, pronounced the following axioms with regard to the celebration of the Sabbath: "The Sabbath is given into your power, but not you into its own," (Treat. Sabbath, fol. 85, b,) or remark with regard to the performance of ceremonies: (Treat. Sanhedrin, 74, a; Yomah, 85, b; Abodah Zarah, 27, b, and 54, a;) "It is said in Leviticus xviii, 4, 'the Lord wills that ye may live by the fulfilment of his statutes,' hence relieves you therefrom, whenever your lives are in danger;" when we consider these sayings of the Scribes, it is quite preposterous to assume that they should have rebuked Christ because his disciples plucked and ate ears, when they were forced to do so by hunger. This narrative is evidently a fiction.

But the least of all, can the Pharisees be charged with having disregarded the words of Hosea vi, 6: "I desire mercy, and not sacrifice," &c. All the principles, which they established with regard to the performance of ceremonies, prove this very fact, that they thoroughly penetrated into the spirit of the Prophets. Nay, the very passage just quoted, they interpret in this way: "The world was, from the very beginning, created only for the sake of benevolence; as it is said, 'I desire mercy, and not sacrifice.'" (Aboth of Rabbi Nathan, Sect. iv.)— Or as it is said Treat. Sota, page 14, a: "The Law commences with charity, and ends with the same."

8. "For the Son of man is Lord even of the Sabbath-day."

That it was the opinion of the Scribes,—and it is well founded in the Bible—that every man was ruler of the Sabbath, I have shown in the preceding verse.

10. "And behold, there was a man, which had his hand withered. And they asked him, saying, Is it lawful to heal on the Sabbath-days? that they might accuse him.

11. And he said unto them, What man shall there be among you, that shall have one sheep, and if it fall into a pit on the Sabbath-day, will he not lay hold on it, and lift it out?

12. How much then is a man better than a sheep? Wherefore, it is lawful to do well on the Sabbath days.

13. Then saith he to the man, Stretch forth thine hand. And he stretched it forth; and it was restored whole, like as the other."

The old narrative, contained in the First Book of the

Kings, relating to us, how a Prophet caused the hand of Jeroboam to wither, and cured it again, by means of a prayer upon the king's request, is anew presented to us with some few variations. Nor can we believe that the Pharisees called him to account, and attempted even to destroy him, because he cured a sick man on the Sabbath-day, since they themselves teach us, (Treat. Sabbath, fol. 109, a,) "If any man should in the least injure his hand or foot, he may pour vinegar or other acids upon the wound," &c. It is utterly impossible, therefore, that they should have found fault with a man, who effected a cure by a mere magic word.

17. "That it might be fulfilled which was spoken by Esaias the Prophet, saying:

18—21. Behold my servant, whom I have chosen; my beloved in whom my soul is well pleased: I will put my spirit upon him, and he shall shew judgment to the Gentiles," &c.

Isaiah speaks of a man, (chap. xlii, 1, &c.,) who should announce salvation unto all Gentiles, and diffuse justice all over the world, Now, as Christ says: (Matth. xv, 24,) "I am not sent but unto the lost sheep of Israel," &c., the prophetic words of Isaiah, though applicable to every champion of truth in the midst of any nation, can, by no means, have reference to Christ, since such a reference would be in contradiction with his own assertion.

22. "Then was brought unto him one possessed with a devil, blind and dumb; and he healed him, insomuch that the blind and dumb both spake and saw."

See my introductory remarks to Chapter viii.

26. "And if Satan cast out Satan, he is divided against himself; how shall then his kingdom stand?"

Whenever a prince, here Satan Beelzebub, orders his subalterns to do something, and counter-orders it after some time, from whatever reason it may be, he can not be charged with being divided against himself, since he acts according to his pleasure, and by virtue of his sovereign power. But even aside from this rather subtle defence, it is now-a-days evident that the whole kingdom of devils ceased to exist with the disappearance of exorcisers and conjurers, and that that kingdom no longer exists, whereever and whenever it is no more welcome. The Old Testament distinctly says, that there is no such kingdom of devils, and that no being besides God can exercise any influence over man's body. Thus we read in Deuteronomy xxxii, 39: "See now that I, I alone, am he, and there is no God with me: I kill, and I make alive; I wound, and I heal: neither is there any that can deliver out of my hand." Isaiah xlv, 6 and 7: "That they may know from the rising of the sun, and from the west, that there is none besides me. I am the Lord, and there is none else. I form the light, and create darkness; I make peace, and create evil: I, the Lord, do all these things." Hence, no mention is made, either in the Old Testament or the Apocrypha, of evil spirits. [35] Christ, therefore, is to be blamed for having availed himself of the false belief entertained by the people at his time, as a means toward establishing his authority, instead of inveighing with all that lay in his power, and with Biblical and philosophical arguments, against the existence of devils, and uprooting this dangerous superstition, with all its miserable offsprings.

29. "Or else, how can one enter into a strong man's house, and spoil his goods, except he first bind the strong man? and then he will spoil his house."

The contents of this verse are imitated after Isaiah xlix, 24 and 25.

30. "He that is not with me, is against me; and he that gathereth not with me, scattereth abroad."

To perceive the futility of the doctrine conveyed here, one needs but give it a practical application. He that is

[35] The term עֲזָאזֵל, which occurs, Levit. xvi, 3, 10 and 25, means not, as some theologians erroneously suppose, "evil spirit," but, as the Septuaginta correctly translates it *Apopompe*, "transportation," "banishment," composed as they probably took the term to be of עַז, ("swift," "fierce,") and אזל, ("to depart," "to leave.") Tradition also relates (Treat. Yomah, fol. 67, a,) that the man who carried the scape-goat to the desert had to precipitate him from a high mountain to cause his death. The spirit of this transaction is this, that the sins of the people which separated them from their God were symbolically carried into an inhospitable desert. It is true the term שֵׁדִים occurs in the Bible, yet is immediately followed, (Deuteronomy xxxii, 17,) by the phrase לא אלה, and (ibid. verse 21,) by the word הבליהם, "nonentities," "follies." From all this we perceive that the Pentateuch repudiates the existence and working of demons as childish phantasmagoria.

not with me, that is to say, whoever does not pursue with me the same way to reach the same place of destination, is against me, does not allow me to continue my journey upon the road which I have taken; and he that gathereth not with me, that is to say, whoever does not acquire wealth with me, scatters it, wastes it, loses it. No man with sound sense will ever make such an assertion. And yet, however great the logical fallacy of this verse is, its dangerous absurdity, clad in the mantle of Religion, has created so much evil, caused so many religious persecutions, has begotten such deep fanaticism, that it could be conquered only by the power of modern civilization. All this is recorded with bloody characters, upon the tear-drenched pages of history.

31. "Wherefore I say unto you, All manner of sin and blasphemy shall be forgiven unto men: but the blasphemy against the Holy Ghost shall not be forgiven unto men."

The doctrine pronounced here, that those who blaspheme the Holy Ghost, that is to say the Law of God, or God-inspired truths, can never obtain forgiveness, is taken from Isaiah lxvi, 24: "And they shall go forth, and look upon the carcasses of men that have transgressed against me: for their worm shall not die, neither shall their fire be quenched;" &c.

32. "And whosoever speaketh a word against the Son of man, it shall be forgiven him: but whosoever speaketh against the Holy Ghost, it shall not be forgiven him, neither in this world, neither in the world to come."

From this it is undeniably evident that Christ did not wish to be held as the same person with the Holy Ghost. For how is it possible to speak against the son of man without speaking against the Holy Ghost, if they constituted one and the same being. Hence, he wishes to be looked upon merely as the son of man, but neither as God, nor, which is the same thing, as the Holy Ghost.

33. "Either make the tree good, and his fruit good; or else make the tree corrupt, and his fruit corrupt: for the tree is known by his fruit."

This sentiment is taken from Sirach xxvii, 7: "The fruit declareth, if the tree have been dressed."

34. "O generation of vipers, how can ye, being evil, speak good things? for out of the abundance of the heart the mouth speaketh."

The sentence, "out of the abundance," &c., is borrowed from Sirach xxvii, 7: "......so is the utterance of a conceit in the heart of man." And if we are guided, in our judgments, by the counseling words of Sirach, the Scribes do not deserve the venomous appellation "generation of vipers." Men, that were filled with such fire for their religion, that they devoted their whole lives to its study; men of whom it is historically confirmed (See Josephus,) that they rebuked even kings, without fear and reserve, for their religious transgressions, and taught and practiced doctrines which breathe self-denial, true nobility of mind and glowing love for truth: such men can never have been filled with that malignity, with which they are charged here.

36. "But I say unto you, That every idle word that men shall speak, they shall give account thereof in the day of judgment."

The Scribes declare, that we have, on some future day, to give account not only of useless words, but also of wasted time, which could be employed for meditation. (Ethics of the Fathers iii, 9.)

37. "For by thy words thou shalt be justified, and by thy words thou shalt be condemned."

The second part of this verse is taken from Job xv, 6, while the first, which is undoubtedly an imitation of the same passage, is an incorrect expression. For nobody can be justified by good and pious words that do not emanate from a good and pious heart; hence the above phrase is generalizing too much.

38. "Then certain of the Scribes and of the Pharisees answered, saying, Master, we would see a sign from thee.

39. But he answered and said unto them, An evil and adulterous generation seeketh after a sign; and there shall no sign be given to it, but the sign of the Prophet Jonas:

40. For as Jonas was three days and three nights in the whale's belly; so shall the son of man be three days and three nights in the heart of the earth."

Whenever a man is called upon, as was here the case, to enlighten doubters, he is bound instantly to give some infallible sign. It is true, Christ could speak of many more things which he intended to perform; but this required to be proven, lest it carried no conviction with it for the moment. Very proper is the remark of the *Fragmentist*: (§ 48,) "Christ himself could perform no miracle unless the people believed beforehand: and whenever knowing people, that is, the Learned and the magistrates of his time, demanded some miracles of him which could be subjected to scrutiny, he began to scold, instead of complying with their demands: hence no one of these classes could believe in him. Thirty to sixty years after the death of Christ, there arose men who proclaimed these wonders to the world, as though they had actually been performed, and this, too, in a language which no Jew in Palestine understood; and, moreover, at a time, when the Jewish nation and commonwealth were in a state of utter disorder and confusion, and there were but few left who knew Jesus. So that there was nothing easier for them than to fabricate wonders, as many as they pleased, without incurring the danger of having their writings known and understood, or confuted. But the converted were from the beginning impressed with the opinion, that it was a virtue and saving action to have faith, and to make reason subservient to the rule of belief; hence there was as much credulity with them, as *pia fraus* with their teachers; and of this pious fraud, it is well known, there was a large stock to be found in the original Christian Church."

The Scribes justly denied Christ even the least authority; since he was unable, though he pretended to be a worker of miracles, to perform a wonder at a moment's bidding, and merely referred to what he intended to do in future.

Moreover, the contradiction between the prophecy of Christ, in this passage, and Matthew xxviii, 1, where we learn that he rose after one day and one night, and not three, proves to us, that we have before us no reports of real events, but fictions.

42. "The queen of the South shall rise up in the judgment with this generation, and shall condemn it: for she came from the uttermost parts of the earth to hear the wisdom of Solomon; and behold, a greater than Solomon is here."

As we have thus far sufficiently shown, Christ taught nothing original that deserved admiration. Whereas, we find upon almost every page of Solomon's writings still extant, rules of wisdom, couched in a Divinely fiery diction, and never before known. Indeed! it required great fertility of imagination on the part of Christ, to demand greater respect than Solomon justly deserves.

43—45. "When the unclean spirit, &c., &c. Then goeth he, and taketh with himself seven other spirits more wicked than himself, and they enter in and dwell there: and the last state of that man is worse than the first. Even so shall it be also unto this wicked generation."

This threat most unjustly directed against the Scribes, as we have shown in our remarks above, is an imitation of Leviticus xxvi, 4 and 28, where we are told that the last punishment of the sinner will be seven times as great as the first.

47. "Then one said unto him, Behold, thy mother and thy brethren stand without, desiring to speak with thee.

48. But he answered and said unto him that told him, Who is my mother? and who are my brethren?"

Such a deportment on the part of Christ with regard to his mother can certainly not be deemed honorable; for a man can, indeed, devote himself to spiritual employments, and yet honor his parents, especially when they do not mean to, nor can throw any obstacles in his way.

50. "For whosoever shall do the will of my Father which is in heaven, the same is my brother, and sister, and mother."

This doctrine is taken from Deuteronomy xxxiii, 9, where we read: "Who said unto his father and to his mother, I have not seen him, neither did he acknowledge his brethren, nor know his own children: for they have observed thy word, and kept thy covenant."

CHAPTER XIII.

3. "And he spake many things unto them in parables, saying, Behold, a sower went forth to sow;

4. And when he sowed, some seeds fell by the way-side, and the fowls came and devoured them up:

5. Some fell upon stony places, where they had not much earth: and," &c., &c.

The materials of this parable are borrowed from Sirach vi, 20—23: "My son gather instruction from thy youth up; so shalt thou find wisdom in thine old age. Come unto her as one that plougheth and soweth, and wait for her good fruits; for thou shalt toil in laboring about her, but thou shalt eat of her fruits right soon," &c.

11. "He answered and said unto them, Because it is given unto you to know the mysteries of the kingdom of heaven, but to them it is not given."

This verse is an imitation of Psalm xxv, 14, where it reads: "The secret of the Lord is with them, that fear Him; and He will cause them to know His covenant." That this was, however, unjustly applied to the teachings of Jesus is evident from my remarks on verse 17, below.

12. "For whosoever hath, to him shall be given, and he shall have more abundance:" &c.

See my remarks on xxv, 14 and 15.

14. "And in them is fulfilled the prophecy of Esaias, which saith, By hearing ye shall hear, and shall not understand; and seeing ye shall see, and shall not perceive."

The attentive reader of Isaiah vi, 9 and 10, must be convinced, that the passage quoted here, can be applied only to the contemporaries of the Prophets, saying: "And he said, Go, and tell this people, Hear ye, indeed, but understand not; and see ye, indeed, but perceive not," &c., &c.

17. "For verily I say unto you, That many Prophets and righteous men have desired to see those things which ye see, and have not seen them; and to hear those things which ye hear, and have not heard them."

We have incontrovertibly proven that Christ taught or

performed nothing worthy of notice which had not long before him been accomplished by Moses and the Prophets. And yet, he presumes to be superior to them, both in intellect and knowledge! This, indeed! is scorning all historical truth. Youth pretends to be wiser than old age!

But least of all is his admonition to strive after the heavenly kingdom original; for it is to be found in almost every passage of the Law and the Prophets. (See Deuteronomy xxx, 19, &c.; Proverbs iii, 13, 14, 15, &c.; viii, 10, 11, 18, 19, &c.)

35. "That it might be fulfilled which was spoken by the Prophet, saying, I will open my mouth in parables; I will utter things which have been kept secret from the foundation of the world."

First of all, this quotation can by no means be applied to Christ, as we have shewn in our remarks upon the preceding verse; and then, the conclusion of the verse, (Psalm lxxviii, 2,) is incorrectly transcribed here, since it reads thus: "I will utter dark sayings of old;" and lastly we find that the Poet Asaph distinctly tells us in the preceding verse, (ibid. 1,) that he speaks of his own person; wherefore, he can not have prophesied of Jesus.

41—45. "The son of man shall send forth his angels," &c.

These verses are composed of the passages Daniel vii, 13 and 14, and ibid. xii, 3, which in order of assuming the show of originality is quoted here with some alteration. But how little this can be applied to Jesus is evident from my illustrations xxiv, 30.

57. "And they were offended in him. But Jesus said unto them, A Prophet is not without honor, save in his own country, and in his own house."

This proves clearly that Christ wished to be regarded as nothing more than a Prophet.

58. "And he did not many mighty works there, because of their unbelief."

Every reasoning man would have expected, in this instance, just the reverse. Even amongst the unbelievers, as Christ calls them, many direct signs must be wrought, to induce them to mend their ways. For these alone stood in the greatest need of a Savior, or, as he himself expresses it somewhere else: "Not the sane, but the sick require a physician."

CHAPTER XIV.

19. "And he commanded the multitude to sit down on the grass, and took the five loaves and the two fishes, and looking up to heaven, he blessed, and brake, and gave the loaves to his disciples, and the disciples to the multitude.

20. And they did all eat, and were filled: and they took up of the fragments that remained twelve baskets full."

This story about Christ's multiplying the loaves, is an apparent imitation of I. Kings xvii, 12, 13, 14, where it is related, that the Prophet Elijah created such a miraculous blessing of flour and oil for the widow of Sarepta, that a handful of meal, and a little oil offered sufficient sustenance to himself, the widow and her family, for many days. A similar miracle is related also to have been performed by the Prophet Elisha. (II. Kings iv, 3, 4, 5, &c.)

Let it not be said that the Evangelist meant these facts, though related in an indubitable, historical tone, to be understood only as figures; for we should then not have any criterion for truth and fiction, untruth and absurdity. Every thing could be interpreted in a symbolical way, but a confusion and chaos of figures would then fill the domain of thought.

23. "And when he had sent the multitudes away, he went up into a mountain apart to pray: and when the evening was come, he was there alone."

From this it is evident, that Christ did not pretend to be the identical being with God; but meant to be looked upon merely as a God-inspired man. If such was not the case, for what purpose, and to whom did he pray?

26. "And when the disciples saw him walking on the sea, they were troubled, saying, It is a spirit; and they cried out for fear."

The founder of the new Religion must equal Moses and the Prophets, in all respects. Now, Moses having led the Israelites, as we are told, "on dry land in the midst of the sea," and the Prophet Elisha having passed the Jordan in the same manner, (II. Kings ii, 14,) a story was to be presented, to relate to us, that Christ, and at least one of his disciples, walked on the sea. It is true, many theologians really regard this story as a fable; but be it as it may, if walking on water proves the Supreme power of a being, every walker on water that in our day exhibits his skill, must be likewise omnipotent and a Divine being; this, however, can not be believed by rational beings.

CHAPTER XV.

1. "Then came to Jesus Scribes and Pharisees, which were of Jerusalem, saying:

2. Why do thy disciples transgress the tradition of the elders? for they wash not their hands when they eat bread."

It is highly improbable that the Scribes should have pronounced this censure; for they permitted the washing of hands in the morning, with the purpose thus to take the meals throughout the day with clean hands; which may have been the case also with the disciples.

3. "But he answered and said unto them, Why do ye also transgress the commandment of God by your tradition?

4. For God commanded saying, Honor thy father and mother: and, He that curseth father or mother, let him die the death.

5. But ye say, Whosoever shall say to his father or his mother, It is a gift, by whatsoever thou mightest be profited by me."

The immoral doctrine which is here charged upon the Scribes (Sopherim) is nowhere to be found throughout their writings still extant. We read, on the contrary: (Treat. Nedarim, fol. 64, a,) "If any one makes a vow, which can not be approved for certain reasons, he is to be reminded of the commandment, 'Honor thy father and thy mother,' which he violates by his very vow. For people will despise his parents, thinking that they gave him a bad education, or were not good examples to him. The pious man makes no vow at all; as Solomon says: 'It is better to make no vow at all,'" &c. We read further, in the same Treatise: "If a man should have made a vow that might be even in the least injurious to his parents, let him be urgently admonished that he is bound to honor his parents, and that vows which tend to set this duty at naught, are null and void in themselves.

14. "Let them alone: they be blind leaders of the blind. And if the blind lead the blind, both shall fall into the ditch.

15. Then answered Peter and said unto him, Declare unto us this parable.

16. And Jesus said, Are ye also yet without understanding?

17. Do not ye yet understand, that whatsoever entereth in at the mouth goeth into the belly, and is cast out into the draught?

18. But those things which proceed out of the mouth come forth from the heart; and they defile the man.

19. For out of the heart proceed evil thoughts, murders, adulteries fornications, thefts, false witness, blasphemies:

20. These are the things which defile a man: but to eat with unwashen hands defileth not a man."

The phrase "blind leaders of the blind," is taken from Isaiah xlii, 19, and is here unjustly applied to the Scribes. For they too, severely censure him who perpetrates the vices enumerated in verse 19, (which, however, are already inveighed against in Exodus xx, 13, 14, 15, 16, &c.,) and most zealously preached true morality. Thus, for instance they established the principle: (Berachoth, fol. 17,) "The aim of wisdom is self-improvement and practical charity;" or: (Ethics of the Fathers i, § 2,) "The world rests upon three things: the Law, Worship of God, and deeds of charity."

If the Sopherim established the washing of the hands, either to prevent the sacred offering, or bread over which grace has been said, from being touched with unclean hands; or to advocate cleanliness, clinging to the principle, that outward cleanliness leads to the purity of morals, and the latter to true piety: who that is in possession of his rational faculties, can blame them therefore? The same custom of washing the hands, before and after meals, we meet also among the ancient Greeks, as we see from Homer, Odyssey i, 136: "And a hand-maid who brought water for washing in a beautiful golden pitcher, on a silver basin, and poured it upon their hands," &c.; and ibid. verse 146: *Toisi De Kerykes Men*

Hydor Epi Cheiras Echenan; "And the heralds poured water over their hands."

How absurd would it have been, if a man had at that time spoken thus: Be moral and pious, and then you need not practise the custom of washing your hands. Indeed! every man would have asked: Pray, are the elements of good manners, and those of piety in conflict with each other? And must we not now address the same question to Christ?

22. "And, behold, a woman of Canaan came out of the same coasts, and cried unto him, saying, Have mercy on me, O Lord, thou son of David; my daughter is grievously vexed with a devil.

23. But he answered her not a word. And his disciples came and besought him, saying, Send her away; for she crieth after us.

24. But he answered and said, I am not sent but unto the lost sheep of the house of Israel.

25. Then came she and worshipped him, saying, Lord, help me.

26. But he answered and said, It is not meet to take the children's bread, and to cast it to dogs."

The history of the Canaanite woman is a tale which had often been told already. This much, however, is evident from its repetition here, *that Christ never meant to establish a universal religion of love as is so often asserted.* For when he uses (chap. x, 5 and 6,) the distinct words: "Go not into the way of the Gentiles, and into any city of the Samaritans enter ye not; but go rather to the lost sheep of the house of Israel," or emphatically expresses himself here (verse 24,) to this effect: "I am not sent but unto the lost sheep of the house of Israel," and would not, therefore, class the heathen woman among his children, but have her regarded as a dog: it can not longer be doubted, that he never intended to found a universal religion of love. Whereas Moses indeed tells us that Divine benevolence is equally accorded to all men. "It shall be an ordinance for ever in your generations: as you are, so shall the stranger be before the Lord." (Numbers xv, 15.) "And if a stranger sojourn with thee in your land, ye shall not vex him. But the stranger that dwelleth with you, shall be unto you as one born among you, and thou shalt love him as thyself."

(Leviticus xix, 33 and 34.) "Ye shall, therefore, keep my statutes and my judgments: which, if a man do, he shall live in them: I am the Lord." (ibid. xviii, 5.) To this verse the *Sifra* remarks: "It reads not *Priests*, *Levites*, or *Israelites*, but "*man*," which means, that a man, of whatever tribe or nation he may be, will participate in eternal salvation, as long as he lives according to the dictates of the Law." Still more distinctly Isaiah expresses himself: "Neither let the son of the strangers, that hath joined himself to the Lord, speak, saying, the Lord hath utterly separated me from his people, &c. Also, the sons of the stranger, that join themselves unto the Lord, to serve him, and to love the name of the Lord, &c. Even them will I bring to my holy mountain, and make them joyful in my house of prayer, &c., for my house shall be called a house of prayer unto all the nations." (Isaiah lvi, 3, 6 and 7.) Again: "Blessed be Egypt my people and Assyria the work of my hands and Israel mine inheritance." (Isaiah xix, 25.) In the same way does the Psalmist express himself. (cii, 19—24.) And, (ibid. cxlv, 9,) "He is good to all, and his tender mercies are all over his works."

Nay, every lover of truth needs only to read Gen. i, 1; vi, 5; vii, 1, &c.; Psalm lxxv, Jonah iii, and he will be convinced, that according to the Mosaism we have to regard God as the ruler and benefactor of the whole human race and not as the only guardian and national God of Israel. For a God, who is represented as the Creator of the whole Universe, who punishes human wickedness and the depravity of the whole mankind, and forgives the sins of the sincere penitents of every nation, and grants them peace, bliss and happiness, was not worshipped as an Israelitish God alone, but as the father of all nations.

The expression אלהי ישראל, means not the Israelitish God, but the God, who is acknowledged and worshipped by Israel. Mankind is the Divine kingdom and Israel is

God's throne, his chosen place from which he will rule over all nations, as it reads Jeremiah iii, 17: "At that time they shall call Jerusalem the [36] throne of the Lord, and all the nations shall be gathered unto it."

It is evident, therefore, that Mosaism is hostile to all pride of nationality: and does not announce Jehovah as the sole God of the Jews, as it is to this day unjustly charged, but as the Father of all mankind. And when the Bible speaks of a chosen people, it does not mean to convey the idea of an exclusively loved, or even preferred nation; but alludes only to its important mission, and peculiar destination, to diffuse, as a priestly nation of God, the true knowledge of the sole original principle unto all the world.

Concerning verses 30 and 31, see my remarks on chapter xi, verse 5.

In verses 32—38 we read again of a miraculous distribution of food, about which compare my remarks on chapter xiv, verses 19 and 20. Peculiar to this narrative, is the mention of the suspicious number *Seven*.

CHAPTER XVI.

Verses 1—5 contain an embellished repetition of chapter xii, 38—41, which see.

11. "How is it that ye do not understand that I spake it not to you concerning bread, that ye should beware of the leaven of the Pharisees and of the Sadducees?"

The term "leaven," is employed in Psalm lxxv, 26, to designate despicable influence, and borrowed from that passage.

15. "He saith unto them, But whom say ye that I am?

16. And Simon Peter answered and said, Thou art the Christ, the Son of the living God."

[36] This metaphor was used by Moses, Exodus xvii, 15, as the Pesikta understood it. כי יד על כס יה מלחמה ל'ה בעמלק מדר דר. To these words the Pesikta adds: פשטה ידו בכסאו של ה'ק'ב'ה וכי ב'ו'ר יש בו כח לפשוט וכ'ו, and renders thus: "Amalek has lifted his hand against the throne of God, (that is Israel,) therefore shall be war for God with Amalek from generation to generation."

The term "Son," must here be taken in the sense of the Hebrew word, which conveys the meaning of "favorite." For if we were to take the term in its literal meaning, Christ should have called himself, however absurd this appellation would be, "Son of God," and not, as he invariably did, "Son of man." To prove that the term "Son," means "favorite," "loved one," "chosen one," we refer to Psalm lxxxix, 26 and 27, where it is said of David: "He shall cry unto me: Thou art my father, my God and the rock of my salvation. I will make him my first-born," &c. II. Samuel vii, 14: "I will be his father, and he shall be my son." Jeremiah xxxi, 9: ". . . . for I am a father to Israel, and Ephraim is my first-born."

17. "And Jesus answered and said unto him, Blessed art thou, Simon Bar-jona: for flesh and blood hath not revealed it unto thee, but my Father which is in heaven."

When Christ tells his disciples, amongst whom was also Simon, in distinct words, (chap. xi, 5,) that the Messianic passage in Isaiah xxxv, 2—10, must be taken literally, and applied to himself, and thus acquainted them with his wish to be regarded as the true Messiah: we can not be led to the delusive belief that a spirit from on high revealed it to Petrus. It was flesh and blood, the son of man himself, who imposed that idea upon him.

18. "And I say also unto thee, That thou art Peter, and upon this rock I will build my church;" &c.

This phraseology is taken from Psalm xviii, 3; or Numbers xxiv, 21.

19. "And I will give unto thee the keys of the kingdom of heaven: and whatsoever thou shalt bind on earth shall be bound in heaven: and whatsoever thou shalt loose on earth shalt be loosed in heaven."

This is an imitation of Isaiah xxii, 22: "And the key of the house of David will I lay upon his shoulder, so he shall open, and none shall shut; and he shall shut, and none shall open." Isaiah prophesied this to Eliakim, the son of Hilkiah, whose name is distinctly mentioned in verse 20. The meaning of that passage is this, that Eliakim should be made first chamberlain of the king,

20. "Then charged he his disciples that they should tell no man that he was Jesus the Christ."

As Christ himself distinctly maintained before large multitudes that he wished to be regarded as the Christ, as it may be seen from chapter xi, 4 and 5, and other passages, but finding that he now and then prohibited his assertion to be repeated as he does here, we can arrive at no other conclusion than this, that it was his intention to make the people still more anxious to spread it about.

21. "From that time forth began Jesus to shew unto his disciples, how that he must go unto Jerusalem, and suffer many things of the elders and chief priests and Scribes, and be killed, and be raised again the third day."

The prophecy pronounced by Christ with regard to his death, could have been proclaimed, under existing circumstances, by even the most humble individual. Hence, we need add no further remarks. As regards, however, the distinct prophecy of his resurrection on the third day, we shall advance our commentary further below.

Verses 24 and 25 have been met and expatiated upon already above, chapter x, 38 and 39.

26. "For what is a man profited, if he shall gain the whole world, and lose his own soul? or what shall a man give in exchange for his soul?"

The first part of this verse is borrowed from II. Maccabees vii, and the second from Psalm xlix, 9.

27. "For the Son of man shall come in the glory of his Father with his angels; and then he shall reward every man according to his works."

This fiction is taken from Daniel vii, 9, 10 and 13. That the phrase כבר אנש, ("like a son of man,") can not, however, be applied to Christ, is evident, beyond all doubt, from verse 14, where we read: "And there was given him dominion, and glory, and a kingdom, that all people, nations, and languages, should serve him: his dominion is an everlasting dominion, which shall not pass away, and his kingdom, that which shall not be destroyed." Nothing of all this took place during the lifetime of Christ, nor has been fulfilled to this day. For almost two thirds of all mankind repudiate Christianity, and even its own professors do not profess the doctrine of Christ, but that of the Apostles. Hence, Christ can not be meant by the phrase כבר אנש, "son of man," however often he may have assumed this name. Besides, this phrase is explained, in Daniel vii, 18, in this wise, that it designates, symbolically, the people of Israel. Furthermore, it is not only unreasonable and irrational to assume, that the all-wise, almighty Creator of the Universe should chose a son of man as his colleague or proxy at the great Judgment, but contradicted in many passages, by the same Prophets to whom Christ so often makes reference. "Behold, the Lord God will come with strong hand, and His arms shall rule for him; behold, his reward is with him, and his work before Him." (Isaiah xl, 10.) "Until the Ancient of days, and judgment was given to the saints of the Most-High," &c. (Daniel vii, 22.) "I beheld, till the thrones were cast down, and the Ancient of days did sit, whose garment was white, as snow, and the hair of his head like the pure wool: his throne was like the fiery flame, and his wheels as burning fire...... thousand thousands ministered unto him,...... the judgment then began," &c. (Daniel vii, 9, 10.) And after the judgment had commenced, thus says Daniel: (ibid. 13,) "I saw in the night visions one like the son of man came with the clouds of heaven, and approached the Ancient of days, and stood before him;" that is to say, to hear also his sentence.

From these and other passages in the Prophets it is evident that God himself, and not the Messiah shall be the Judge of the Universe. And how can it be otherwise? It is God alone who, as we read in Jeremiah xvii, 10: "can search the heart, and try the reins, even to give every man according to his ways, and according to the fruits of his doings."

Could we authenticate our objections to Christ and his system by no other proof, the manner in which he expresses himself in the verse under consideration, would be sufficient to show, that he was not the Messiah.

28. "Verily I say unto you, There be some standing here, which shall not taste of death, till they see the Son of man coming in his kingdom."

I have to add nothing to what the anonymous *Fragmentist* has remarked on this verse. He says: (pages 118 and 119,) "No more distinct assertion can be made with regard to Christ's visible and glorious return — an assertion, moreover, which fixes this event upon, and within the limits of a not far distant period. The persons themselves that then stood around Christ on the same spot, shall not all have departed hence; but some of them see him appear in his kingdom. But since Christ, unfortunately, has not appeared within heavenly clouds, either during that period, or many centuries afterwards, it is in our day attempted to remedy the evident fallacy of this prophecy, by most artificial, or poor interpretations of Christ's words," &c. "Indeed! the first coming of the Messiah is not fixed upon so distinct a period in the Elder Testament, as in the New. And a Jew can advance far more reasonable and proper commentaries and objections, with the view of showing that his Messiah has not yet come, than a Christian could attempt to save himself and his Christianity by the assertion, that his Messiah has not returned." (Page 123.)

How firmly Christ's disciples believed that their Master would return, even during their life-time, is evident from I. Thessalonians iv, 13—18, v, 1—5; Epistle of James v, 7—9. But it is a fact, founded upon history, that the Disciples and the first Christians waited in vain for the return of their Master; hence there is no promise found more evidently false than this, and the belief is useless and erroneous, as Paul himself tells us, if Christ should not return to reward the faithful in his kingdom.

CHAPTER XVII.

2. "And was transfigured before them: and his face did shine as the sun, and his raiment was white as the light.

3—7. And, behold, there appeared unto them Moses and Elias talking with him," &c.

In comparing the vision spoken of in these verses, with those of Moses, Isaiah, Ezekiel, and others, we must declare the former very insignificant. It seems, besides, to be borrowed from Exodus xxxiv, 29.

Concerning verse 5, see my remarks on chapter iii, verse 17.

10. "And his disciples asked him, saying, Why then say the Scribes that Elias must first come?

11. And Jesus answered and said unto them, Elias truly shall first come, and restore all things:

12. But I say unto you, That Elias is come already, and they knew him not, but have done unto him whatsoever they listed. Likewise shall also the Son of man suffer of them.

13. Then the disciples understood that he spake unto them of John the Baptist."

If Christ accords full authority to the doctrine conveyed in Malachi iii, 3 and 4, he can by no means assert, that the Prophets referred to John the Baptist. For if the latter had been the person that was to appear in the spirit of Elijah, he should have effected, according to the contents of the same prophecy, general repentance and improvement. The narrative of the exorcism of the devil that haunted the lunatic, (verse 14—19,) is one of those stories, upon which I expatiated above, in my introductory remarks to chapter viii.

20. "...... for verily I say unto you, If ye have faith as a grain of mustard-seed, ye shall say unto this mountain, Remove hence to yonder place; and it shall remove; and nothing shall be impossible unto you."

This contents of this verse are borrowed from the famous old Greek proverb, " If God be with us, every thing that is impossible becomes possible," and the metaphor used here is occasioned by Psalm cxiv, 3 and 4, where the royal bard relates, that the sea had fled, that the

Jordan was driven backward, that the mountains skipped like rams, and the hills like little lambs before the God-believing Israelites.

22. "....The Son of man shall be betrayed into the hands of men."

Every one, even without being gifted with the power of prophecying could at that time foresee, that Christ would endanger his life by going to Jerusalem.

23. "And they shall kill him, and the third day he shall be raised again. And they were exceeding sorry."

As regards the resurrection here spoken of, see my remarks on chapter xxvii, 65, below. I must, however, mention one point, that this fiction was prominently occasioned by Hosea, vi, 1 and 2, where we read, relative to the relief of Israel from his heavy, political disease, as follows: "Come and let us return unto the Lord; for he hath torn, and he will heal us: he hath smitten, and He will bind up our wounds. He will revive us after two days: on the third day he will raise us up, and we shall live in His presence."

27. "Notwithstanding, lest we should offend them, go thou to the sea, and cast an hook, and take up the fish that first cometh up; and when thou hast opened his mouth, thou shalt find a piece of money: that take, and give unto them for me and thee."

The history of this miracle is an imitation of I. Kings xvii, 6. As there it is related that ravens delivered Elijah by the brook of Kerith from his distress, and provided him with bread and flesh, so it was necessary that some species of the animal kingdom should come to the rescue of Christ also.

CHAPTER XVIII.

3. "And said, Verily I say unto you, Except ye be converted, and become as little children, ye shall not enter into the kingdom of heaven.

4. Whosoever therefore shall humble himself as this little child, the same is greatest in the kingdom of heaven."

The same doctrine is taught in Psalm li, 19: "The sacrifices of God are a broken spirit; a broken and a contrite heart, O God, wilt Thou not despise." Or, Isaiah lxvi, 2: "For all these things my hand hath made, that all these things came into being, saith the Lord; but upon such a one will I look, upon the poor, and him who is of a contrite spirit, and who trembleth at my word."

6. "But whoso shall offend one of these little ones which believe in me, it were better for him that a mill-stone were hanged about his neck, and that he were drowned in the depth of the sea."

Why Christ accords such great importance to his individual teachings, we can not conceive; for as far as we have hitherto shown, we can not discover, that he taught better moral doctrines, nor more instructive lessons than those proclaimed by the Prophets.

7. "Wo unto the world because of offences! for it must needs be that offences come; but wo to that man by whom the offence cometh!"

On this point we find sufficient information in Ps. xxxvii With regard to verses 8 and 9, compare my remarks on chapter v, 29 and 30.

10. "Take heed that ye despise not one of these little ones; for I say unto you, That in heaven their angels do always behold the face of my Father which is in heaven."

The assertion that the pious are placed under the protection of guardian spirits, is borrowed from Psalm xci, 11 and 12, where it is said: "For His angels will He give charge concerning thee, to guard thee on thy ways. Upon their hands shall they bear thee, that thou mayest not dash against a stone, thy foot."

11. "For the son of man is come to save that which was lost."

Every attentive reader must here ask: By what means? Has Christ perchance shown a new, hitherto unknown way toward salvation? As yet we have not discovered it in his speeches. Or does perchance the mere belief, that this son of man is the Annointed, or Messiah, comprise already all salvation?

First then, we have shown in several passages, with incontrovertible arguments, that Christ could not have been the Messiah. And even aside from this, of what avail was his appearance, since neither human desires for evil were decreased, nor any new mode of remedying them was taught. It is true, there are such who still believe, that Christ was commissioned, or intended to lead those to salvation that were subject to the original sin; but since he was unable to remove the original sin itself,—that is, human evil desires,—which can indeed, not be done without stripping man of his human nature, a task impossible, in his hands: every one is still bound to obtain salvation by following the best moral lessons and precepts, and strive himself to conquer that original sin as it continues to be waging war against him.

12. "How think ye? If a man have an hundred sheep, and one of them be gone astray, doth he not leave the ninety and nine, and goeth into the mountains, and seeketh that which is gone astray?"

The subject of this parable is borrowed from Ezekiel xxxiv, 16: "That which was lost will I seek for," &c.

15. "Moreover if thy brother shall trespass against thee, go and tell him his fault between thee and him alone: if he shall hear thee, thou hast gained thy brother."

The same lesson is taught already in Leviticus xix, 17. Also, Sirach xix, 13: "Admonish thy friend, it may be he hath not said it: and if he have, that he speak it not again."

16. "But if he will not hear *thee, then* take with thee one or two more, that in the mouth of two or three witnesses every word may be established."

Thus also do the Scribes teach: (Treat. Yomah, fol. 87, a,) "If a man have trespassed against his brother, and the latter be not willing to listen to an apology, let him take," &c.

18. "Verily I say unto you," &c.

See my remarks on chapter xvi, verse 19.

20. "For where two or three are gathered together in my name, there am I in the midst of them."

This verse contains again nothing more than what the Sophrim had already taught: "When ten men are assembled, and occupy themselves with the Law, ... and whence is it inferred that the same is the case with two? because it is said: (Malachi iii, 16,) 'Then conversed they that fear the Lord one with the other: and the Lord listened and heard it;' nay! whence is it inferred that the same is the case even with one? it is said: (Exodus xx, 21,) 'In every place where my name shall be mentioned, I will come down to thee, and bless thee.'" (Ethics of the Fathers iii, 7.)

21. "Then came Peter to him, and said, Lord, how oft shall my brother sin against me, and I forgive him? till seven times?"

The answer given by Christ, "I say not unto thee, Until seven times: but, until seventy times seven," could have easily been found in Leviticus xix, 17. For the Law therein contained is violated whenever we refuse pardoning our offender. More obvious, it is taught by the Sophrim in the Mechilta, where it reads: "The rule which shall regulate all our actions should be, that we always remember the words of Exodus xxii, 27, 'for I am gracious.' The meaning is: Because, says the Lord, out of mercy I called the universe in existence, and, therefore, it behoves my creatures to act kindly and indulgently toward each other. For to that purpose they are created and according to the use they make of this virtue I will treat them."

23—35. "Therefore is the kingdom of heaven likened," &c.

The simile, as it occurs here, representing God as king, and man as His servants, is often employed by the Prophets, and, therefore, borrowed from them. The moral Law conveyed in it: that God will not grant forgiveness to a man who would not forgive his brother, is taken from Sirach xxviii, 2.

CHAPTER XIX.

3. "The Pharisees also came unto him, tempting him, and saying unto him, Is it lawful for a man to put away his wife for every cause?

4. And he answered and said unto them, Have ye not read, that He which made them at the beginning made them male and female,

5. And said, For this cause shall a man leave father and mother, and shall cleave to his wife: and they twain shall be one flesh? —(Genesis ii, 24.)

6. Wherefore they are no more twain, but one flesh. What therefore God hath joined together, let not man put asunder."

Whoever reads attentively the passage adduced here from the Pentateuch, shall find, that it by no means contains a Commandment, but simply states the reason why a man should leave his parents, his flesh and blood, and cleave to a strange person. Entirely incorrect, however, is the conclusion in verse 5, "What God hath joined," &c. For whenever man and wife can not live together in harmony, it is evident, that the Lord has not joined them together, as the poet most beautifully expresses it:

"The bond not sanctified on earth by love,
"Was not forever blessed by God above,"

and can, therefore, be put asunder by man. And granted even, that every matrimonial bond is effected by the providence of God, the irreconcilable discord between man and wife shows, that divorce also is ordained for them by God, and can, and should be performed by men.

7. "They say unto him, Why did Moses then command to give a writing of divorcement, and to put her away?

8. He saith unto them, Moses because of the hardness of your hearts suffered you to put away your wives: but from the beginning it was not so."

It is impossible that Moses, the strict teacher, who never allowed the passions of the people to influence him, should have yielded to the hardness of their hearts, and given a Law to favor them. On the contrary; from Deuteronomy xxiv, 1, where we read: "When a man hath taken a wife, and married her, and it come to pass, that, if she find no favor in his eyes, because he hath found some scandalous thing in her, he may write her a bill of divorcement," &c., it is evident, that the Mosaic Law does not leave divorcements to the arbitrariness and passions of a man, and that mere dislike, and, as we are justified in concluding *analogically*, other causes proceeding from hardness of the heart, such as jealousy, harshness, difference of tastes, disparity of temperaments, &c., are no sufficient grounds for divorcements. Hence, the Law permits divorces only, when a peculiar act, violating the rights of husband or wife, has been proven. The Biblical passage in question has been interpreted in the same manner by the Academy of Shamai.

Since also, as we have just proven, even important grounds, that are difficult to substantiate, are not sufficient for divorcements, nay! when jealousy has stepped between man and wife, a mysterious ceremony (Numbers v, 10—30,) must be resorted to, ere separation can be effected: it is but natural to conclude, that the Biblical phrase, "because he hath found some scandalous things in her," can refer only to such cases, as natural Law itself demands; to wit: adultery, intentional abandonment, cruel treatment, &c.

9. "And I say unto you, Whosoever shall put away his wife, except it be for fornication, and shall marry another, committeth adultery: and whoso marrieth her which is put away doth commit adultery."

By thus limiting the right of divorcement to adultery alone, Christ violates not only the Law of Moses which, as he asserts himself, (Matth. v, 17,) he had not come to destroy, &c., but also the Law of nature, as we have shown in our commentary on verses 7 and 8.

Should some reply, that the will of Christ was that of the Deity, we would ask: Can God be pleased to violate the sacred Law of Nature?

16. "And, behold, one came and said unto him, Good Master, what good thing shall I do, that I may have eternal life?

17. And he said unto him, Why callest thou me good? there is none good but one, that is, God: but if thou wilt enter into life, keep the commandments."

Christ teaches here, in unequivocal terms, that there is but one, unique God, that there is no triune God, and that he was no part of the Divinity; saying: "there is none,"—not excepting himself—"good, but one, that is, God."

18. "He saith unto him, Which? Jesus said, Thou shalt do no murder, Thou shalt not commit adultery, Thou shalt not steal, Thou shalt not bear false witness,

19. Honor thy father and thy mother: and, Thou shalt love thy neighbor as thyself."

From these words of Christ it must be seen, that he knew no better moral lessons to inculcate, than those of Moses; (Exodus xx, 12—17; Leviticus xix, 18;) and these, therefore, suffice for the acquisition of eternal salvation. However, he could have expressed his views in a far more concise manner, by addressing the youth in the words of Michah: (vi, 8 and 9,) "He hath told thee, O man, what is good, and what the Lord doth require of thee: nothing but to do justice, to exercise charity, and walk humbly with thy God."

21. "— — —If thou wilt be perfect," &c.

With regard to the lesson conveyed in this verse, that we should be benevolent, and ought not regard temporal treasures as the highest things to be acquired, see above, chapter vi, 20, and compare also Psalm cxix, 72, and lxii, 11.

24. "And again I say unto you, It is easier for a camel to go through the eye of a needle, than for a rich man to enter into the kingdom of God."

So also it is observed in Deuteronomy xxxii, 15, that wealth and high-life lead to haughtiness and self-conceit, and thus cause man to violate God's Laws, on account whereof the Lord visits him with misfortunes with the view of inducing him to improve and repent.

28. "And Jesus said unto them, Verily I say unto you, That ye which followed me in the regeneration, when the Son of man shall sit in the throne of his glory, ye also shall sit upon twelve thrones, judging the twelve tribes of Israel."

We have proven above, chapter xvi, 28, that Christ did not appear in glory, as he maintains here; hence, his promise, given to his disciples and based upon his return is but empty talk. It is true that they saw this afterwards, and attempted, as we clearly perceive from their writings, (for instance, II. Peter iii, 8,) to console themselves by subtle interpretations; yet, common sense repudiates such absurd fictions.

30. "But many that are first shall be last; and the last shall be first."

To the same effect the Sophrim express themselves: "A reverse order of things will be found in Paradise. Many that occupy high places on earth, will be low hereafter; and many that were here held low, will be raised high there."

CHAPTER XX.

1. "For the kingdom of heaven is like unto a man that is an householder, which went out early in the morning to hire laborers into his vine-yard.

2. And when he had agreed with the laborers for a penny a day, he sent them into his vine-yard.

3. And he went out about the third hour, and saw others standing idle in the market-place,

4. And said unto them; Go ye also into the vine-yard, and whatsoever is right I will give you. And they went their way.

5. Again he went out about the sixth and ninth hour, and did likewise," &c., &c.

Israel is often represented by the Prophets, (Isaiah v, 1; Psalm lxxx, 9, &c.,) by the symbol of a vine-yard. The above parable is certainly borrowed from them, to symbolise the Church.

The same simile is found also in the Jerusalem Talmud, Treat. Berachoth, together with its *tertium comparationis:* That there are who distinguish themselves in a shorter space of time, than others.

The originality in the Talmud is evident from the simple style, so peculiar to the Sophrim. The simile is somewhat remodelled and colored in Matthew, in order to adapt it to the intended comparison: that a man should not rely upon his merits, nor do good with the view of receiving reward for it. This doctrine, however, is not new, but was, long before Christ, an axiom of the Scribes: "Be not like unto servants, that serve their masters with the view of receiving payment; but be as servants that serve their master without expecting payment; and let the fear of God be on you." (Ethics of the Fathers i, 3.)

18. "Behold, we go up to Jerusalem; and the Son of man shall be betrayed unto the chief priests, and unto the Scribes, and they shall condemn him unto death,

19. And shall deliver him to the Gentiles to mock, and to scourge, and to crucify him: and the third day he shall rise again."

The prophecy of Christ, with the exception of the reputed resurrection upon which we shall expatiate hereafter, can be regarded only as a plausible supposition. For, accused of blasphemy and demagoguism, he could expect nothing else than that the Highpriests and Scribes, as soon as they should take hold of him, would deliver him up to the Gentiles, who, as the former had no longer any jurisdiction over life and death, would crucify him according to the Roman Law.

23. "And he saith unto them, Ye shall drink indeed of my cup, and be baptized with the baptism that I am baptized with: but to sit on my right hand, and on my left, is not mine to give, but it shall be given to them for whom it is prepared of my Father."

From this verse we can again perceive that Christ never meant to be looked upon as a Divine being. Nay, when we remember his pious words, contained in chapter xix, verse 17, it is incredible, that he ever entertained the sinful thought, that the Supreme Being and Intelligence had become incarnate in him, to vegetate, for a brief space of time, on a grain of the endless Universe, and preach again ancient morals to a few human beings. Hence we may justly conclude, that all verses which speak of Christ's almighty power, glory, and universal judgeship, are but interpolations of later times.

26. "But it shall not be so among you: but whosoever will be great among you, let him be your minister."

The lesson that we should be modest, and could reach the kingdom of heaven only in the way of humility, is taught in Proverbs xvi, 5: "An abomination of the Lord is every one that is proud of heart: though hand joined in hand, he shall not be unpunished;" or ibid. xxix, 23: "The pride of man will humble him, but the humble in spirit will attain to honor;" or Michah vi, 8: "It hath been told thee, ... and to walk humbly before thy God."

27. "And whosoever will be chief among you, let him be your servant."

The same is remarked in Treat. Horioth, 9: "When Rabbi Gamaliel offered offices to two Scholars, and these declined from aversion to every kind of power, he said to them: 'Do you think that I meant to accord you power? I intended to impose a burden upon you!'"

28. "Even as the Son of man came not to be ministered unto, but to minister, and to give his life a ransom for many."

We have already proven, in our remarks upon chapter iii, verse 15, that Christ thought himself as much liable to sin, as any other man; nor held himself, as it is perceptible from many passages, but especially chapter xix, 17, to be a Divine, but a frail, weak, human being. How then can the Evangelist now make him say, that he gave his life a ransom for many? How can he, who himself stands in need of mercy and atonement, represent himself a trespass-offering for others? From the deportment and speeches of Christ during his last moments, it can indeed be clearly seen, that this so-called work of redemption or expiatory death lay not in the least in his plan. For when on his entering Jerusalem he perceived that the multitudes would, unlike his disciples, cry "Hosanna," and the Supreme Tribunal determined to have him taken up, he left the Temple, concealed himself in secret places, outside of Jerusalem, and held merely nocturnal meetings, so that he might not be easily detected and taken. And when he, at last, had reason to suspect one of his disciples of treason, he began to tremble and fear, because he held his life to be in danger. Still more; when he was taken, and, after a short trial, crucified, he exclaimed in despair: "My God, my God, why hast Thou forsaken me?"

Now, why did he exhibit such anguish and pain, if death was the aim and mission of his life? Indeed! the most subtle interpretations can not solve these contradictions! Whereas the old scriptural Writings most beautifully teach us, that the Lord forgives the Repentant even without sacrifices and expiatory practices, and that improvement is more pleasing to God, than sacrifices. (Psalms xxv, 6—20; xl, 7—9; li, 18, 19; ciii, 5—19; Proverbs xxi, 3; xvi, 6; Hosea xiv, 2—4; Isaiah i, 11—20; lviii, 3, &c.; Joel xii, 12, 13: Sirach vii, 9; xxxiv, 20; xxxv, 1—4.) For though as asserted by the Scholastic *Anselmus*, (eleventh century,) we offend the Infinite Holiness of the Supreme Being, by our sins, so that Divine

Justice demands a punishment proportional to our guilt, it is nevertheless evident that the Lord in His infinite Justice and mercy can, whenever he thinks proper, spare the sinner his punishment, because this forgiveness of Sin is more in accordance with the Divine holiness and justice, than the infliction of punishment. Only the partial opinions of the purpose of Divine punishment, and the mistake of human, for Divine justice, could call forth the absurd doctrine of mediation, or expiation through Christ. Since, however, this doctrine has been so often refuted, by Christian theologians, by means of philosophical, ethic and exegetic arguments, we deem it unnecessary further to expatiate upon the subject, and call the attention of our readers only to the absurd quintessence of it: that the Lord, with the view of doing justice to his purposes, sacrificed himself.

With regard to our verse, I conclude with the words of Luther, on I. Corinthians xv: "The worldlings look upon this as folly, and think it can not be true, that God should act and judge so foolishly, to condemn the whole world, without distinction, for the sake of one man; or, again for the sake of one man, accord salvation to all, without their co-operation. For according to their understanding we should judge in this wise: 'Every one lives and dies by virtue of his own merits.'" Compare with this Ezekiel, chapter xviii.

Verses 30—34 contain again a narrative, to the effect that Christ cured two blind men. Why so many stories of his having cured the blind, dumb and lame are presented to us, is easily to be perceived, when we consider that Christ meant, according to Matthew xi, 5, literally to fulfil the poetic words of Isaiah xxxv, 5. But how little consideration such stories deserve, I have shown in my introductory remarks to chapter viii, as well as chapter ix, 8 and 33.

CHAPTER XXI.

2. "Saying unto them, Go into the village over against you, and straightway ye shall find an ass tied, and a colt with her: loose them and bring them unto me.
3. And if any man say aught unto you, ye shall say, The Lord hath need of them; and straightway he will send them.
4. All this was done, that it might be fulfilled which was spoken by the Prophet, saying,
5. Tell ye the daughter of Zion, Behold, thy king cometh unto thee, meek, and sitting upon an ass, and a colt the foal of an ass."

Christ attempts here to apply the prophecy of Zechariah ix, 9, to himself. By tearing disjointed phrases from their context, one may easily substantiate the most absurd things by Holy Writ. We could, for instance, as the ingenious Maimonides remarks, "prove, by wrenching phrases from the Biblical text, without regarding their connection, that we must worship idols." Take for instance Deuteronomy xi, 16. By leaving out the first clause, "Take heed to yourselves, that your heart be not deceived," and quoting only the clause, "and serve other Gods," you will at once have the commandment to worship idols. Thus we can see, how necessary it is, whenever we wish to find the real meaning of a quoted passage, first to examine it in its context; which we shall do here.

The Prophet Zechariah, after having announced (ix, 1—9,) to all the enemies of Israel, the Syrians, Philistines, Tyrians and Sidonians, the punishment to be inflicted upon them by God, and their ultimate conversion to Judaism, he prophecied to Jerusalem a blissful, paradisical time of peace, when all the implements of war, horses, (in mountainous Palestine, horses were used only for war-purposes, and asses alone served as burden-beasts,) chariots and battle-bows should no more be seen, while the king, himself an humble, just and benevolent man, should be seen riding upon an ass; [37] for he shall be

[37] That, however, it was customary for people in high positions, to ride on foals of asses, can be seen in Judges x, 4.

in peace with all the nations, and his dominion extend from sea to sea, and from the rivers to the ends of the earth. Nothing of all this is applicable to Christ and his time. The mere riding on a foal of an ass, can not yet constitute the sign of Messiahship.

12. "And Jesus went into the Temple of God, and cast out all them that sold and bought in the Temple, and overthrew the tables of the money-changers, and the seats of them, that sold doves."

The story in this verse is founded on Zechariah xiv, 21, where it reads: "In that day there shall be no Canaanite, (merchant,) any more in the House of the Lord of hosts." This prophecy, however, is very erroneously referred to the time of Christ:

1. Because the Prophet does not say that such a fact will take place by tumultuous and forcible means, but, as it is literally said in the same verse, by the holiness and piety of all the citizens of Jerusalem and Juda.

2. Of all the events which Zechariah announced in the quoted chapter, nothing was fulfilled in the time of Jesus.

18. "Now in the morning as he returned into the city, he hungered.

19. And when he saw a fig-tree in the way, he came to it, and found nothing thereon, but leaves only, and said unto it, Let no fruit grow on thee henceforward for ever. And presently the fig-tree withered away."

From these verses also, we can see that Christ was not a Divine being, but a common mortal; otherwise he would at once have known that the tree bore no fruits, nor would he have hungered. Now, he being as humble a man as any other, we must doubt this very much, that he could have destroyed, by his curse, the vitality of the tree.

22. "And all things whatsoever ye shall ask in prayer, believing, ye shall receive."

This is taught in Psalm cxlv, 18 and 19: "The Lord is nigh unto all who call upon Him, unto all who call upon Him in truth. The desire of those who fear Him will He fulfil, and their cry will He hear, and save them."

27. "And they answered Jesus, and said, We can not tell. And he said unto them, Neither tell I you by what authority I do these things."

The fact that Christ, instead of performing some miracle at a moment so important, resorted to such a child-like evasion, proves how little credence can be attributed to the stories of his miracles.

33. "Hear another parable: there was a certain householder, which planted a vine-yard, and hedged it round about, and digged a wine-press in it, and built a tower, and let it out to husband-men, and went into a far country."

This parable is borrowed from Isaiah v, 1—7, but somewhat remodelled toward its close.

The stiffneckedness charged upon the Jewish nation, is an imitation of Jeremiah ii, iii. Yet, such a charge was the least just at the time of Christ. For when a nation emphatically repudiates such reformers whose reforms do not consist in improved rituals, or the establishment of better moral doctrines, but in the intention of being regarded as Prophets, by merely repeating the beautiful and unsurpassably sublime morals of ancient time with some unimportant alterations, nay! even frequent errors: we can not charge it with stubbornness, but must acknowledge that it acts from a due sense of Religion.

42. "Jesus saith unto them, Did ye never read in the Scriptures, The stone which the builders rejected, the same is become the head of the corner: this is the Lord's doing, and it is marvelous in our eyes?"

The two verses, Psalm cxviii, 22 and 23, which Christ attempts to apply to himself, were, as is evident from verse 10, meant by David as relating to himself.

The former shepherd-boy, after having gained many victories, and subjugated all neighboring tribes, who now is clad in royal attire, could indeed exclaim, in his enthusiasm: "All nations encompassed me about; but in the name of the Lord I will surely cut them off," which can, by no means, be applied to Christ, who lived and died in the midst of Jews. And as the whole Psalm speaks of David and his victorious expeditions, every reasonable man must perceive, that two verses of that chapter can not refer to a strange person and his mission, since this would be a destruction of the connection. Besides, the verses next following could, in this case, then only be brought into harmony with their two predecessors, if we would substitute absurdities for interpretation.

43. "Therefore say I unto you, The kingdom of God shall be taken from you, and given to a nation bringing forth the fruits thereof."

Prophets, whose predictions Christ himself declared to be Divine, contradict the contents of this verse. "And yet for all that, though they (the Jews) be in the land of their enemies, will I not cast them away, neither will I loathe them to destroy them utterly, to break my covenant with them; for I am the Lord their God." (Leviticus xxvi, 44,) See also: Isaiah lx, 10—22; Zechariah viii, 20—23, where we read especially in the last verse, as follows: "Thus hath said the Lord of hosts, In those days, ten men out of all the languages of the nations shall take hold—yea, they shall take hold of him that is a Jew, saying, Let us go with you; for we have heard that God is with you." (Compare also Daniel vii, 27.)

44. "And whosoever shall fall on this stone, shall be broken: but on whomsoever it shall fall, it will grind him to powder."

This verse is an imitation of Isaiah viii, 14 and 15, ". . . . but also for a stone of stumbling, and for a rock to fall, ... that many shall stumble over them, and fall, ..."

CHAPTER XXII.

Verses 1—14. The form of this parable, speaking of a king who made a wedding for his son, seems to have been occasioned by Isaiah lxii, 5, where Israel is represented as a bride-groom, and Jerusalem, as his bride. Compare also: Isaiah lxi, 10 and 11.

19. "Shew me the tribute-money. And they brought unto him a penny.
20. And he saith unto them, Whose is this image and superscription?
21. They say unto him, Cæsar's. Then saith he unto them, Render, therefore, unto Cæsar, the things which are Cæsar's; and unto God, the things that are God's."

It is highly improbable that the Scribes put the question to Christ, whether tribute should be paid to Cæsar. Considering that the Prophet Jeremiah (xl, 9,) had taught the people: "Seek the welfare of the city," &c., and the Sophrim themselves taught these principles: "The Law of the land is the Law of Religion," Treat. Bava Kamma, fol. 112. "The government never decrees Laws unless they were dictated from above," and "Tribute can not be withheld from the government:" considering all this, the question above would have been rather easily and simply answered.

Admitted, however, that the question was indeed addressed to Christ, with the view of enticing him into some rebellious remark, it is not clear, why he should have evaded the answer by a subtle and manifest untruth, instead of referring them to the Laws of Moses and the Prophets. It is highly absurd to assert that the money of Cæsar, because he had it coined, should be returned to him, even though it had been acquired by honest means. We may as well maintain, that a manufacturer, after having sold his manufactures stamped with his sign, or given them to his laborers as wages, could re-demand them solely because he had them manufactured. Can any man declare such a course to be just? If the right of governments to impose taxes upon their citizens were based upon no more rational principle than that advanced in the above verses, even the most humble mind could not rest satisfied. However incorrect verse 21 is, it nevertheless offered a first basis to Christianity in monarchical countries. History teaches us that even the most enlightened, liberal and un-Christian monarchs ardently desired, and most earnestly strove to establish a so-called Christian state; for they were not inclined to give up the golden rule: "Render unto Cæsar the things that are Cæsar's!" This also is the reason why the Jews were, and are to this very day hated, oppressed, and persecuted, by all monarchical governments, not on account of their peculiar, otherwise entirely harmless ceremonies, but on account of the republican and cosmopolitical nature of *their* Bible. The professors of Judaism, regarding as they do their Bible as holy and inviolable, which recognizes God alone as king, and knows no other tribute than that to be paid to the poor and needy; the Jews sacrificing as they do their life and substance for the observance of the doctrines of a Bible, that places the monarchical government on a level with slavery, (see I. Samuel viii, 7—19,) must naturally be a stumbling block in the way of all tyrants. Earthly Rulers do not regard Religion as the highest concern of man, but as a tool for their own ambition, as a handmaid of their government. And though it is but the superstition of thousands of years, for which they struggle, they nevertheless think themselves justified in their course of action. For this superstition is highly useful for their governments, serves as a cover for the oppressive taxes and inhuman extortions, and especially canonizes human bondage. Hence it can not at all be wondered at, that all those are oppressed and banished from the higher ranks of human society, who would not do homage to such cruel nuisance, but openly profess, standing upon the platform of their truly enlightening Bible, the monstrosity thereof.

30. "For in the resurrection they neither marry nor are given in marriage, but are as the angels of God in heaven."

The view expressed here, has been anticipated by the Psalmist: (xvii, 15,) "In righteousness shall I behold Thy face; and be satisfied, when I awake, with contemplating Thy likeness." "The bodies of those that shall rise, will be so perfect, that they, in eternal purity, will undisturbedly enjoy the rays of the primitive source of light." (See Treat. Chagigah, fol. 15.)

31. "But as touching the resurrection of the dead, have ye not read that which was spoken unto you by God, saying,

32. I am the God of Abraham, and the God of Isaac, and the God of Jacob? God is not the God of the dead, but of the living."

Instead of adducing such a sophistical proof for the resurrection of the dead, Christ might have cited: Deuteronomy xxxii, 39: "I kill, and I make alive," or I. Samuel ii, 6: "The Lord killeth, and maketh alive: he bringeth down to the grave, and bringeth up." And indeed! the Sophrim attempt to prove by these passages, that the doctrine of the resurrection is really contained in the Bible. They say: "Both phrases, 'I wound and heal,' and its parallel, 'I kill and make alive,' are alike applicable only to the same person. But we find it distinctly expressed in Isaiah: (xxvi, 9,) 'Thy dead shall live, my dead bodies shall arise .... and the earth shall cast out the departed;' or in Daniel: (xii, 2,) 'And many of those that sleep in the dust of the earth shall awake, some to everlasting life and some to disgrace and everlasting ignominy,' and ibid. verse 13: 'But thou, go toward thy dissolution, rest, and arise for thy lot at the end of days.'"

Verses 36—40 contain doctrines well known from Deuteronomy vi, 5, and Leviticus xix, 18, by the faithful observance of which, as Christ himself admits, (according to Luke x, 28,) eternal life may be acquired. [38]

42. "What think ye of Christ? whose son is he? They say unto him, The son of David.

43. He saith unto them, How then doth David in spirit call him Lord, saying,

44. The Lord said unto my Lord, Sit thou on my right hand, till I make thine enemies thy footstool?

45. If David then called him Lord, how is he his son?

46. And no man was able to answer him a word, neither durst any man from that day forth ask him any more questions."

The cx. Psalm, cited here treats, by no means of the Messiah, but of King David, or some other king. This is evident particularly from verse 5, where it is said: "The Lord hath crushed kings at thy right hand on the day of His wrath." If it had been intended here to allude to the Messiah, the verb must have been in the future tense, instead of the preterit; since the fact represented here as past, could have been past only after the appearance

[38] Compare Treat. Sabbath, fol. 31, a. (Here we read the following: A heathen came to Rabbi Hillel with the singular request to teach him the Jewish Religion, while he was standing *on one foot*. Hillel said: "Do not do unto others, as thou wishest not to be done to; this is the whole Law, all the rest is commentary."—*Translator*.)

of the Messiah. But it may be said, how can David call himself "Lord?" To this we reply:

1. David is not the author of this Psalm. The phrase לדוד מזמור, is of no account, as a proof, *pro* or *con*, since it may just as well mean, "A Psalm *on*, or *dedicated to* David," as, A Psalm *of* David. The first meaning is the more probable one, so that this Psalm, like many others, was composed by some unknown author, who could well call David, "my Lord."

2. If David had composed this Psalm, he could never have said, "The Lord said unto me," or "unto David," because the Psalms were destined to be recited by Levites in the Temple, who could not have made use of such an expression. For this reason we find that David uses the third person, in Psalm lxi, 7—8, although he is the author of that sacred song. [39]

CHAPTER XXIII.

2. "The Scribes and Pharisees sit in Moses' seat:

3. All therefore whatsoever they bid you observe, that observe and do; but do not ye after their works: for they say and do not."

Christ teaches here, in unequivocal terms, that the ceremonial Laws of Moses should be for ever held inviolate.

8. "But be not ye called Rabbi: for one is your Master, even Christ; and all ye are brethren."

Christ could not have expressed himself more distinctly, that he did not wish to be regarded as more than the most distinguished teacher. Passing over the venemous appellations which he lavishes upon the most educated of his people, we will only remark that his picture of their character is certainly false, and can be applied only to the degenerate class of Pharisees, whom the Scribes themselves repudiate. (Treat. Sotah 23.) This our assertion is based upon their writings, though we

[39] See *Disputatio Rab Nachmanides cum fratre Paulo.*

are not inclined to defend all their innumerable religious enactments, which owe their origin partially to temporary wants, and partially to too scrupulous piety. We find among the Scribes innumerable models of modesty, faithfulness, disinterestedness, benevolence, &c. (See Treat. Sotah 40; Ketuboth 105, &c.) Such a miserable body of teachers, as Christ represents the Sanhedrin to have been, could never have produced such nobleminded disciples. *Audiatur et altera pars.*

16—22. "Wo unto you, ye blind guides, which say, Whosoever shall swear by the temple, it is nothing; but whosoever shall swear by the gold of the temple, he is a debtor...... And whosoever shall swear by the altar, it is nothing, but whosoever sweareth by the gift that is upon it, he is guilty," &c.

These verses contain such barefaced, false accusations against the Pharisees, that I have to remark nothing more, than to beg my readers, in order to ascertain the truth of my assertion, to cast a glance at the doctrines of the Pharisees, relative to vows and oaths, as they may be found in Treatise Shabuoth, fol. 20, and Nedarim, fols. 10 and 12.

This deportment of Christ, who boasted of himself that he was wiser than Solomon, is utterly inexcusable, preaching to his people, as he did, in this instance, untruths and calumnies, with the view of stirring them up against their leaders and venerable teachers.

23. "Wo unto you, Scribes and Pharisees, hypocrites! for ye pay tithe of mint, and anise, and cummin, and have omitted the weightier matters of the Law, judgment, mercy, and faith: these ought ye to have done, and not to leave the other undone."

From this verse it is again evident, that Christ did not only not mean to abolish the ceremonial Law of Moses, but held it to be indispensable. This can not be more clearly expressed than he does here: "These ought ye to have done, and not to leave the other undone," both the moral and ceremonial Laws ought to be practised with equal zeal.

34. "Wherefore, behold, I send unto you Prophets, and wise men, and Scribes; and some of them ye shall kill and crucify," &c.

It is a historical fact, that crucifixion was the capital

punishment which the Romans inflicted on rebels, but not so, with the Sophrim and Pharisees; hence the prophecy in this verse contains an untruth.

35. "That upon you may come all the righteous blood shed upon the earth, from the blood of righteous Abel unto the blood of Zacharias, son of Barachias, whom ye slew between the temple and the altar."

This verse shows as clearly as the sun at noon, that the whole account given by our historiographer in regard to the Pharisees, is merely a fiction, composed with the view to decry, and render them obnoxious to the people. For

1. Zacharias the son of Barachias belonged to the head-leaders and founders of the school of the Sophrim, and was honored and respected by all his contemporaries until the last moments of life. (See Treat. Yomah, page 9, b.)

2. If any one should object, that the Evangelist, although he explicitly says the son of Barachias nevertheless means Zechariah the son of Jehojadah, (II. Chron. xxiv, 22,) it is a nonsensical statement, that the all-righteous God should punish men for a crime which was committed many hundred years ago, by the King Joash, with whom they stood in no connexion whatever. Especially as Joash was punished for his crime, (see II. Chronicles xxiv, 25,) and the whole Israelitish nation had atoned for the crime committed in the first Temple during the destruction of it. (See Lamentations ii, 20.) Compare also the old Jewish legend about the punishment of the murder of Zechariah, son of Jehojadah, during the destruction of the first Temple. (Treatise Gittin, page 57, b.)

37. "O Jerusalem, Jerusalem, thou that killest the Prophets, and stonest them which are sent unto thee, how often would I have gathered thy children together, even as a hen gathered her chickens under her wings, and ye would not!"

The announcement of the destruction of Jerusalem as the punishment for the sins of the nation, is an imitation of Jerem vii, 13—15. Even the phrase, "as a hen," &c., is borrowed from Isaiah xxxi, 5.

CHAPTER XXIV.

2. "And Jesus said unto them, See ye not all these things? verily I say unto you, There shall not be left here one stone upon another, that shall not be thrown down."

After the religious factions had wasted and broken, in useless contentions, the otherwise rather weak political power of Palestine; after Pompey had appeared there as arbitrator between Aristobulus and Hyrcanus, and appointed the latter Highpriest, while he sent the former with his sons as captive to Rome; every attentive observer even without being endowed with prophetic power, could already then with certainty foresee the destruction of Jerusalem and the Temple by the Romans. Hence we can not regard Christ's announcement of the destruction of the holy city and Temple as a prophecy; the less so, because Christ did not even so far surpass common politicians, as to announce the time and day of the event.

Verses 5—12. These verses are borrowed from ancient Jewish legends. (See Treat. Sotah, 49, b.)

13. "But he that shall endure unto the end, the same shall be saved."

This verse is taken from Daniel xii, 12: "Happy is he that waiteth," &c.

20. "But pray ye that your flight be not in the winter, neither on the Sabbath-day."

From this verse we see clearly, that Christ did not intend to abolish the Sabbath, or transfer it to some other day. As he tells his disciples, although speaking of the end of days, "pray ye, that your flight be not on the Sabbath-day," it is evident, that he believed in the preservation of the Mosaic Sabbath to the end of days. Wherefore, Dr. Luther also observes: (Works iii, page 643,) "But who means to regard the Sabbath as commanded by God, must celebrate Saturday, but not Sunday; for the former, and not the latter was instituted for the Jews, as the Sabbath-day," &c. We have said above, that Christianity was not Christ's, but the Apostles' institution; now, however, we think ourselves justified in asserting even this, that Christianity is not even the Religion of the Apostles, but of some Popes. For the former celebrated the Sabbath-day in common with the Jews, which was done also by most Christians, till the thirteenth century. (See Johann Meyer, *De temp. sacr. etc.* 2, 9, and 10, § 11; and Benj. Otto, *De flumine Sabbatico*, § 10.)

21. "For then shall be great tribulation, such as was not since the beginning of the world to this time, no, nor ever shall be."

This verse is borrowed from Daniel xii, 1: "And at that time . . . . and there will be a time of distress, such as hath never been since the existence of any nation until that same time."

28. "For wheresoever the carcass is, there will the eagles be gathered together."

This verse is borrowed from Habakkuk i, 8: ". . . . and their horseman will come from afar; they will fly like the eagle hastening to eat;" or from Job xxxix, 30: "His young ones also sip some blood; and where the slain lie, there is he." The allegory of Habakkuk is ingenious; representing the wicked in Israel by a carcass, and their enemies by an eagle. It is, however, very strange, that Christ who never forgot to raise his own individuality as high as possible, here compares himself to a carcass, and his disciples to an eagle.

29. "Immediately after the tribulation of those days shall the sun be darkened, and the moon shall not give her light, and the stars shall fall from heaven, and the powers of the heavens shall be shaken."

This is borrowed from Isaiah xiii, 10: "For the stars of the heaven and their orbits shall not give forth their light; the sun shall be dark at his rising; and the moon shall not shed abroad her radiance;" or from Ezekiel xxxii, 7 and 8: "And I will cover up the heaven, when thou art gone, and darken their stars," &c.

30. "And then shall appear the sign of the Son of Man in heaven: and then shall all the tribes of the earth mourn, and they shall see the son of man coming in the clouds of heaven with power and great glory."

This passage undoubtedly refers to Daniel vii, 13 and 14: "I looked in the nightly vision, and, behold, with the clouds of heaven came one like a son of man, and he attained as far as the Ancient of days, and they brought him near before Him. And there were given him dominion, and dignity, and government, and all people, nations, and languages had to serve him," &c.

But this passage can, by no means, be applied to Christ, since Daniel himself, in interpreting his vision, declares, (verse 27,) that the "Son of man," referred to the holy people of Israel, whose kingdom is an everlasting kingdom."

31. "And he shall send his angels with a great sound of a trumpet," &c.

This is an imitation of Isaiah xxvii, 13: "And it shall come to pass on that day, that the great cornet shall be blown," &c.

34. "Verily I say unto you, This generation shall not pass, till all these things be fulfilled."

Since Christ maintained, (verses 29 and 30) that he should return upon a cloud of heaven immediately after the tribulation of those days, that is to say, the destruction of Jerusalem, and evidently for this reason recommended watchfulness to his disciples, we conclude that the phrase, "this generation shall not pass," means to convey the idea, that all these things shall be fulfilled during its lifetime. Knowing as we do, that Christ has, after so many centuries, not yet re-appeared, either in body or soul; and that vice is still in existence with unbroken power, by the side of virtue, we can not fail to observe the fallacy of this prophecy.

35. "Heaven and earth shall pass away, but my words shall not pass away."

This verse is an imitation of Isaiah xl, 8: "The grass withereth, the flower fadeth, but the word of God will remain for ever;" or ibid. li, 6: "For the heavens shall vanish away like smoke, and the earth shall wear out like a garment," &c.

36. "But of that day and hour knoweth no man, no, not the angels of heaven, but my Father only."

This speech again shows that Christ never meant to be regarded as God, or God-man. For as he says, "of that day and hour knoweth no man, no, not even the angels of heaven," and, according to Mark xiii, 32, "neither the Son, but the Father alone," it is evident, that he did not desire to represent himself either as one being with God, or as God-man, but simply as a mortal. Hence, we are again compelled to conclude, that all passages which represent Him as the Supreme Being, are interpolations.

43. "But know this, that if the good man of the house had known in what watch the thief would come, he would have watched, and would not have suffered his house to be broken up.

44. Therefore be ye also ready: for in such an hour as ye think not the Son of man cometh."

Verse 43 is borrowed from Jeremiah ii, 26, with this alteration, that in the latter verse the sinner, and in the former, Christ himself is compared with a thief. Thus we act when we borrow plumage from others: we disfigure ourselves with our own hands.

45—51. "Who then is a faithful and wise servant, whom his Lord hath made ruler over his household, to give them meat in due season?" &c.

The form of this parable is occasioned by the fact, that Moses and the Prophets employ the term "food," "meat," to symbolize the Law. For instance: Isaiah lv, 1; Proverbs ix, 5. The moral of this parable seems to be borrowed from Jeremiah xxiii, 1—3, and Michah iii, 1—12.

CHAPTER XXV.

1. "Then shall the kingdom of heaven be likened unto ten virgins, which took their lamps, and went forth to meet the bride-groom.

2. And five of them were wise, and five were foolish.

3. They that were foolish took their lamps, and took no oil with them:

4. But the wise took oil in their vessels with their lamps.

5. While the bride-groom tarried, they all slumbered and slept.

6. And at midnight there was a cry made, Behold, the bride-groom cometh; go ye out to meet him."

This parable seems to be of a very ancient date, and was, therefore, generally known among the Scribes. Thus we read in Treat. Sabbath, fol. 153, a: "The kingdom of heaven is like unto a king who invites his servants to a banquet without, however, appointing the time and hour. The wise among them adorned themselves and waited before the gate of the palace. 'For,' said they, 'does the king stand in need of anything? He may call us at any moment.' The foolish among them, attended to their ordinary labors. 'For,' said they, 'every banquet requires preparations.' All at once, the king caused all of them to be called to table. The wise appeared in their festive garments, while the foolish were clad in ragged and filthy clothes. Wherefore the king was pleased with the wise, but angry with the foolish, and said: 'Those that prepared themselves and put on their festive garments may sit down; but those that have appeared unadorned, shall stand up, and look at the banqueting of the others.' Mark, therefore, this lesson: 'Mend thy ways on the day previous to thy death,' that is to say, every day.'" The same parable is found also, only with a few formal alterations, in Treat. Sabbath, fol. 152, b.

14. "For the kingdom of heaven is as a man traveling into a far country, who called his own servants, and delivered unto them his goods.

15. And unto one he gave five talents, to another two, and to another one; to every man according to his several ability; and straightway took his journey," &c.

The moral lesson contained in these parables, is taught also in Ethics of the Fathers iii, § 19: "Every thing is seen by God, yet free will is given. The world is judged by goodness, and all things according to the multitude of works." Spiritual and physical faculties, given as they are by God, should ever be manifested by good deeds.

29. "For unto every one that hath shall be given, and he shall have abundance: but from him that hath not shall be taken away even that which he hath."

This verse is founded on Daniel ii, 21: "......he giveth wisdom unto the wise, and knowledge to them that know understanding." Or it is occasioned by Exodus xxxi, 6: "....and in the hearts of all that are wise-hearted, I have put wisdom," Compare also Treat. Berachoth 55, a.

Concerning verse 31, see my remarks on chapter xvi, 27, above.

32. "And before him shall be gathered all nations: and he shall separate them one from another, as a shepherd divideth his sheep from the goats."

This is an imitation of Ezekiel xxxiv, 17: "And as for you, O my flock, thus saith the Lord Eternal, Behold, I will judge between lamb and lamb, between the wethers and he-goats."

35—45. "For I was an hungred, and ye gave me meat: I was thirsty, and ye gave me drink: I was a stranger, and ye took me in:" &c., &c.

These passages are occasioned by Proverbs xix, 17: "Whoso hath compassion on the poor, lendeth unto the Lord," &c. See also Isaiah lviii, 7, and Ezekiel xviii, 7

46. "And these shall go away into everlasting punishment: but the righteous into life eternal."

This verse is borrowed from Daniel xii, 2 and 3: "....some to everlasting life, and some to disgrace and shame. And the wise shall shine brilliantly like the brilliance of heaven," &c.

CHAPTER XXVI.

15. "And said unto them, What will ye give me, and I will deliver him unto you? And they covenanted with him for thirty pieces of silver.
16. And from that time he sought opportunity to betray him."

The subject of this story is borrowed from Zechariah xi, 12, where the Prophet represents himself as the shepherd of Israel, and receives, according to the price fixed in Exodus xxi, 32, for a servant, thirty pieces of silver for his wages.

18. "And he said, Go into the city to such a man, and say unto him,

The Master saith, My time is at hand; I will keep the Passover at thy house with my disciples."

This order given by Christ proves how strictly he adhered to the Mosaic Ceremonial Laws. He causes, as the Anonymous Fragmentist, of Wolfenbuttel, justly remarks, the paschal lamb to be prepared for himself and his disciples; eats unleavened cakes, drinks the customary *calicem benedictionis*, and sings the usual hymns of praise. Nor can it appear strange that Christ, who loved to speak in parables, symbolized his approaching death, while he was partaking the paschal supper in commemoration of the delivery of the Jews from the Egyptian bondage, and expressed the wish, according to Luke xxii, 19, and I. Corinthians xi, 23, that his disciples should, in future, whenever they celebrated the Passover feast, remember also their departed teacher. He, however, did by no means intend, to introduce an entirely novel, and, as is to-day erroneously asserted, extraordinarily holy ceremony. Had this indeed been his intention, he would have, in the first place, distinctly told them, henceforth to discontinue the paschal supper, after which he, otherwise, so fervently longed, and which he celebrated as a true orthodox Jew, but to institute in its stead another ceremony commemorative of his death; and then, this fact would not have been passed over in silence by his most distinguished disciple, John.

28. "For this is my blood of the new testament, which is shed for many for the remission of sins."

This verse is evidently occasioned by Isaiah liii, 11 and 12, where the Prophet tells the people, that they had to suffer for the sins of many. But that Isaiah represents by "the man of pains," the Jewish nation, is incontrovertibly perceptible from verse 10, where we read: "But when he hath sacrificed himself as the trespass-offering, then shall he see his seed, live many days," &c.

Besides, Christ here runs into contradiction with himself. For, if the sins of many should be atoned for, by his death, he necessarily meant to be looked upon as the most immaculate being, since, otherwise, he should have himself required some self-atonement. Now, he himself says: (Matthew xix, 17,) "Why callest thou me good? There is none good, but one, that is, God," and shows unequivocally, that he did not deem himself innocent and perfect, which stands in diametrical contradiction to the assertion under consideration. (Compare also my commentary on chapter xx, verse 28, above.)

31. ". . . . All ye shall be offended because of me this night: for it is written, I will smite the Shepherd, and the sheep of the flock shall be scattered abroad."

The verse cited here, is taken from Zechariah xiii, 7, and reads thus: "Awake, sword of vengeance! against my shepherd, against the man whom I have associated with me, saith the Lord of hosts. Smite the shepherd, that the sheep be scattered, but I shall take the feeble ones under my protection." Not only the beginning and conclusion of this verse, but the whole connection of the whole chapter clearly shows, that Zechariah merely speaks of the false prophets in Israel. It is strange, that Christ applies such a passage to himself.

39. "And he went a little farther, and fell on his face, and prayed, saying, O my Father, if it be possible, let this cup pass from me: nevertheless not as I will, but as thou wilt."

This verse again distinctly shows, that Christ did not mean to be regarded as God, or God-man. For, why should he have found it necessary in this case, to pray and prostrate himself? Nay, how could he speak of a different will between himself and his Father?

42. "He went away again the second time, and prayed, saying, O my Father, if this cup may not pass away from me, except I drink it, thy will be done.

43. And he came and found them asleep again: for their eyes were heavy.

44. And he left them, and went away again, and prayed the third time, saying the same words."

Here we are forcibly reminded of certain historiographers, who describe, *verbatim*, some dialogue, which neither of the acting parties could ever have related. Now, if the disciples' eyes were heavy, if they were asleep and

Christ did not disturb them: who heard his prayer? Besides, we are not told, nor is it probable, that he communicated it to any one.

46. "Rise, let us be going: behold, he is at hand that doth betray me."

It is quite natural that when Christ, who had gone out to the Mount of Olives, as related in verse 30, all at once missed Judas, he began to fear and tremble at the thought that the latter might soon betray him—perhaps also, in order to avoid popular commotion—during the very night, all of which was soon verified, to his great horror.

53. "Thinkest thou that I can not now pray to my Father, and he shall presently give me more than twelve legions of angels.

54. But how then shall the Scriptures be fulfilled, that thus it must be?"

Kind Reader! which passage of the Scriptures was to be fulfilled? Is it Psalm xxii, 7, as Luther supposes? Look at that passage, and you shall find, as is clearly perceptible from verse 5, but especially verses 25 and following, that that Psalm refers exclusively to David. The twelve legions of angels, of whom Christ here speaks, seem not to have been ready at his command; for, as the Scriptural passage, to which he refers, was but a shallow excuse, we see no reason, why he should not have availed himself of those angels.

65. "Then the Highpriest rent his clothes, saying, He hath spoken blasphemy; what further need have we of witnesses? behold, now we have heard his blasphemy."

It is certainly blasphemy, when a man in all earnest maintains, that he should on some future day judge the world together with God Himself. And Christ even authenticated his assertion by miracles,—which, however, we emphatically deny,—he could not have thereby proved anything, since we read of far greater miracles of the Prophets, (compare for instance Christ's prediction of Peter's threefold denial before the cock crow, with Isaiah xxxvii, 30, 36, and xxxviii, 8, &c.,) and yet, they deemed themselves not even perfect enough to appear before

God, much less, therefore, to be His adjuncts, on the bench of Judgment.

CHAPTER XXVII.

3. "Then Judas, which had betrayed him, when he saw that he was condemned, repented himself, and brought again the thirty pieces of silver to the chief priests and elders.

4. Saying, I have sinned in that I have betrayed the innocent blood. And they said, What is that to us? see thou to that.

5. And he cast down the pieces of silver in the Temple, and departed, and went and hanged himself.

6. And the chief priests took the silver pieces, and said, It is not lawful for to put them into the treasury, because it is the price of blood.

7. And they took counsel, and bought with them the potter's field, to bury strangers in.

8. Wherefore that field was called, The field of blood, unto this day."

These historical notes of the Evangelist are contradicted by Acts i, 18 and 19, where we read: "Now this man, (Judas,) purchased a field with the reward of iniquity; and falling head-long, he burst asunder in the midst, and all his bowels gushed out. And it was known unto all the dwellers at Jerusalem; insomuch as that field is called in their proper tongue, *Aceldama*, that is to say, The field of blood." Hence, Judas did not repent of his deed, nor return the money to the priests, for which they bought a piece of land to bury strangers in, but is said to have bought, "with the reward of iniquity," a field for himself. Thus we have another proof, how little *Fides humana* and *historica* can be ascribed to the Writings of the New Testament, since men who could, and ought to have known better than any others, all that they report, contradict themselves in such a direct manner. We are, therefore, justified to assert, that all reports of the Evangelists are mere fictions. The fiction contained in verse 7 is occasioned by Zechariah xi, 13, whose words are not only distorted—(compare my remarks on verse 9, below,)—but even falsely interpreted, since the term יוצר, which signifies the same as אוצר, "treasure," is rendered by "potter."

9. "Then was fulfilled that which was spoken by Jeremy the Prophet, saying, And they took the thirty pieces of silver, the price of him that was valued, whom they of the children of Israel did value;

10. And gave them for the potter's field, as the Lord appointed me."

Not Jeremiah, but Zechariah speaks (xi, 12 and 13,) of thirty pieces of silver, which he received as reward, but cast them according to God's command, into the treasury of the Temple. Besides, these verses have quite a different reading from that introduced here. They read literally thus: "And I said unto them, if it be pleasing to you, give me my reward, and if not, forbear. So they weighed out as my reward, thirty pieces of silver. And the Lord said unto me, Cast unto the treasures, the precious price which I am prized at by them. And I took the thirty pieces of silver, and cast them into the house of the Lord unto the treasury." We see, that the Evangelist did not care for truth, since he did not inquire whether the passage quoted by him would suit his subject. He often alters the reading of Holy Writ to adapt it to his purposes, and thus makes every Prophet say what he (the Evangelist) pleases.

34. "They gave him vinegar to drink, mingled with gall: and when he had tasted thereof, he would not drink."

This narration is borrowed from Psalm lxix, 22, where David symbolically tells us, that his enemies gave him gall to eat and vinegar to drink. This also proves to us, that the description of Christ's execution contains many traces of complete fiction.

35. "And they crucified him, and parted his garments, casting lots: that it might be fulfilled which was spoken by the Prophet, They parted my garments among them, and upon my vesture did they cast lots."

Every unbiased reader will admit that the Psalmist said all this of himself distinctly, adding in the verse following, (xxii, 20,) that the Lord shall deliver him from the hands of these men, that cast lots for his garments; which can not be applied to Christ.

42. "He saved others; himself he can not save. If he be the King of Israel, let him now come down from the cross, and we will believe him."

This would certainly have been a convincing and decisive proof to win over a whole nation;—a result which Christ so ardently wished to accomplish, but was unable to produce. When we consider, moreover, that history furnished him with so many examples, how workers of miracles most easily obtained their end by sudden, amazing wonders: (Daniel iii, 14—30; vi, 16—28; I. Kings xviii, 21—41;) it is rather surprising, that he did not improve this important moment. The power of Christ can not, therefore, have been so great as it appeared to the imagination of his biographer.

45. "Now from the sixth hour there was darkness over all the land unto the ninth hour."

This story is either an imitation of notices given by Greek and Roman authors when having reported the decease of rulers, &c., (see Wettstein,) as for instance, *Serv. ad Virgil Georg.* i, 465, *seq.*, says: "*Constat, occiso Caesare in senatu pridie idus Martias, solis fuisse defectum ab hora sexta usque ad noctem.*" "It is evident, Cesar having been slaugthered on the fourteenth of March in the Senate, the sun was eclipsed from the sixth hour until night;" or it is borrowed from Jewish legends. (See Treat. Succah, Midrash Echa, chapter i, &c.)

63. "Saying, Sir, we remember that that deceiver said, while he was yet alive, After three days I will rise again.

64. Command therefore that the sepulchre be made sure until the third day, lest his disciples come by night, and steal him away, and say unto the people, He is risen from the dead: so the last error shall be worse than the first.

65. Pilate said unto them, Ye have a watch: go your way, make it as sure as ye can."

Already the Anonymous Fragmentist of Wolfenbuttel has incontrovertibly proved, however many objections may have been made to his arguments, that the history of Christ's resurrection is the invention of Matthew. Hence, it would be idle to add anything. Yet, as these fragments are scarcely to be found in private and public libraries, and even in book-stores, I shall introduce here some passages from them.

Page 372. "Since not a single person, except Matthew, makes mention anywhere of this story,—though opportunity often presented itself,—either in speech or writing, either as proof or defence, it can not in any way be the true record of a real occurrence. To be in possession of a valid proof that so often presents itself, to know of it and, at the same time, to be called upon to make use of it, and yet, never to refer to it, but merely adduce absurdities: this is a contradiction that can not be mistaken. Thus, then, it is at once clear, that Matthew has invented this story, since he wished to give some reply to the accusation, and could find out nothing better. But how abortive this invention proved to be, is shown by the repeated contradictions, into which Matthew has fallen with the story itself, with himself and other Evangelists.

1. "It is a contradiction that the Highpriests should have known of the resurrection, even before it took place, whereas the Apostles themselves, of whom it is said that the mysteries of God's kingdom were revealed to them, had no knowledge whatever of that occurrence. Of them it is distinctly said, that they knew not the prophecy of his resurrection. And that such was really the case, is proved by their whole conduct. They complain, that their hope for the redemption of Israel had been destroyed by his very death; they went to the grave with spices, believing that he like other deceased men would remain dead, and pass through the process of decomposition;—nay! when they found that the corpse was no more in the grave, they do not in the least dream of his resurrection, but conclude, that he must have been taken out, and carried to some other place;—a portion of them are not even inclined to believe the report of his resurrection,—in a word: up to the death of Christ, and some time after it, his disciples had in no way known, heard, or thought of his resurrection. How then can it be supposed that the Highpriests and Scribes had knowledge thereof? and that they, therefore, had taken the precautionary step to set a watch on the sepulchre.

2. "It is incredible that the Highpriests and the whole

body of the Senate publicly repaired to Pilate on the first day of Passover, and then went in procession with the Roman Sentinels through the city-gates, and had the Sepulchre sealed up. Not to mention other circumstances, it was a violation of Jewish Law and custom, to attend on the day of the Feast, on which they had to be particularly quiet and clean, to such a work, to mingle with heathens, and touch a grave. If, as we read, the disciples of Christ kept quiet during the Feast, according to Law, how could the Highpriests commit, before the very face of the people, such violations, especially touch a grave whereas all graves were on the approach of the Festivals, whitewashed, in order that they could be observed at the distance, and caution the people against rendering themselves unclean by touching them.

3. "Even aside from the consideration of what the Jews were by Law permitted to do, it can not be supposed that a whole body of Judges should ever have so rudely acted against the public welfare, and publicly repaired *in corpore* to the heathens, and moved in procession, together with the soldiers, through the city, although they could have obtained their object by quietly sending a deputation to Pilate.

4. "And again.—Why should they have gone to Pilate and thus given the heathens still more power over their people? Joseph to whom the grave belonged, and had it within the precincts of his garden, could as Jew and Member of the Senate not prevent sentinels from being placed at the grave; nay! it is even natural that he desired and requested that precaution, in order that he publicly removed all suspicion of deception on his part, with which he must have necessarily been charged with others.

5. "And what is the final result? The whole Senate, a body of seventy magistrates, are represented, in this story, as rogues, who considerately agree to commit a falsehood and call even Roman guards to their aid for that purpose. Properly speaking, this was impossible.

But what about Joseph, what about Nicodemus? Are they also represented as rogues? Do now the Pharisean and Sadducean Members of the Senate agree to deny the doctrine of resurrection by an invented falsehood, though the Apostles otherwise knew in so masterly a manner to represent them as disagreeing with regard to this point so far that the Pharisees defended it in opposition to the Sadducees?

6. "Can so many intelligent men resort to such a monstrous falsehood: that all Roman soldiers slept on their posts, so that a number of Jews could pass by them, roll away the large stone from the grave, and carry off the corpse? All this was done, *incognito*, without the least noise, and secretly, so that not one of the soldiers awoke, or traces remained of those that took the corpse off?

7. "If then, lastly, Matthew puts, in this manner, the blame from himself upon the Senate, and charges them of a flagrant and public falsehood: whence does it come that the deception of the Apostles has become a common saying among the Jews until this day, whereas all Apostles and Evangelists are everywhere silent with regard to the deception practised by the Jewish Sanhedrin? It strikes me, that all these things are contradictory, and bear the stamp of untruth upon their very faces."

Page 406. "Tell me, before God, my Readers, if ye are conscientious and honest, can you regard this testimony in so important a case as unanimous and honest, which is so variously and evidently contradictory with regard to the acting persons, to time, place, manner, purpose, speeches and reports?"

Page 407. "They do not act as other honest men who have but truth in view, and can boldly refer to other people, that saw him come, depart and walk about; no! all at once he is with them without having come,—he comes in a manner, imperceptible to human eyes, through closed doors, through a key-hole, and disappears again in the same way;—not a person in the street sees him come and go. Nay, throughout all the fifty days, after his resurrection, during which he is said to have gone about, not one of his disciples makes the least mention thereof to a stranger; they keep the thing secret, lest some one might have said to them: "show him to us, and then we will believe that he is alive." No, they make him first revive for themselves, appear invisible to all, and rise to heaven, from the Mount of Olives, before their own eyes, yet unknown to all in the city; and then they go and say: he was here and there."

Page 409. "Indeed! if we had no other reason for disbelieving the story of Christ's resurrection, this one alone, that Christ did not appear publicly, would suffice to confute its credibility; for such a course could never correspond with the purpose of Christ's coming into this world."

We abstain from all further remarks on the story of Christ's resurrection, and conclude with the words of the Fragmentist:

Page 105. "Nay, even if he had risen from death, it would not follow that he was indeed the Savior. For we read in the Scriptures also of others whom the Lord awoke from death, without, however, appointing them Messiahs for the people. And even the report that he rose again, we can not so easily accept as truth. Witnesses to this report are, as we learn, his adherents and disciples: and it is even they, who are, in our opinion, not beyond suspicion. The Senate of Jerusalem distinctly cautioned us through their deputies, and said, that these same disciples had secretly gone to the grave and stolen the corpse, and now went about and said, that he had risen. We know none of these disciples; hence, we can not be found fault with, if we accord, in this case, more credence to the Sanhedrin in Jerusalem, than to such unknown and suspicious witnesses."

APPENDIX.

ILLUSTRATION OF SOME OLD-BIBLICAL PASSAGES, THAT ARE REGARDED AS CONTAINING MESSIANIC PROPHECIES.

Although we have sufficiently proved above, (chapter iv,) that the founder of Christianity can not be regarded either as the Messiah or Savior of the human race, we will now, in order to remove by the light of truth, every shadow of proof for his Divine mission, consider the respective so-called Messianic passages, and even those that have been made such by the imaginations of idle minds.

We read in Treat. Sanhedrin, fol. 98, b: "What is the name of the Messiah? The disciples of Rabbi Shiloh maintain: "Shiloh is his name; for thus said our Patriarch Jacob: (Genesis xlix, 10,) עד כי יבא שילה, 'until Shiloh come.'" Hence the passage in question is generally rendered thus: "The sceptre shall not depart from Judah, nor the Law-giver from between his feet, until Shiloh come, and to whom all nations shall gather." From this verse Christianity concludes as follows: "Since the Israelites are scattered all over the earth, and the sceptre has been, for a long time, no more in the hands of Judah, it is certain that the Messiah has already come according to the prophecy of the Patriarch; and this Messiah was no other than Jesus Christ, the Nazarene."

However simple this argument seems to be, yet, every one that examines the verse in question with an unbiased eye, will find that it has been incorrectly interpreted, and thus given rise to illogical conclusions. Nay, we shall find, that even the Talmudic view which makes this Biblical passage a Messianic one, can not at all be taken into consideration.

Let us then first quote *in extenso*, the above mentioned passage from Treat. Sanhedrin: "What is the name of the Messiah? The disciples of Rabbi Shiloh said: 'Shiloh; for it is said,' &c.; the disciples of Rabbi Yinoi maintain: 'Yinon; as it is said,' &c.; the disciples of Rabbi Chaninah assert: 'Chaninah,' &c.; Rab said: 'If there be one of the living worthy of being the Messiah, it is our holy teacher, (Rabbi Jehudah Hanasi,) if he be among the dead, it is Daniel.'" We now see that every party accorded the name of its own Rabbi to the Messiah, whence we must conclude, that there is no question at all about a real name of the Messiah, but that every party merely intended to pay a compliment to its teacher, and regarded him as the most pious and the purest man of the age, so that he was most worthy to be the Messiah or Savior of his contemporaries. This is the more clearly perceptible from another passage in the Talmud, which flatly contradicts the assertion that Jacob alluded at all to the Messiah. In Treat. Pesachim we read: "Rabbi Simon, son of Pasi, taught: 'When the Patriarch Jacob attempts to prophesy of the Messianic time, the Divine spirit removed away from him.'"

How incorrect, on the other hand, the common, above quoted translation is, has been shown already by the learned and ingenious Dr. I. M Wise, (*Israelite*, Vol. I., 1854,) where, among the important and interesting remarks, he observes: "How can our Patriarch have meant to convey the idea of sceptre, by the term שבט, when he never saw one, and no archeologist can prove, that a sceptre then existed. And how could our inspired Patriarch have repeated the same thing in two different verses? Had he not said already in verse 8: 'But thou, Jehudah, unto thee thy brothers will render homage, ... thy father's children shall bow down unto thee.'" And I would add, that it would be strange that Jacob, who pronounced his benedictions in parallelisms should have changed his style in verse 10. Or was he so at a loss for words, just when he arrived at the phrase עד כי יבא שילה, that he could not find a parallelism? How absurd this would be? We remove all these difficulties by adopting Dr. Wise's translation, שבט, "tribe," מחקק, "ruler," "leader," and שילה, "Shiloh," signifying the first capital of Palestine after its conquest by the Israelites. The translation of the verse under consideration would then read thus: "No tribe shall depart from Judah, nor a ruler from between his feet, until he shall have come to Shiloh, [1] and the nations be submitted to him."

But admitted that the passage really refers to a future Messiah, named Shiloh, what has this to do with Jesus? Why does the Evangelist make Joseph dream, that the new-born child should be named Jesus, and not Shiloh? Besides, history would necessarily lead to this conclusion: Since as it asserted, that Jacob prophesied that the Messiah would come as soon as the sceptre departed from Judah, he ought to have appeared long before Christ, that is immediately after King Zedekiah had been carried as captive to Babylon, and thus the reign of Judah ceased to exist.

Now, as no Messiah appeared at that time, it is evident, that Jacob did not prophesy of any, and least of all, allude to Christ.

Again. It is concluded from Daniel ix, 24, that Christ was the Messiah, because it is said: "he will cause the oblations and sacrifices to cease." The train of argument is this: Since it is said that after the appearance

[1] I am of the opinion that שילה could be rendered also by "Peace," "Rest," derived from שלה, "to be quiet," so that the passage in question would read thus: "Until peace shall come." So translated we find this term also in Treat. Sanhedrin, fol. 119, where we read: "Thou hast, as yet not come to rest and to the inheritance; rest, that is Shiloh," &c.

of the Messiah the sacrifices shall cease, and they have really been discontinued for a long time, it is certain, that the Messiah must have come already. To show the incorrectness of this argument, we will transcribe here the whole passage from Daniel, (ix, 24—27,) in which the Prophet gives Divine information with regard to the future fate of his people and country. The passage reads literally thus: "Seventy weeks are fixed for thy people and thy holy city, to destroy the transgression, to annihilate sin, and atone for iniquity, whereupon everlasting righteousness will be again brought about, and the vision and prophecy will be fulfilled, and the most holy thing annointed. Know therefore and comprehend that from the going forth of the word to restore and build Jerusalem until the annointed prince will be seven weeks: and during sixty and two weeks will it be again built with streets and ditches even in the pressure of the times. And after the sixty and two weeks will an annointed one be cut off without a successor to follow him; and the city and the Sanctuary will the people of the prince that is coming destroy; but his end will come in a violent overflow; but until the end of the war devastations will be remaining. And though he will make a strong covenant with the high for one year-week, but already in the half of this year-week will he cause the sacrifices and oblations to cease, and the wings of crime will rise victoriously, until destruction and devastation shall strike also the devastator."

All commentators assert, that Daniel merely refers to the state of affairs during the period of the Second Temple, and prophesied its destruction, and show conclusively, that these predictions were fulfilled. How can verse 24 be applied to Christ? Has he ever restituted everlasting justice? Has vice ceased among mankind? Do we not read in Isaiah ii, 2—5: "And it shall come to pass in the last days, (that is, at the time of the Messiah,) &c., the Lord will judge among the nations, &c., nation shall not lift up sword against nation, and they shall not learn war any more!" Well, has this prophecy been fulfilled? Is no war carried on any longer? Is it abolished everywhere? Besides, we hear, from verse 26, that the city—Jerusalem—will remain waste until the end of all wars, (the time of Messiah.) The abolition of sacrifices—verse 27—is evidently not a sign of the post-Messianic time, but an event which really took place at the destruction of the Temple, and was predicted by Daniel. But such a sign for the Messianic time is presented by Daniel: (xii, 2,) "And many of those that sleep in the dust of the earth shall awake, some to everlasting life, and some to shame and everlasting ignominy." Hence, a general resurrection [2] of the dead shall take place at the time of the Messiah, in a manner, that those who have risen shall no more die. Now, as this event has, to this day, not occurred, Christ can not be regarded as the Messiah.

Others attempt to apply also the second Psalm to Christ; an attempt which we can confute by the following arguments:

1. The ninth verse of that Psalm would have no sense. It reads thus: "Thou shalt break them (the nations) with a rod of iron; like an earthern vessel shalt thou dash them in pieces." Which nation then did Christ crush by the sword? Nay, does not his very system reject such war-like purposes? since he says: (Matthew xxvi, 52,) "For all they that take the sword, shall perish with the sword."

2. The Messiah has nothing to do with kings and princes exclusively, but is sent for the whole human race. Why then is it expected only of Rulers, that they should do homage to the son or favorite of God? Every reasonable man must, therefore perceive, that this is the correct interpretation of the chapter in question, as pronounced by most commentators: The Psalm relates to King David

[2] The passage in Daniel most likely suggested Matthew's invention of the fable of the resurrection of the dead, which the other Evangelists do not mention, although this would have been a decisive evidence for the mission of Jesus; but he misinterpreted the prophecy of Daniel, telling of a resurrection in the vicinity of Jerusalem only, which is not contained in that prophecy.

or Solomon. The phrase: (verse 7,) "The Lord hath said unto me: Thou art my son!" is an allusion to the words of the Prophet, (II. Samuel vii, 14,) to whom the Lord said with regard to Solomon: "I will be his father, and he shall be my son;" or to Psalm lxxxix, 27, where David exclaims: "Thou art my Father," &c.

Nor can Isaiah, chapter xi, be applied to Christ. We read there: "And there shall come forth a scion out of the stem of Jesse, and a branch shall grow out of his roots . . . . The wolf shall dwell with the lamb, and the leopard shall lie down with the kid; and the calf and the young lion and the fatling together," &c. This chapter can not be applied to Christ, for two reasons:

1. Because it prognosticates a golden time, peace and undisturbed harmony, which was not that of Christ; nay! he even tells us that he meant to accomplish just the reverse saying: "I have not come to send peace, but the sword."

2. The Prophet continues (verse 12,) thus: "And the Lord shall set up an ensign for the nations, and shall assemble the outcasts of Israel, and gather together the dispersed of Judah from the four corners of the earth." This did not occur, as history proves, at the time of Christ; hence he can not have been the Messiah.

As regards the renowned passage in Isaiah lii and liii, in which Christian theologians think to find some prophecy relative to Christ, I have already shown, that it can not be applied to Christ, because the tenth verse tells us that "he shall see his seed—and the pleasure of the Lord shall succeed in his hand," nothing of which is in the least applicable to Christ. This much only I have to add here, that according to the opinion of the Talmud, Treat. Sanhedrin, fol. 98, b, Daniel,—according to modern Christian theologians, (Isaiah himself, Staudlin,) the Jewish nation, or at least the better portion of it,—(Eckerman, Paulus and Schuster,) King Usiah,—(Augusti,) the order of the Prophets, (Rosenmuller, Gabler, and De Wette,) must be understood as alluded to in the chapter quoted. The last opinion is the most plausible one.

At the conclusion of our investigation, we would call the attention of our readers to one of the Christian doctrine, which is intimately connected with the Messiahship, and was invented merely to prove, by Scriptural passage, that Christ was the Messiah: we mean the theory of *Original Sin*. Although it is attempted to base it on Genesis, chapter iii, it is entirely foreign to Judaism. Dr. Bretschneider says: (Dogmatics ii, page 53,) "We have mentioned already, (vol. I., page 689 and following,) that the Mosaic records know nothing of the doctrine that the image of God was destroyed, and understanding and will were depraved in consequence of our first parents having eaten of the forbidden fruit; but that that very narrative rather tells us just the reverse. Nor has any dogmatist as yet been able to prove that theory from the Mosaic narrative," &c.

This Christian dogma, as we have just remarked has been evidently invented for this reason, to justify and embellish the sufferings and death of Christ. Without, however, further investigating the matter, I will transcribe here some passages from the papers of the Anonymous (Wolfenbuttel) Fragmentist. He says: (page 223,) "Since the distortion of the Scriptural passages mentioned would not suffice, to justify the obedience of blind belief to the detriment of common sense, the deplorable fall of our first parents, and the corruption of our natural powers thereby caused, were called into requisition. While yet in the state of Innocence, so it is maintained, man was endowed with an innate likeness of God, that is a profound perception of God, the world and himself, with perfect wisdom, justice and holiness. But in consequence of the fall, he has forfeited all these virtues, and thus propagated all physical and spiritual corruption to all posterity. Now sheer ignorance, darkness and blindness rule the very nature of man, and his will is, from his very birth, inclined to evil, and dead for all that is good. So that, according to this theory the nature of the human race has undergone a complete change, and our noblest faculty, reason itself, is corrupt, at least in spiritual matters. But I must confess: when I contemplate with unbiased mind the Mosaic history of the first human pair in Paradise, I can by no means perceive, that they were in the least superior to us in spiritual perfection. For, before their fall, they appear to have sufficiently known neither God nor the devil, neither Nature nor themselves, since they allowed themselves to be misled by the outward charms of a beautiful apple, and the persuasion of a treacherous serpent or the devil, and act against the direct prohibition of God, and to do what was indeed evil. They sin even in this, that they do not follow the dictates of reason, but precipitately obey their deceptive senses and treacherous persuasions. Now, if the first human beings, though they were in a state of perfect innocence and free from original sin, could sin like ourselves, and this too from the same cause, that is by their inability to make their appetites and desires subservient to reason: how can a corruption of our noblest nature be derived from that narrative, and particularly reason be charged with it, because it was blind to the knowledge of Divine matters, and that, therefore, its use is dangerous. On the contrary, the neglect of its use is the very way that leads away from the true knowledge of God, and the obedience which we owe to His commandments, that way on which our first parents went toward their sin.

Would that every one gather so much strength, as to try his present reason and see, whether he could not, by his natural knowledge, judge far better of his God and the Paradise, than the human pair are said to have judged. Indeed! mere reason sufficiently informs us of the truth, wisdom, goodness and power of God that, if he would directly make his will known to us, to eat of all the trees but one, we should never entertain the thought, that God had not said, or meant it; that he knew better, that it was good to eat of that forbidden tree, since it would render us intelligent, and wise as He is Himself, and enable us to discern good from evil. Although we could not fathom the reason of the prohibition, we would nevertheless never suspect God of having pronounced that prohibition from envy or malevolence, lest we become equal to him, but we would certainly entertain the belief, that that particular fruit was injurious to us, and forbidden, therefore, for our own good. Thus every one, who is endowed with natural understanding and wishes to employ it, could be convinced, that his natural reason has not decreased in the knowledge of God's perfections, nor become more subservient and liable to the rule of sensual appetites, as we find it in the history of the first human pair."

Thus then we find that the dogma of Original Sin, and the corruption of the human race thereby produced, has no foundation in the Bible, but has been invented by theologians, to show the necessity of a suffering Messiah, and the redemption of mankind from eternal condemnation. How untenable, however, this theory of Original Sin is, has been already proved, also by Christian theologians. "Admitted," says Dr. Bretschneider, "that the punishment as far as it was inflicted upon Adam and Eve, was just, how can it be right, that all their posterity should forfeit their Divine likeness and immortality, on account of the recklessness of their first parents? Was it just, that God punish in a manner as to render the whole world unhappy? Could he have chosen a punishment that destroyed His purposes with regard to the human society? And granted, God was morally bound to punish in such a severe manner, ought He, knowing beforehand as he did, how Adam and Eve would act, not to have at once removed all temptation, or tempted them then only, when they had sons and daughters, so that the salvation of their posterity was secured? This is so simple, that all counter-arguments are abortive." (Dogmatics, page 57.)

Here then, kind reader, is an instance, by which you

may judge all Christian theories, which, as you will find on some reflection, hang on delicate threads of cobwebs that disfigure the Temple of Truth and Wisdom.

CONCLUDING OBSERVATIONS.

In tendering my warmest thanks to the reviewer, Rev. Dr. Wise, for his indulgent criticism on my "Guide," (contained in the *Asmonean*, 1853,) I will add a few words concerning my description of the Sadducean System, (above page 65.) According to the learned Philo, who lived some years before Christ, and followed mostly the doctrines of Plato; God and Matter are the Principles that existed from all eternity. Thus we see that the theory of Two Original Principles was adopted by many Jews long before Simon Magus, (the Sorcerer.)

It is true that the Stoics regard Matter as something passive; yet, Zeno, the founder of the Stoic system, nevertheless regards the natural bodies and powers as being of Divine kind, permeated as they are by Divine reason, so that the Deity dwells, as it were in Matter; and he, therefore, admits the worship of more than one God.

Now, as the Talmud often advances Stoic assertions, for instance: מן מלכי? רבנן "Who are the kings? the learned,—similar to the Stoic of description of a wise man,—the wise man alone is happy, is king," &c., so that it can not be denied that our ancient Sages were acquainted with Stoic philosophy; as שתי רשויות, (two principles,) are often mentioned or must be supposed, whenever Jewish idolators are spoken of: (see Jerus. Talmud, sect. 9; Babyl. Talmud, Treat. Menachoth, fol. 110; Pesachim, fol. 55,) I have arrived at the conclusion, that the Sadduceans who, as I have shown from Treat. Chagigah were held to be idolators, probably adopted the Stoic system. I doubt not that this hypothesis, which rests on logical conclusions, will be found correct upon investigations of modern Jewish historians.

ERRATA.

"By," instead of "under," in sixth line of page - - - -	4
"Yet," instead of "but," in fourth line from foot of page - -	7
"וערבן," instead of "ופרבן," in twenty-ninth line of page - -	10
"His view," instead of "it," in fifth line of page - - -	21
"It is," instead of "This," in twenty-first line of page - -	22
"5," instead of "25," in third line of page - - - - -	28
"Even," instead of "ever," in seventeenth line of page - -	31
"Required," instead of "applicable," in 19th line of page - -	42
"Folio," instead of "¶," in seventh line of page - - -	63
"Was," after "combination," in twenty-fifth line of page - -	63
"And had no," instead of "nor had any," in 15th line of page -	70
"And yet was," instead of "as," in eleventh line of page - -	75
"A," instead of "as," in third line of page - - - -	118
"The," should be omitted in the 25th line of page - -	139
"The whole," should be omitted in the 30th line of page -	139
"The," instead of "This," before contents in 34th line of page	145

www.ingramcontent.com/pod-product-compliance
Lightning Source LLC
LaVergne TN
LVHW011210110826
845150LV00006B/1393

* 9 7 8 1 4 2 5 5 1 7 4 0 3 *